Volume A

UNDERSTANDING AND USING

ENGLISH GRAMMAR

Second Edition

Betty Schrampfer Azar

PRENTICE HALL REGENTS
Englewood Cliffs, New Jersey 07632

Library of Congress Cataloging-in-Publication Data

Azar, Betty Schrampfer, (date)
    Understanding and using English grammar / by Betty Schrampfer
Azar. -- 2nd ed.
    p. cm.
    Includes index.
    ISBN 0-13-943663-4 (v. A). -- ISBN 0-13-943671-5 (v. B)
    1. English language--Textbooks for foreign speakers. 2. English
language--Grammar--1950- I. Title.
PE1128.A97 1989b
428.2'4--dc19   88-37396
                                                       CIP

To my mother,

FRANCES NIES SCHRAMPFER

and my father,

WILLIAM H. SCHRAMPFER

Editorial/production supervision and
    interior design: *Ros Herion Freese*
Cover design: *Joel Mitnick Design*
Manufacturing buyer: *Laura Crossland*

© 1989 by Prentice-Hall, Inc.
A Division of Simon & Schuster
Englewood Cliffs, New Jersey 07632

Printed in the United States of America

10 9 8 7 6 5 4 3 2

ISBN   0-13-943614-6

ISBN   0-13-943663-4   {VOL. A}

ISBN   0-13-943671-5   {VOL. B}

Prentice-Hall International (UK) Limited, *London*
Prentice-Hall of Australia Pty. Limited, *Sydney*
Prentice-Hall Canada Inc., *Toronto*
Prentice-Hall Hispanoamericana, S.A., *Mexico*
Prentice-Hall of India Private Limited, *New Delhi*
Prentice-Hall of Japan, Inc., *Tokyo*
Simon & Schuster Asia Pte. Ltd., *Singapore*
Editora Prentice-Hall do Brasil, Ltda., *Rio de Janeiro*

Contents

Preface to the Second Edition

The second edition of *Understanding and Using English Grammar* contains changes directed primarily toward clarification of structure presentations in the charts and improvements in the exercises. The revisions are based in large part upon the many wonderful and graciously offered suggestions from teachers and students familiar with the original text. A few new short grammar units have been included. One grammar area (comparisons) has been moved from *Understanding and Using English Grammar* to the second edition of *Fundamentals of English Grammar*. Additional notes on structure differences between American and British English have been included in the second edition.

The text remains a developmental skills text for students of English as a second or foreign language. While focusing on grammar, it promotes the development of all language skills in a variety of ways.

As in the original edition, the charts consist of examples accompanied by explanations and are intended to be easily understood by the students. Terminology is kept to a minimum.

The exercises reflect an eclectic approach, not only because there are many effective ways of teaching language, but also because certain structures simply tend to lend themselves to one approach rather than another. The exercises may be directed toward listening skills, oral production, writing skills, or reading comprehension—or any combination thereof. Some of the exercises have a straightforward, controlled concentration on form and meaning. These are followed by other more complicated and challenging exercises that engender creative, independent use of target structures. The exercise contexts reflect realistic, typical language use and are relevant to the students' concerns, daily lives, and life experiences. Items in the exercises are variously designed to encourage students to talk about themselves and their activities, to promote vocabulary development, to be informative, to engender cross-cultural comparisons, to be thought-provoking, to cause a smile or a chuckle, or to stimulate short discussions on a variety of topics.

In order to meet the needs of different teachers in different teaching situations, the revision of *Understanding and Using English Grammar* is available in two formats: in a single volume or in split volumes. The restructuring of the organization was designed principally to accommodate splitting the text into two volumes, with Volume A focusing on verb forms and Volume B focusing on complex structures. As in the original edition, each chapter is a self-contained unit; the teacher may present the chapters in the given order or rearrange the order of presentation to suit his/her needs and purposes.

Appendix 1 (*Supplementary Grammar Units*) has been expanded and now includes exercises. Information about parts of speech and basic structures such as questions and negatives is in the appendix so that students may have these units available whether using the single-volume text or the split volumes. The teacher can fit these units in as s/he deems appropriate in the syllabus. A teacher may, for example, choose to teach the question unit either prior to or in the course of teaching the verb tense chapter, may teach it in conjunction with the noun clause chapter, or may simply refer to it as needed in connection with tenses, modals, the passive, or any other unit. Much of the material in Appendix 1 is review from the other two texts in the series, but not all. As with any other grammar units in the text, the Appendix 1 material seeks to consolidate previous understandings as the basis upon which to expand usage ability.

Understanding and Using English Grammar (blue cover) is intended for upper-level students. It is part of a series of three grammar books. *Fundamentals of English Grammar* (black) is directed toward mid-level students, and *Basic English Grammar* (red) is designed for lower-level students.

WORKBOOKS

The second edition is accompanied by student workbooks: *Understanding and Using English Grammar—Workbooks A and B*. They contain not only Self-study Practices (answers given) for independent out-of-class work by the students, but also Guided Study Practices (answers not given) for classwork, homework, and individualized instruction as the teacher sees the need. In addition, there are suggestions for oral and/or writing activities, an emphasis on vocabulary development, and two practice tests for each chapter.

TEACHER'S GUIDE

The second edition of *Understanding and Using English Grammar* is also accompanied by a much expanded *Teacher's Guide* that contains: presentation suggestions; specific techniques for handling the varied types of exercises; background grammar notes; item notes on cultural content, vocabulary, and structure usage; problems to anticipate; suggestions for oral and written student-centered activities; and answers to the exercises.

ACKNOWLEDGMENTS

First of all, I would like to express my appreciation to Donald A. Azar for his irreplaceable encouragement, partnership, good humor, and computer expertise. He is the co-author of the *Workbooks* and also has served as an advisor on the revision. A person of myriad skills, he has eased the way through a demanding project during a busy time in our lives, making the work I enjoy even more enjoyable.

I wish also to express my great appreciation to Barbara Matthies, the writer of the accompanying *Teacher's Guide*, for her continuing support both as a colleague and a friend—and for a wonderful time in Kathmandu, where we spent hours tossing around ideas. To me, there is nothing better than a good friend/colleague who likes to talk about English grammar and the teaching of ESL/EFL.

I wish to express my gratitude to the following colleagues for their suggestions, interest, keen perceptions, and cheerful repartee: Irene Juzkiw, Rachel Spack (Shelley) Koch, Jeanie Francis, Susan Jamieson, Phyllis Mithin, Larry Francis, Barbara Leonhard, Nancy Price, Maureen Burke, Steve Molinsky, Bill Bliss, and Candace Matthews. An additional special thanks goes to Shelley, Jeanie, Susan, and Barbara Andrews for their wonderful contributions to and interest in the workbook project.

The many other colleagues I have spoken with about the revision are too numerous to name, but I thank all of them for sharing their ideas with me. I would like to say a special thank you to the teachers I met in Puerto Rico. And to all of those who so conscientiously and scrupulously responded to the questionnaire on revising the text, my heartfelt thanks.

The reviewers of the revised manuscript have been exceptionally helpful. In particular, I wish to thank Mr. Richard Eisman; Ms. J. Rajah; Ms. Mohana K. Nambiar; Dr. Dagmar Buhring Acuna, Universidad Interamericana de Puerto Rico; Mr. James E. Purpura, Institute for North American Studies, Barcelona, Spain; Ms. Teresa Pica, University of Pennsylvania, Graduate School of Education; Prof. Habibah HJ. Ashari, Coordinator, TESL Program, Center of Preparatory Education, MARA Institute of Technology, Malaysia; Mr. Richard L. Coe, State University of New York at Buffalo, Cooperative Education Program in Malaysia; Ms. Lynne Sarkisan Cresitello; Mr. Nicholas J. Dimmitt, University of Bahrain, Isa Town, Bahrain; Ms. Cheryl Engber, Indiana University; Ms. Linda A. Moody, Associate Director, The English Center for International Women, Mills College; Mr. William R. Slager, Department of English, University of Utah; and Ms. Shirley Wu, Singapore.

I must say a special thank you to Lilian and Leonard Feinberg, who graciously made available to me language teaching materials they had written. They are much appreciated as friends and mentors.

My gratitude also goes to Tina Carver, editor and friend, and to Ed Stanford, Andy Martin, Gil Muller, Noel Carter, Ros Herion Freese, Sylvia

Moore, Don Martinetti, and all of the others with Prentice Hall Regents who made this project possible and enjoyable.

I wish to thank Chelsea Parker for her willing, cheerful, and able office assistance. She is also a great joy and delight in my life.

Finally, I thank my mother for inputting and editing, my father for being a veritable wellspring of ideas for entries, and both of them for helping with the tedious job of reading proof. Throughout my life, they have been and still are ever ready to assist me in my various endeavors—for which I am truly grateful.

BETTY S. AZAR
Langley, Washington

CHAPTER 1
Verb Tenses

☐ **EXERCISE 1—ORAL:** Interview another student in the class. Take notes during the interview, and then introduce this student to the rest of the class. Possible topics for the interview follow. As a class, discuss what questions you might ask to elicit this information.

1. name
2. spelling of name
3. country of origin
4. residence at present
5. length of time in (*this city or country*), both past and future
6. reason for coming here
7. field of study or work
8. spare-time activities and interests
9. general well-being and adjustment to living here
10. comments on living here

☐ **EXERCISE 2—WRITTEN:** Write a short autobiographical paragraph telling who you are, what you have done in the past two years, and what your plans are for the next two years.

☐ **EXERCISE 3—ORAL (BOOKS CLOSED):** Ask a classmate a question using ***what*** + *a form of **do*** (e.g., *What are you doing? What did you do? What have you done?*). Use the given time expressions.

Example: every morning
Student A: What do you do every morning?
Student B: I (go to classes/eat breakfast/etc.) every morning.

1. every day before you come to school
2. last night
3. since you got up this morning
4. right now
5. at (*this exact time*) yesterday
6. for the past five minutes
7. tomorrow
8. at (*this exact time*) tomorrow
9. by the time you got to class this morning
10. by the time you go to bed tonight

***AN OVERVIEW OF ENGLISH VERB TENSES FOLLOWS IN CHARTS 1-1
THROUGH 1-5.*** The diagram shown below will be used in the tense descriptions:

1-1 THE SIMPLE TENSES

TENSE	EXAMPLES	MEANING
SIMPLE PRESENT ✗✗✗✗✗✗✦✗✗✗✗✗	(a) It **snows** in Alaska. (b) I **watch** television every day.	In general, the simple present expresses events or situations that *exist always, usually, habitually*; they exist now, have existed in the past, and probably will exist in the future.
SIMPLE PAST ✗	(c) It **snowed** yesterday. (d) I **watched** television last night.	*At one particular time in the past*, this happened. It began and ended in the past.
SIMPLE FUTURE ✗	(e) It **will snow** tomorrow. (f) I **will watch** television tonight.	*At one particular time in the future*, this will happen.

1-2   THE PROGRESSIVE TENSES★

Form:	**be + -ing** (*present participle*)	
Meaning:	The progressive tenses give the idea that an action is *in progress* during a particular time. The tenses say that an action *begins before*, *is in progress during*, and *continues after* another time or action.	

PRESENT PROGRESSIVE	(a) He *is sleeping* right now.	He went to sleep at 10:00 tonight. It is now 11:00 and he is still asleep. His sleep began in the past, *is in progress at the present time*, and probably will continue.
PAST PROGRESSIVE	(b) He *was sleeping* when I arrived.	He went to sleep at 10:00 last night. I arrived at 11:00. He was still asleep. His sleep began before and *was in progress at a particular time in the past*. It probably continued.
FUTURE PROGRESSIVE	(c) He *will be sleeping* when we arrive.	He will go to sleep at 10:00 tomorrow night. We will arrive at 11:00. The action of sleeping will begin before we arrive and it *will be in progress at a particular time in the future*. Probably his sleep will continue.

★The progressive tenses are also called the continuous tenses: *present continuous*, *past continuous*, and *future continuous*.

1-3 THE PERFECT TENSES

Form: *have* + *past participle*

Meaning: The perfect tenses all give the idea that one thing *happens before* another time or event.

PRESENT PERFECT ―×eat――now―×― (time?)	(a) I *have* already *eaten*.	I *finished* eating sometime *before now*. The exact time is not important.
PAST PERFECT ―×eat―×arrive――――	(b) I *had* already *eaten* when they arrived.	First I finished eating. Later they arrived. My eating was completely *finished before another time in the past*.
FUTURE PERFECT ――――×eat―×arrive―	(c) I *will* already *have eaten* when they arrive.	First I will finish eating. Later they will arrive. My eating will be completely *finished before another time in the future*.

1-4 THE PERFECT PROGRESSIVE TENSES

Form:	**have** + **been** + **-ing** (*present participle*)	
Meaning:	The perfect progressive tenses give the idea that one event is *in progress immediately before, up to, until another time or event*. The tenses are used to express the *duration* of the first event.	
PRESENT PERFECT PROGRESSIVE 2 hrs.	(a) I **have been studying** for two hours.	Event in progress: studying. When? *Before now, up to now.* How long? For two hours.
PAST PERFECT PROGRESSIVE 2 hrs.	(b) I **had been studying** for two hours before my friend came.	Event in progress: studying. When? *Before another event in the past.* How long? For two hours.
FUTURE PERFECT PROGRESSIVE 2 hrs.	(c) I **will have been studying** for two hours by the time you arrive.	Event in progress: studying. When? *Before another event in the future.* How long? For two hours.

1-5 SUMMARY CHART OF VERB TENSES

SIMPLE PRESENT The world *is* round. I *study* every day.	PRESENT PROGRESSIVE I *am studying* right now.
SIMPLE PAST I *studied* last night.	PAST PROGRESSIVE I *was studying* when they came.
SIMPLE FUTURE I *will study* tomorrow.	FUTURE PROGRESSIVE I *will be studying* when you come.

PRESENT PERFECT	PRESENT PERFECT PROGRESSIVE
I have already *studied* Chapter One.	I *have been studying* for two hours.
PAST PERFECT	PAST PERFECT PROGRESSIVE
I *had* already *studied* Chapter One before I began to study Chapter Two.	I *had been studying* for two hours before my friends came.
FUTURE PERFECT	FUTURE PERFECT PROGRESSIVE
I *will* already *have studied* Chapter Four before I study Chapter Five.	I *will have been studying* for two hours by the time you arrive.

□ **EXERCISE 4—ORAL (BOOKS CLOSED):** Practice using tenses by answering the questions in complete sentences.

1. What do you do every day?
2. What did you do yesterday?
3. What will you do tomorrow?
4. What are you doing right now?
5. What were you doing at this time yesterday?
6. What will you be doing at this time tomorrow?
7. What have you done since you got up this morning?
8. What had you done before you went to bed last night?
9. What will you have done by the time you go to bed tonight?
10. What are you doing? How long have you been doing that?
11. What were you doing before I walked into the classroom today? How long had you been doing that?
12. What will you be doing before I walk into the classroom tomorrow? How long will you have been doing that?

□ **EXERCISE 5—SPELLING PRETEST (BOOKS CLOSED):** You will be using many verbs in their *-ing* and *-ed* forms in this chapter. Use this pretest to check yourself on spelling rules. On another piece of paper, write the words that your teacher says.

Example: (cry + *-ed*)
Teacher: Cried. I cried because I was sad. Cried.
Written Response: cried

1. (hope + *-ed*)
2. (dine + *-ing*)
3. (stop + *-ed*)
4. (plan + *-ing*)
5. (rain + *-ed*)
6. (wait + *-ing*)
7. (listen + *-ing*)
8. (happen + *-ed*)
9. (begin + *-ing*)
10. (occur + *-ed*)
11. (start + *-ing*)
12. (warn + *-ed*)
13. (enjoy + *-ed*)
14. (play + *-ing*)
15. (study + *-ing*)
16. (worry + *-ed*)
17. (die + *-ed*)
18. (lie + *-ing*)

1-6 SPELLING OF -ING AND -ED FORMS

(1) VERBS THAT END IN -E	(a) hope date injure	hoping dating injuring	hoped dated injured	**-ING FORM:** If the word ends in -e, drop the -e and add -ing.* **-ED FORM:** If the word ends in -e, just add -d.
(2) VERBS THAT END IN A VOWEL AND A CONSONANT	**ONE-SYLLABLE VERBS**			
	(b) stop rob beg	stopping robbing begging	stopped robbed begged	*1 vowel → 2 consonants**
	(c) rain fool dream	raining fooling dreaming	rained fooled dreamed	*2 vowels → 1 consonant*
	TWO-SYLLABLE VERBS			
	(d) listen offer open	listening offering opening	listened offered opened	*1st syllable stressed → 1 consonant*
	(e) begin prefer control	beginning preferring controlling	(began) preferred controlled	*2nd syllable stressed → 2 consonants*
(3) VERBS THAT END IN TWO CONSONANTS	(f) start fold demand	starting folding demanding	started folded demanded	If the word ends in two consonants, just add the ending.
(4) VERBS THAT END IN -Y	(g) enjoy pray buy	enjoying praying buying	enjoyed prayed (bought)	If -y is preceded by a vowel, keep the -y. If -y is preceded by a consonant: **-ING FORM:** keep the -y, add -ing. **-ED FORM:** change -y to -i, add -ed.
	(h) study try reply	studying trying replying	studied tried replied	
(5) VERBS THAT END IN -IE	(i) die lie tie	dying lying tying	died lied tied	**-ING FORM:** Change -ie to -y, add -ing. **-ED FORM:** Add -d.

*Exception: If a verb ends in -ee, the final -e is not dropped: *seeing, agreeing, freeing.*
**Exception: -w and -x are not doubled: *plow → plowed; fix → fixed.*

EXERCISE 6: Give the correct *-ing* form for the following.

1. hold → *holding*
2. hide
3. run
4. ruin
5. come
6. write
7. eat
8. sit
9. act
10. pat
11. open
12. begin
13. earn
14. fry
15. die
16. employ

EXERCISE 7: Give the correct *-ing* and *-ed* forms for the following.

1. boil → *boiling, boiled*
2. try
3. stay
4. tape
5. tap
6. offer
7. prefer
8. gain
9. plan
10. tie
11. help
12. study
13. admit
14. visit
15. hug
16. rage

EXERCISE 8: Give the correct *-ed* form for the following.

1. bore
2. jar red
3. jeer
4. intensify ied
5. sob
6. loot
7. point
8. ripen
9. refer red
10. destroy ed

EXERCISE 9: Give the correct *-ing* form for the following.

1. raid
2. ride
3. bid
4. bury
5. lie
6. argue
7. tame
8. teem
9. trim
10. harm

1-7 SIMPLE PRESENT

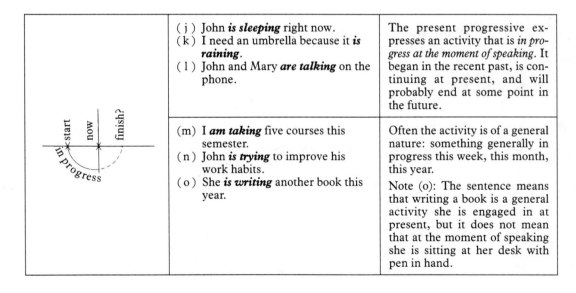

	(a) Water **consists** of hydrogen and oxygen. (b) Most animals **kill** only for food. (c) The world **is** round.	The simple present says that something was true in the past, is true in the present, and will be true in the future. It is used for *general statements of fact.*
	(d) I **study** for two hours every night. (e) My classes **begin** at nine. (f) He always **eats** a sandwich for lunch.	The simple present is used to express *habitual or everyday activity.*
	(g) I **have** only a dollar right now. (h) I **don't recognize** that man. (i) He **needs** a pen right now.	Certain verbs are not used in the progressive tenses. (See Chart 1-9.) With these verbs, the simple present may indicate a situation that exists right now, at the moment of speaking.

1-8 PRESENT PROGRESSIVE

	(j) John **is sleeping** right now. (k) I need an umbrella because it **is raining**. (l) John and Mary **are talking** on the phone.	The present progressive expresses an activity that is *in progress at the moment of speaking.* It began in the recent past, is continuing at present, and will probably end at some point in the future.
	(m) I **am taking** five courses this semester. (n) John **is trying** to improve his work habits. (o) She **is writing** another book this year.	Often the activity is of a general nature: something generally in progress this week, this month, this year. Note (o): The sentence means that writing a book is a general activity she is engaged in at present, but it does not mean that at the moment of speaking she is sitting at her desk with pen in hand.

tik

⊠ **EXERCISE 10:** Use either the SIMPLE PRESENT or the PRESENT PROGRESSIVE of the verbs in parentheses.

1. Diane can't come to the phone because she (*wash*) ___*is washing*___ her hair.

2. Diane (*wash*) ___washes___ her hair every other day or so.

3. Kathy (*sit, usually★*) ___usually sits___ in the front row during class, but today she (*sit*) ___is sitting___ in the last row.

4. Please be quiet. I (*try*) ___am trying___ to concentrate.

5. (*Lock, you, always★*) ___you always lock___ the door to your apartment when you leave?

6. I wrote to my friend last week. She hasn't answered my letter yet. I (*wait, still★*) ___am still waiting___ for a reply.

7. After three days of rain, I'm glad that the sun (*shine*) ___is shining___ again today.

8. Every morning, the sun (*shine*) ___shines___ in my bedroom window and (*wake*) ___wakes___ me up.

9. A: Look! It (*snow*) ___is snowing___.

   B: It's beautiful! This is the first time I've ever seen snow. It (*snow, not★*) ___doesn't snow___ in my country.

10. Mike is a student, but he (*go, not★*) ___is not going___ to school right now because it's summer. He (*attend*) ___attends___ college from September to May every year, but in the summers he (*have, usually★*) ___usually has___ a job at the post office. In fact, he (*work*) ___is working___ there this summer.

☐ **EXERCISE 11—ORAL:** On a piece of paper, write one direction that you want a classmate to follow. Examples: *Stand up. Smile. Open the door. Sneeze.*

   (*To the teacher: Collect and then redistribute the directions. Ask each student in turn to perform the required action, and have another student use the present progressive to describe this action.*)

★See Appendix 1 for usual placement of midsentence adverbs (Chart A-4), for question forms (Chart B-1), and for negative forms (Chart C-1).

1-9 NONPROGRESSIVE VERBS

NONPROGRESSIVE (a) Ali **knows** this grammar.	Some verbs are *nonprogressive*: they are not used in any of the progressive tenses. These verbs describe states (i.e., conditions that exist); they do not describe activities that are in progress. In (a): "Ali knows" describes a mental state that exists.
PROGRESSIVE (b) Kim **is reading** about this grammar.	COMPARE: In (b): "Kim is reading" is an activity in progress. Progressive tenses can be used with the verb **read** but not with the verb **know**.

COMMON NONPROGRESSIVE VERBS

(1) MENTAL STATE	know	believe	imagine	want
	realize	feel	doubt	need
	understand	suppose	remember	prefer
	recognize	think★	forget	mean
(2) EMOTIONAL STATE	love	hate	fear	mind
	like	dislike	envy	care
	appreciate			
(3) POSSESSION	possess	have★	own	belong
(4) SENSE PERCEPTIONS	taste★ smell★	hear feel★	see★	
(5) OTHER EXISTING STATES	seem	cost	be★	consist of
	look★	owe	exist	contain
	appear★	weigh★		include

★Verbs with an asterisk are also commonly used as progressive verbs, with a difference in meaning, as in the following examples:

	NONPROGRESSIVE (existing state)	PROGRESSIVE (activity in progress)
think	I **think** he is a kind man.	I **am thinking** about this grammar.
have	He **has** a car.	I **am having** trouble. She **is having** a good time.
taste	This food **tastes** good.	The chef **is tasting** the sauce.
smell	These flowers **smell** good.	Don **is smelling** the roses.
see	I **see** a butterfly. **Do** you **see** it?	The doctor **is seeing** a patient.
feel	The cat's fur **feels** soft.	Sue **is feeling** the cat's fur.
look	She **looks** cold. I'll lend her my coat.	I **am looking** out the window.
appear	He **appears** to be asleep.	The actor **is appearing** on the stage.
weigh	A piano is heavy. It **weighs** a lot.	The grocer **is weighing** the bananas.
be	I **am** hungry.	Tom **is being** foolish.★★

★★COMPARE:

(a) *Bob is foolish.* = Foolishness is one of Bob's usual characteristics.

(b) *Tom is being foolish.* = Right now, at the moment of speaking, Tom is doing something that the speaker considers foolish.

The verb **be** (+ *an adjective*) is used in the progressive to describe a temporary characteristic. Very few adjectives are used with **be** in the progressive; some of the most common are: *foolish, nice, kind, lazy, careful, patient, silly, rude, polite, impolite.*

□ **EXERCISE 12:** Use either the SIMPLE PRESENT or the PRESENT PROGRESSIVE of the verbs in parentheses.

1. I can't afford that ring. It (*cost*) _____ **costs** _____ too much.

2. Look. It (*begin*) _is beginning_ to rain. Unfortunately, I (*have, not★*) _don't have_ my umbrella with me. Tom is lucky. He (*wear*) _is wearing_ a raincoat.

3. I (*own, not*) _don't own_ an umbrella. I (*wear*) _wear_ a waterproof hat on rainy days.

4. Right now I (*look*) _am looking_ around the classroom. Yoko (*write*) _is writing_ in her book. Carlos (*bite*) _is biting_ his pencil. Wan-Ning (*scratch*) _is scratching_ his head. Ahmed (*stare*) _is staring_ out the window. He (*seem*) _seems_ to be daydreaming, but perhaps he (*think*) _is thinking_ hard about verb tenses. What (*think, you*) _do you think_ Ahmed (*do*) _is doing_ ?

★A form of **do** is usually used in the negative when the main verb is **have** (especially in American English but also commonly in British English); e.g., *I don't have a car.* Using **have** without a form of **do** is also possible but less common: *I haven't a car.*

5. There's a book on my desk, but it (*belong, not*) _does not belong_
_____ to me.

6. Dennis (*fix*) _is fixxing_ the roof of his house today, and he
(*need*) _needs_ some help. Can you help him?

7. Barbara (*tutor, often*) _often tutors_ other students in her math
class. This afternoon she (*help*) _is helping_ Steve with his math
assignment because he (*understand, not*) _doesn't understand_ the
material they (*work*) _are working_ on in their class this week.

8. Right now I (*look*) _am looking_ at Janet. She (*look*) _looks_
angry. I wonder what's the matter. She (*have*) _is having (has)_
a frown on her face. She certainly (*have, not*) _doesn't have_
any fun right now.

9. A: Who is that woman who (*stand*) _is standing_ next to
the window?

B: Which woman? (*Talk, you*) _you're talking_ about the
woman who (*wear*) _is wearing_ the blue and gold dress?

A: No, I (*talk, not*) _am not talking_ about her. I (*mean*)
mean the woman who (*wear*) _is wearing_
the blue suit.

B: Oh. I (*know, not*) _don't know_. I (*recognize, not*) _don't_
recognize her.

10. A: Close your eyes. Now listen carefully. What (*hear, you*) _are do_
you hearing hear? What (*do, I*) _am I doing_?

B: I (*believe*) _believe_ you (*rub*) _are rubbing_
the top of your desk with your hand.

A: Close, but not exactly right. Try again. (*Listen, you*) _are you listening_
_____ carefully?

B: Aha! You (*rub*) _are rubbing_ your hands together.

A: Right!

☐ **EXERCISE 13—WRITTEN:** Go to a place where there are many people (or imagine yourself to be in such a place). Describe the activities you observe. Let your reader see what you see; draw a "picture" by using words.

   Use present tenses. Begin your writing with a description of your own immediate activities; e.g., *I am sitting on a bench at the zoo.*

1–10 USING THE PRESENT PROGRESSIVE WITH *ALWAYS*

(a) Mary **always leaves** for school at 7:45.	In sentences referring to present time, usually the simple present is used with **always** to describe habitual or everyday activities, as in (a).
(b) Mary **is always leaving** her dirty socks on the floor for me to pick up! Who does she think I am? Her maid?	In special circumstances, a speaker may use the present progressive with **always** to complain, i.e., to express annoyance or anger, as in (b).★
(c) I **am always/forever/constantly picking** up Mary's dirty socks!	In addition to **always**, the words **forever** and **constantly** are used with the present progressive to express annoyance.

★COMPARE: "*Mary is always leaving her dirty socks on the floor*" expresses annoyance.
"*Mary always leaves her dirty socks on the floor*" is a statement of fact in which the speaker is not necessarily expressing an attitude of annoyance. Annoyance may, however, be included in the speaker's tone of voice.

☐ **EXERCISE 14—ORAL:** Assume you have a roommate named Jack who has many bad habits. These bad habits annoy you. Pretend you are speaking to a friend and complaining about Jack. Use the present progressive. Use *always, constantly,* or *forever* in each sentence. Say your sentence aloud with some annoyance, impatience, or anger in your voice.

   Here is a list of some of Jack's bad habits:

   1. He messes up the kitchen. → *He's always messing up the kitchen!*
   2. He leaves his dirty dishes on the table.
   3. He borrows my clothes without asking me.
   4. He brags about himself.
   5. He tries to show me that he's smarter than I.
   6. He cracks his knuckles while I'm trying to study.

7. I like fresh air and like to have the windows open, but he closes the windows.

8. *Complete the following with your own words.*

A: I really don't know if I can stand to have Sue for a roommate one more day. She's driving me crazy.

B: Oh? What's wrong?

A: Well, for one thing she's always _____.

B: Really?

A: And not only that. She's forever _____.

B: That must be very inconvenient for you.

A: It is. And what's more, she's constantly _____. Can you believe that? And she's always _____.

B: I think you're right. You need to find a new roommate.

1-11 REGULAR AND IRREGULAR VERBS

REGULAR VERBS: The simple past and past participle end in *-ed*.				English verbs have four principal parts:
SIMPLE FORM	SIMPLE PAST	PAST PARTICIPLE	PRESENT PARTICIPLE	(1) simple form (2) simple past (3) past participle (4) present participle
hope	*hoped*	*hoped*	*hoping*	
stop	*stopped*	*stopped*	*stopping*	
listen	*listened*	*listened*	*listening*	
study	*studied*	*studied*	*studying*	
start	*started*	*started*	*starting*	
IRREGULAR VERBS: The simple past and past participle do not end in *-ed*.				Some verbs have irregular past forms. Most of the irregular verbs in English are given in the following alphabetical list.
SIMPLE FORM	SIMPLE PAST	PAST PARTICIPLE	PRESENT PARTICIPLE	
break	*broke*	*broken*	*breaking*	
come	*came*	*come*	*coming*	
find	*found*	*found*	*finding*	
hit	*hit*	*hit*	*hitting*	
swim	*swam*	*swum*	*swimming*	

AN ALPHABETICAL LIST OF IRREGULAR VERBS

SIMPLE FORM	SIMPLE PAST	PAST PARTICIPLE	SIMPLE FORM	SIMPLE PAST	PAST PARTICIPLE
arise	arose	arisen	forbid	forbade	forbidden
be	was, were	been	forecast	forecast	forecast
bear	bore	borne/born	forget	forgot	forgotten
beat	beat	beaten/beat	forgive	forgave	forgiven
become	became	become	forsake	forsook	forsaken
begin	began	begun	freeze	froze	frozen
bend	bent	bent	get	got	gotten*
bet	bet	bet*	give	gave	given
bid	bid	bid	go	went	gone
bind	bound	bound	grind	ground	ground
bite	bit	bitten	grow	grew	grown
bleed	bled	bled	hang	hung	hung
blow	blew	blown	have	had	had
break	broke	broken	hear	heard	heard
breed	bred	bred	hide	hid	hidden
bring	brought	brought	hit	hit	hit
broadcast	broadcast	broadcast	hold	held	held
build	built	built	hurt	hurt	hurt
burst	burst	burst	keep	kept	kept
buy	bought	bought	know	knew	known
cast	cast	cast	lay	laid	laid
catch	caught	caught	lead	led	led
choose	chose	chosen	leave	left	left
cling	clung	clung	lend	lent	lent
come	came	come	let	let	let
cost	cost	cost	lie	lay	lain
creep	crept	crept	light	lit/lighted	lit/lighted
cut	cut	cut	lose	lost	lost
deal	dealt	dealt	make	made	made
dig	dug	dug	mean	meant	meant
do	did	done	meet	met	met
draw	drew	drawn	mislay	mislaid	mislaid
eat	ate	eaten	mistake	mistook	mistaken
fall	fell	fallen	pay	paid	paid
feed	fed	fed	put	put	put
feel	felt	felt	quit	quit	quit*
fight	fought	fought	read	read	read
find	found	found	rid	rid	rid
fit	fit	fit*	ride	rode	ridden
flee	fled	fled	ring	rang	rung
fling	flung	flung	rise	rose	risen
fly	flew	flown	run	ran	run

Vaginal
Penis
anus

Touch

I will undertake that it will not transpine : tôi bảo
đảm rằng điều đó sẽ ❏ bị lộ ra.

SIMPLE FORM	SIMPLE PAST	PAST PARTICIPLE	SIMPLE FORM	SIMPLE PAST	PAST PARTICIPLE
say	said	said	sting	stung	stung
see	saw	seen	stink	stank/stunk	stunk
seek	sought	sought	strive	strove	striven
sell	sold	sold	strike	struck	struck/stricken
send	sent	sent	string	strung	strung
set	set	set	swear	swore	sworn
shake	shook	shaken	sweep	swept	swept
shed	shed	shed	swim	swam	swum
sing shine	shone/shined	shone/shined	swing	swung	swung
shoot	shot	shot	take	took	taken
show	showed	shown/showed	teach	taught	taught
shrink	shrank/shrunk	shrunk	tear	tore	torn
shut	shut	shut	tell	told	told
sing	sang	sung	think	thought	thought
sit	sat	sat	throw	threw	thrown
sleep	slept	slept	thrust	thrust	thrust
slide	slid	slid	understand	understood	understood
slit	slit	slit	undertake	undertook	undertaken
speak	spoke	spoken	upset	upset	upset
speed	sped/speeded	sped/speeded	wake	woke/waked	woken/waked
spend	spent	spent	wear	wore	worn
spin	spun	spun	weave	wove	woven
spit	spit/spat	spit/spat	weep	wept	wept
split	split	split	win	won	won
spread	spread	spread	wind	wound	wound
spring	sprang/sprung	sprung	withdraw	withdrew	withdrawn
stand	stood	stood	wring	wrung	wrung
steal	stole	stolen	write	wrote	written
stick	stuck	stuck			

*The following are some differences in verb forms between American English and British English:

American	British
bet-bet-bet	bet-bet-bet OR bet-betted-betted
fit-fit-fit	fit-fitted-fitted
get-got-gotten	get-got-got
quit-quit-quit	quit-quitted-quitted

American: burn, dream, kneel, lean, leap, learn, smell, spell, spill, spoil are usually regular: burned, dreamed, kneeled, leaned, leaped, etc.

British: simple past and past participle forms of these verbs can be regular but more commonly end with -t: burnt, dreamt, knelt, leant, leapt, learnt, smelt, spelt, spilt, spoilt.

ill-treat = abuse =(v)= bạc đãi

An ill-timed remark : 1 sự nhận xét ❏ đúng lúc

☐ **EXERCISE 15—ORAL:** Practice pronouncing the following past forms of regular verbs.

GROUP A: Final *-ed* is pronounced /**t**/ after voiceless sounds:

1. looked
2. asked
3. helped
4. laughed

5. pushed
6. watched
7. dressed
8. boxed

GROUP B: Final *-ed* is pronounced /**d**/ after voiced sounds:

9. sobbed
10. believed
11. filled
12. poured

13. roamed
14. judged
15. enjoyed
16. dried

GROUP C: Final *-ed* is pronounced /ə**d**/ after *-d* and *-t*:

17. needed
18. defended
19. added
20. loaded

21. waited
22. rested
23. counted
24. halted

Practice the following sentences aloud.

25. My friend jumped up and down and shouted when she heard the news.
26. The concert lasted for two hours.
27. With the coming of spring, the river flooded and inundated several villages.
28. She tapped the top of her desk.
29. He described his house.
30. They demanded to know the answer.
31. The airplane departed at six and landed at eight.
32. Alice pushed and I pulled.
33. He handed me his dictionary.
34. Jack tooted his horn.
35. They asked us to help them.

☐ **EXERCISE 16—ORAL (BOOKS CLOSED):** This and the following three exercises are quick oral reviews of irregular verbs. In this exercise, answer with "yes" and a complete sentence.★

★Usually a short answer is given to a yes/no question. *Example:*
    A: *Did you sit down?*
    B: *Yes, I did. (short answer)*
In this exercise you are asked to give a full answer so that you can review the simple past of irregular verbs. Which irregular verbs come easily for you? Which ones are a little more troublesome? Which ones don't you know?

Example: Did you sit down?
Response: Yes, I sat down.

1. Did you drink some coffee before class?
2. Did you bring your books to class?
3. Did you forget your briefcase?
4. Did you shake your head?
5. Did you catch the bus this morning?
6. Did you drive to school?
7. Did you lose your book?
8. Did you find your book?
9. Did you wind your watch this morning?
10. Did you understand what I said?
11. Did you tell your friend the news?
12. Did you spread the news?
13. Did you fall on the ice?
14. Did you hurt yourself when you fell?
15. Did you fly to (*this city*)?
16. Did you wear a coat to class?
17. Did you hang your coat on a hook?
18. Did you eat lunch?
19. Did you take chemistry in high school?
20. Did you ride the bus to school?
21. Did you swear to tell the truth?
22. I made a mistake. Did you forgive me?
23. Did you write a letter to your family?
24. Did you bite the dog???

□ **EXERCISE 17—ORAL (BOOKS CLOSED):**   Answer, ''No, Someone else . . . .''

Example: Did you shut the door?
Response: No, someone else shut the door.

1. Did you make a mistake?
2. Did you break that window?
3. Did you steal my wallet?
4. Did you take my piece of paper?
5. Did you draw that picture?
6. Did you sweep the floor this morning?
7. Did you teach class yesterday?
8. Did you dig that hole in the garden?
9. Did you feed the cat?
10. Did you hide my book from me?
11. Did you blow that whistle?
12. Did you throw a piece of chalk out the window?
13. Did you tear that piece of paper?
14. Did you build that house?
15. Did you speak to (. . .)?

☐ **EXERCISE 18—ORAL (BOOKS CLOSED):** Answer with "yes."

> *Example:* Did you sit down?
> *Response:* Yes, I sat down.

1. Did you give me some money?
2. Did you stand at the bus stop?
3. Did you choose the blue pen?
4. Did you run to class this (*morning*)?
5. Did you sleep well last night?
6. Did you hear that noise outside the window?
7. Did you withdraw some money from the bank?
8. Did you wake up at seven this morning?
9. Did you swim in the ocean?
10. Did you go home after class yesterday?
11. Did you bend your elbow?
12. Did you send a letter?
13. Did you sing a song?
14. Did you stick your hand in your pocket?
15. Did you grind the pepper?
16. Did you strike the desk with your hand?
17. Did you light a match?
18. Did you mean what you said?
19. Did you hold your hand up?
20. Did you speak to (. . .)?

☐ **EXERCISE 19—ORAL (BOOKS CLOSED):** Answer with "yes."

> *Example:* Did the students come to class?
> *Response:* Yes, they came to class.

1. Did class begin at (*nine*)?
2. Did the sun rise at six this morning?
3. Did you cut your finger?
4. Did it bleed when you cut it?
5. Did the grass grow after the rain?
6. Did a bee sting you?
7. Did the telephone ring?
8. Did the water freeze?
9. Did your friend quit school?
10. Did the soldiers fight?
11. Did the thief creep into the room?
12. Did the policeman shoot at the thief?

13. Did the thief flee?
14. Did your team win the game yesterday?
15. Did your car slide on the ice?
16. Did the door swing open?
17. Did the children blow up some balloons?
18. Did the balloons burst?
19. Did the radio station broadcast the news?
20. Did you know all of the irregular verbs?

☐ **EXERCISE 20:** Some of the verbs in the irregular verb list can be troublesome. Many native speakers find some of these verbs troublesome, too, especially *lay* and *lie*. Study the examples. (See Appendix 1, Chart A-1 for more information about transitive and intransitive verbs.)

TRANSITIVE (followed by an object)	INTRANSITIVE (not followed by an object)
(a) *raise, raised, raised* Tom raised his head.	(b) *rise, rose, risen* The sun rises in the east.
(c) *set, set, set* I will set the book on the desk.	(d) *sit, sat, sat* I sit in the front row.
(e) *lay, laid, laid* I am laying the book on the desk.	(f) *lie,★ lay, lain* He is lying on his bed.
(g) *hang, hung, hung* I hung my clothes in the closet. (h) *hang, hanged, hanged* They hanged the criminal by the neck until he was dead.	

★*Lie* is a regular verb (*lie, lied*) when it means "not tell the truth": *He lied to me about his age.*

Choose the correct word in parentheses.

1. The student (raised, rose) his hand in class.
2. Hot air (raises, rises).
3. Ann (set, sat) in a chair because she was tired.
4. I (set, sat) your dictionary on the table a few minutes ago.
5. Hens (lay, lie) eggs.
6. Al is (laying, lying) on the grass in the park right now.
7. Jan (laid, lay) the comb on top of the dresser a few minutes ago.
8. If you are tired, you should (lay, lie) down and take a nap.
9. San Francisco (lay, lies) to the north of Los Angeles.
10. We (hanged, hung) the picture on the wall.

1-12   SIMPLE PAST

	(a) I **walked** to school yesterday. (b) He **lived** in Paris for ten years, but now he is living in Rome. (c) I **bought** a new car three days ago.	The simple past indicates that an activity or situation *began and ended at a particular time in the past.*
	(d) I **stood** under a tree *when it* **began** *to rain.* (e) *When she* **heard** *a strange noise,* she **got** up to investigate. (f) *When I* **dropped** *my cup,* the coffee **spilled** *on my lap.*	If a sentence contains **when** and has the simple past in both clauses, the action in the "**when** clause" happens first. In (d): 1st: The rain began. 2nd: I stood under a tree.

1-13   PAST PROGRESSIVE

	(g) I **was walking** down the street when it began to rain. (h) While I **was walking** down the street, it began to rain. (i) I **was standing** under a tree when it began to rain. (j) At eight o'clock last night, I **was studying**. (k) Last year at this time, I **was attending** school.	In (g): 1st: I was walking down the street. 2nd: It began to rain. In other words, both actions occurred at the *same* time, but *one action began earlier and was in progress when the other action occurred.* In (j): My studying began before 8:00, was in progress at that time, and probably continued.
	(l) While I **was studying** in one room of our apartment, my roommate **was having** a party in the other room.	Sometimes the past progressive is used in both parts of a sentence when two actions are in progress simultaneously.
	(m) It **rained** this morning. (n) It **was raining** this morning.	In some cases, the simple past and the past progressive give almost the same meaning, as in (m) and (n).

□ **EXERCISE 21:** Use the SIMPLE PAST or the PAST PROGRESSIVE in the following.

    1. I am sitting in class right now. I (*sit*) _____ *was sitting* _____ in class at this

    exact same time yesterday.

2. I don't want to go to the zoo today because it is raining. The same thing happened yesterday. I (*want, not*) ___didn't want___ to go to the zoo because it (*rain*) ___was raining___.

3. I (*call*) ___called___ Roger at nine last night, but he (*be, not*) ___wasn't___ at home. He (*study*) ___was studying___ at the library.

4. I (*hear, not*) ___didn't hear___ the thunder during the storm last night because I (*sleep*) ___were sleeping___.

5. It was beautiful yesterday when we went for a walk in the park. The sun (*shine*) ___was shining___. A cool breeze (*blow*) ___was blowing___. The birds (*sing*) ___were singing___.

6. My brother and sister (*argue*) ___were arguing___ about something when I (*walk*) ___were walking___ into the room.

7. I got a package in the mail. When I (*open*) ___were opening___ it, I (*find*) ___found___ a surprise.

8. Tommy went to his friends' house, but the boys (*be, not*) ___weren't___ there. They (*play*) ___were playing___ soccer in the vacant lot down the street.

9. Stanley (*climb*) ___was climbing___ the stairs when he (*trip*) ___triped___ and (*fall*) ___fell___. Luckily, he (*hurt, not*) ___didn't hurt___ himself.

10. While Mrs. Emerson (*read*) ___was reading___ the little boy a story, he (*fall*) ___fell___ asleep, so she (*close*) ___closed___ the book and quietly (*tiptoe*) ___tiptoed___ out of the room.

11. I really enjoyed my vacation last January. While it (*snow*) ___was snowing___ in Iowa, the sun (*shine*) ___was shining___ in Florida. While you (*shovel*) ___were shoveling___ snow in Iowa, I (*lie*) ___were lying___ on the beach in Florida.

12. While Ted (*shovel*) ___was shoveling___ snow from his driveway yesterday, his wife (*bring*) ___brought___ him a cup of hot chocolate.

☒ **EXERCISE 22:** Use the SIMPLE PAST or the PAST PROGRESSIVE.

1. I (*have, almost*) almost had a car accident last night. I (*drive*) was driving down Washington Avenue when suddenly I (*see*) saw a car in my lane. It (*come*) was coming right at my car. I (*step*) stepped on the brakes and (*swerve*) swerved to the right. The other car (*miss, just*) just missed my car by about an inch.

2. Ten years ago, the government (*decide*) decided to begin a food program. At that time, many people in the rural areas of the country (*starve*) was starving due to several years of drought.

3. It was my first day of class. I (*find, finally*) finally found the right room. The room (*be, already*) was already full of students. On one side of the room, students (*talk, busily*) were talking loudly to each other in Spanish. Other students (*speak*) were speaking Japanese, and some (*converse*) were conversing in Arabic. It sounded like the United Nations. Some of the students, however, (*sit, just*) just sitting quietly by themselves. I (*choose*) chose an empty seat in the last row and (*sit*) sat down. In a few minutes, the teacher (*walk*) walked into the room and all the multilingual conversation (*stop*) stopped.

4. A: (*Hear, you*) Did you hear what she just said?
   B: No, I (*listen, not*) wasn't listening. I (*think*) was thinking about something else.

5. A: Why weren't you at the meeting?
   B: I (*wait*) was waiting for an overseas call from my family.

6. A: I'm sure you met Carol Jones at the party last night.
   B: I don't remember her. What (*wear, she*) was she wearing? or did she wear?

7. A: What's wrong with your foot?

   B: I (step) _____Stepped_____ on a bee while I (run) ____was____ (con on)

   _____running_____ barefoot through the grass. It (sting) _____

   _____stung_____ me.

8. A: How (break, you) ____did you break____ your arm?

   B: I (slip) _____Slipped_____ on the ice while I (cross) ____was____

   _____crossing_____ the street in front of the dorm.

1–14 USING EXPRESSIONS OF PLACE WITH PROGRESSIVE TENSES

(a) Kay *is studying **in her room***. (b) Kay *is **in her room** studying*. (c) Jack *was **in bed** reading* a book when I came.	An expression of place can sometimes come between the auxiliary ***be*** and the ***-ing*** verb in a progressive tense, as in (b) and (c).

☒ **EXERCISE 23:** In the following, change the position of the expression of place.

1. Sally is listening to music in her room. → *Sally is in her room listening to music*.
2. Roy is taking a nap on the couch.
3. Anita was attending a conference in England last month.
4. The teacher is correcting papers at her desk.
5. Some of the students were late to class because they were playing soccer at the park.

Complete the following: Use the PRESENT PROGRESSIVE or the PAST PROGRESSIVE. Use the expression of place in parentheses.

6. A: Where's Joan? (*at the library*)

   B: _____ ***She's at the library studying for a test.*** _____

7. A: Is Mark here? (*upstairs*)

   B: Yes. _He's standing beside upstairs_

8. A: Have you seen Professor Marx? (*in her office*)

   B: Yes. _I ___ ___ professor Marx in her office_

9. A: Where's your mother, Jimmy? (*in the kitchen*)

   B: _My mother is cooking in the kitchen_

10. A: Ahmed was absent yesterday. Where was he? (*at home*)

    B: _He was staying home._

11. A: Was Mr. Rivera out of town last week? (*in New York*)

    B: Yes. _he was in NewYork to visit his parents_

Add expressions of place between **be** *and the* **-ing** *verb.*

12. My sister is visiting some relatives. → *My sister is in Chicago visiting some relatives.*
13. I'm back to work now, but a month ago I was lying in the sun.
14. We are studying English grammar.
15. No one could see the thief because he was hiding from the police.
16. When I saw Diana, she was trying to find out what she was supposed to do.

☐ **EXERCISE 24:** Come to class prepared to do a pantomime. While you are doing your pantomime, the rest of the class will try to determine what you are doing and then, when you are finished, will describe what you did, step by step.

Examples of subjects for a pantomime:

   (a) threading a needle and sewing on a button
   (b) washing dishes, and perhaps breaking one
   (c) bowling
   (d) reading a newspaper while eating breakfast

(To the teacher: Suggested time limit for each pantomime: two minutes. In all, each pantomime and the oral description should take no more than four or five minutes. The intention is that a few pantomimes be presented each day for the rest of the time spent working on verb tenses.)

☐ **EXERCISE 25—WRITTEN:** In writing, describe one or more of the pantomimes that are performed by your classmates. Give a title to the pantomime, and identify the pantomimist. Use a few "time words" to show the order in which the actions were performed; e.g., *first, next, then, after that, before, when, while.*

1-15 PRESENT PERFECT

(time?)	(a) They **have moved** into a new apartment. (b) **Have** you ever **visited** Mexico? (c) I **have** already **seen** that movie. (d) I **have** never **seen** snow.	The present perfect expresses the idea that something happened (or never happened) *before now, at an unspecified time in the past.* The exact time it happened is not important. If there is a specific mention of time, the simple past is used: *I saw that movie last night.*
	(e) We **have had** four tests so far this semester. (f) I **have written** my wife a letter every other day for the last two weeks. (g) I **have met** many people since I came here in June. (h) I **have flown** on an airplane many times.	The present perfect also expresses the *repetition of an activity before now.* The exact time of each repetition is not important.
	(i) I **have been** here *since seven o'clock.* (j) We **have been** here *for two weeks.* (k) I **have had** this same pair of shoes *for three years.* (l) I **have liked** cowboy movies ever *since I was a child.* (m) I **have known** him *for many years.*	The present perfect also, when used with **for** or **since**, expresses a situation that *began in the past and continues to the present.* In the examples, notice the difference between **since** and **for**: **since** + a particular time **for** + a duration of time

□ **EXERCISE 26:** Use the SIMPLE PAST or the PRESENT PERFECT. In some sentences, either tense is possible but the meaning is different.

1. I (*attend, not*) __*haven't attended*__ any parties since I came here.

2. Al (*go*) __went__ to a party at Sally's apartment last Saturday night.

3. Bill (*arrive*) __arrived__ here three days ago.

4. Bill (*be*) __has been__ here since the 22nd.

5. Try not to be absent from class again for the rest of the term. You (*miss, already*) __have missed__ too many classes. You (*miss*) __missed__ two classes just last week.

6. Last January, I (*see*) __saw__ snow for the first time in my life.

7. In her whole lifetime, Anna (*see, never*) __has never seen__ snow.

8. I (*know*) __have known__ Greg Adams for ten years.

9. So far this week, I (*have*) __have had__ two tests and a quiz.

10. Up to now, Professor Williams (*give*) __have given__ our class five tests.

□ **EXERCISE 27—ORAL (BOOKS CLOSED):** Answer the question in a complete sentence.

Example: How many tests have you taken since the beginning of the (*semester*)?

Response: I have taken (*three, several, many*) tests since the beginning of the (*semester*). OR: I haven't taken any tests since the beginning of the (*semester*).

1. How many books have you bought since the beginning of the (*semester*)?
2. How many letters have you gotten so far this month/week?
3. How many letters have you written since the beginning of the month/week?
4. How many questions have I asked so far?
5. How many times have you flown in an airplane?
6. How many people have you met since you came here?

7. How many classes have you missed since the beginning of the (*semester*)?
8. How many cups of coffee have you had since you got up this morning?
9. How many classes have you had so far today?
10. How many times have you eaten (*your native*) food/eaten at a restaurant since you came here?

☐ **EXERCISE 28:** Complete the sentences with any appropriate time expressions.

1. Today is _____the 14th of June_____. I bought this book _____two weeks_____ ago.

   I have had this book since _____June 1_____.

   I have had this book for _____two weeks_____.

2. I have a pen. I bought it _____two months_____ ago.

   I have had this pen for _____two months_____.

   I have had this pen since _____july 7ᵗʰ_____.

3. Today is _____the 7ᵗʰ of September_____. I moved to this city _____nine months ago_____.

   I have been in this city since _____October 11ᵗʰ 1992_____.

   I have been here for _____9 months_____.

4. It is 19_93_. I started going to school in 19_71_.

   I have been a student for _____twenty-two years_____.

   I have been a student since _____1971_____.

5. I first met our teacher _____in 1990_____.

   I have known her/him for _____three years_____.

   I have known her/him since _____1990_____.

☐ **EXERCISE 29—ORAL (BOOKS CLOSED):** Answer the questions in complete sentences.

To the teacher: Following is an example of a possible exchange.

To Student **A:** *When did you come to (this city/country)?*
--I came here on June 2nd.

To Student **B:** *How long has (Student A) been here?*
--He/she has been here for two weeks.
Or, using **since**?
--He/she has been here since June 2nd.

1. **A.** When did you arrive (*in this city/country*)? **B.** How long has (*he/she*) been here?

2. **A:** When did you get to class today? **B:** How long has (*he/she*) been in class?

3. **A:** What time did you get up this morning? **B:** How long has (. . .) been up?

4. Who in this class owns a car/bicycle? **A:** When did you buy it? **B:** How long has (. . .) had a car/bicycle?

5. Who is wearing a watch? **A:** When did you get it? **B:** How long has (. . .) had his/her watch?

6. Who is married? **A:** When did you get married? **B:** How long has (. . .) been married?

7. **A:** Do you know (. . .)? When did you meet him/her? **B:** How long has (. . .) known (. . .)?

8. **A:** Is that your pen/notebook/pencil sharpener? When did you buy it? **B:** How long has (. . .) had his/her pen/notebook/pencil sharpener?

□ **EXERCISE 30—ORAL (BOOKS CLOSED):** To practice irregular past participles, begin your response with ''I have never . . . .''

    Example: see that movie
    Response: I've never seen that movie.

1. drive a truck
2. buy an airplane
3. read that book
4. break a window
5. draw a picture of yourself
6. ride a horse
7. eat paper
8. teach English
9. catch a butterfly
10. make apple pie
11. win a lottery
12. fly an airplane
13. sleep in a tent
14. write a letter to the President of the United States
15. lose your wallet
16. have a car accident
17. speak to (*a local personage*)
18. steal anything
19. fall off a mountain
20. bring a friend to class
21. hold a snake
22. feed a lion
23. build a house
24. forget your name
25. wear a kimono
26. drink Turkish coffee
27. understand Einstein's theory of relativity
28. leave your umbrella at a restaurant

□ **EXERCISE 31—ORAL (BOOKS CLOSED):** *Student A:* Ask a question beginning with "Have you ever . . . ." *Student B:* Answer the question.

Example: break your arm.
Student A: Have you ever broken your arm?
Student B: Yes, I have. OR: No, I haven't.

1. climb a mountain
2. write a book
3. be in (*Japan*)
4. tell a lie
5. smoke a cigar
6. ride a motorcycle
7. teach (*a particular subject*)
8. see a ghost
9. meet (. . .)'s parents
10. give a speech in English
11. eat (*Thai*) food
12. study biology
13. play a violin
14. go to (*a particular landmark in this city*)
15. walk on the moon
16. watch (*a particular TV show*)
17. take a course in chemistry
18. drive (*a particular kind of car*)
19. fall asleep during class
20. have (*a particular kind of food*)

□ **EXERCISE 32—ORAL:** *Have* and *has* (used as auxiliary verbs, not as main verbs) are usually contracted with personal pronouns in both speaking and informal writing. *Have* and *has* are often contracted with nouns and other words in informal speaking but not in writing. (See Appendix 1, Chart A-8.) Practice pronouncing contracted *have* and *has* in the following sentences.

1. You've been there. They've been there. She's been there. We've all been there.
2. Mary has never been there. → *"Mary's" never been there.*
3. The weather has been nice lately.
4. My neighbors have asked me over for dinner.
5. The teacher has never eaten hot Vietnamese food.
6. The teacher has a red tie. (*No contraction;* **has** *is the main verb.*)
7. My parents have lived in the same house for over thirty years.
8. My parents have a house.
9. Where have you been?
10. What have you done with my books?

☒ **EXERCISE 33:** Use the SIMPLE PAST or the PRESENT PERFECT.

1. What (*learn, you*) _have you learned_ since you (*come*) _came_ here? How many new friends (*make, you*) _have you made_ ? I hope you (*meet, already*) _have already met_ a lot of interesting people.

2. Since classes began, I (*have, not*) _haven't had_ much free time. I (*have*) _have had_ several big tests to study for.

3. Last night my roommate and I (*have*) _had_ some free time, so we (*go*) _went_ to a show.

4. I admit that I (*get★*) _have gotten_ older since I last (*see*) _saw_ you, but with any luck at all, I (*get, also*) _also got_ wiser.

5. The science of medicine (*advance*) _advanced_ a great deal in the nineteenth century.

6. Since the beginning of the twentieth century, medical scientists (*make*) _have made_ many important discoveries.

7. Libraries today are different from those in the 1800s. For example, the contents of libraries (*change*) _have changed_ greatly through the years. In the 1800s, libraries (*be*) _was_ simply collections of books. However, today most libraries (*become*) _have become_ multimedia centers that contain tapes, computers,

---

★COMPARE:

(a) I **have gotten** (British: **have got**) four letters so far this week.	In (a): **have gotten** (**have got**) is present perfect.
(b) I **have got** a problem.	In (b): **have got** is NOT present perfect. In (b), **have got** means **have**: *I've got a problem.* = *I have a problem.* The expression **have got** is common in informal spoken English. Its meaning is present; it has no past form.

Complete the following by writing two sentences. Use the PRESENT PERFECT PROGRESSIVE in the first sentence; then make another sentence that might typically follow in this situation.

4. The baby is crying. She . . . *has been crying for almost ten minutes. I wonder what's wrong.*

5. It's raining. It _has been raining since six o'clock this morning_ . _I wish that it stops soon ._

6. I'm studying. I _have been studying for three o'clock . I can't stop my studing right now because I have a test in tomorrow —_

7. I'm waiting for my friend. I _have been waiting for my friend for two hours . I think I should phone to his office ._

8. Bob is sitting in the waiting room. He _have been sitting in the waiting room all this morning . Perhaps he want to meet me this is a important person_

☒ **EXERCISE 35:** Use the **PRESENT PERFECT** or the **PRESENT PERFECT PROGRESSIVE**. In some sentences, either tense may be used with little or no change in meaning.

1. It (*snow*) _has been snowing_ all day. I wonder when it will stop.

2. We (*have*) _have had_ three major snowstorms so far this winter. I wonder how many more we will have.

3. It's ten P.M. I (*study*) _have been studying_ for two hours and probably won't finish until midnight.

4. I (*write*) _have written_ them three times, but I still haven't received a reply.

5. I (*live*) _have lived_ _or (have been living)_ here since last March.

6. The telephone (*ring*) _has rung_ four times in the last hour, and each time it has been for my roommate.

7. The telephone (*ring*) _has been ringing_ for almost a minute. Why doesn't someone answer it?

8. The little boy is dirty from head to foot because he (*play*) _has been playing_ in the mud. _(but easy)_

perfect

1. A: (*Be, you*) _have been being_ able to reach Bob on the phone
   yet?

   B: Not yet. I (*try*) _have been trying_ for the last twenty
   minutes, but the line (*be*) _has been_ busy.

2. A: Hi, Jenny. I (*see, not*) _haven't seen_ you for weeks.
   What (*do, you*) _have you been doing_ lately?

   B: Studying.

3. A: What are you going to order for dinner?

   B: Well, I (*have, never*) _have never had_ pizza, so I think I'll
   order that.

4. A: What's the matter? Your eyes are red and puffy. (*Cry, you*) _Why_
   have you cried ?

   B: No. I just finished peeling some onions.

5. A: Dr. Jones is a good teacher. How long (*be, he*) _have he been_
   at the university?

   B: He (*teach*) _have been teaching_ here for twenty-five years.

☐ **EXERCISE 37—ORAL/WRITTEN:** Complete the following with your own words.

1. . . . since 8 o'clock this morning.
   → *I have been sitting in class since 8 o'clock this morning.*
   I have had three classes since 8 o'clock this morning.
2. . . . since I came to . . . .
3. . . . since 19 . . . (*year*).
4. . . . since (*month*).
5. . . . since (*day*).
6. . . . since . . . o'clock this morning/afternoon/evening.
7. . . . since the beginning of the 20th century.
8. . . . since . . . .

1-17 PAST PERFECT

	(a) My parents **had** already **eaten** by the time I got home. (b) Until yesterday, I **had** never **heard** about it. (c) The thief simply walked in. Someone **had forgotten** to lock the door.	The past perfect expresses an activity that was *completed before another activity or time in the past.*
	(d) Sam **had** already **left** *when* we got there. (e) Sam **had left** *before* we got there. (f) Sam **left** *before* we got there. (g) *After* the guests **had left**, I went to bed. (h) *After* the guests **left**, I went to bed.	In (d): *First*: Sam left. *Second*: We got there.★ If either **before** or **after** is used in the sentence, the past perfect is often not necessary because the time relationship is already clear. The simple past may be used, as in (f) and (h). Note: (e) and (f) have the same meaning; (g) and (h) have the same meaning.

★COMPARE: Sam **left** *when* we got there. = *First*: We got there.
    Second: Sam left.

1-18 PAST PERFECT PROGRESSIVE

	(i) The police **had been looking** for the criminal *for* two years before they caught him. (j) The patient **had been waiting** in the emergency room *for* almost an hour before a doctor finally treated her. (k) He finally came at six o'clock. I **had been waiting** for him *since* four-thirty.	The past perfect progressive emphasizes the *duration* of an activity that was *in progress before another activity or time in the past.*
	(l) When Judy got home, her hair was still wet because she **had been swimming**. (m) Her eyes were red because she **had been crying**.	This tense also may express an activity *in progress recent to another time or activity in the past.*

□ EXERCISE 38—ORAL: *Had* (used as an auxiliary verb, not a main verb) is usually contracted with personal pronouns in both speaking and informal writing. *Had* is often contracted with nouns and other words in informal speaking but not in writing. (See Appendix 1, Chart A-8.) Practice pronouncing contracted *had* in the following sentences.

1. We'd never seen it before. He'd never seen it. They'd never seen it.
2. I'd never seen it before. I'd like to see it again.*
3. We got home late. The children had already fallen asleep.
4. My roommates had finished dinner by the time I got home.
5. My roommates had dinner early.
6. We couldn't cross the river. The flood had washed away the bridge.
7. You were at Jim's at eight. Where had you been before that?
8. Who had been there before you?

□ EXERCISE 39: Use the SIMPLE PAST or the PAST PERFECT. Are there some blanks where either tense is possible?

1. He (be) _had been / was_ a newspaper reporter before he (become) _became_ a businessman.

2. I (feel) _felt_ a little better after I (take) _had taken / took_ the medicine.

3. I was late. The teacher (give, already) _had already given_ a quiz (immediately after) when I (get) _got_ to class.

4. The anthropologist (leave) _left_ the village when she (collect) _had collected_ enough data. (= tài liệu, = tiền từ để biết)

5. It was raining hard, but by the time class (be) _was_ over, the rain (stop) _had stopped_.

□ EXERCISE 40: Use the SIMPLE PAST or the PAST PERFECT.

1. Class (begin, already) _had already begun_ by the time I (get) _got_ there, so I (take, quietly) _quietly took_ a seat in the back.

---

*COMPARE: *I'd been = I had been* ('d + past participle = past perfect)
          I'd like = I would like ('d + simple form = *would*)

2. Millions of years ago, dinosaurs (*roam*) _roamed_ the earth, but they (*become*) _had become_ extinct by the time humankind first (*appear*) _appeared_.

3. I (*see, never*) _had never seen_ any of Picasso's paintings before I (*visit*) _visited_ the art museum.

4. I almost missed my plane. All of the other passengers (*board, already*) _had already boarded_ by the time I (*get*) _got_ there.

5. Yesterday at a restaurant, I (*see*) _saw_ Pam Donnelly, an old friend of mine. I (*see, not*) _had not seen_ her in years. At first, I (*recognize, not*) _didn't recognize_ her because she (*lose*) _had lost_ at least fifty pounds.

☐ **EXERCISE 41:** Use the **PRESENT PERFECT PROGRESSIVE** or the **PAST PERFECT PROGRESSIVE.**

1. It is midnight. I (*study*) _have been studying_ for five straight hours. No wonder I'm getting tired.

2. It was midnight. I (*study*) _had been studying_ for five straight hours. No wonder I was getting tired.

3. Jack suddenly realized that the teacher was asking him a question. He couldn't answer because he (*daydream*) _had been daydreaming_ for the last ten minutes.

4. Wake up! You (*sleep*) _have been sleeping_ long enough. It's time to get up.

5. At least two hundred people were waiting in line to buy tickets to the game. Some of them (*stand*) _had been standing_ in line for more than four hours. We decided not to try to get tickets for ourselves.

☐ **EXERCISE 42:** Discuss the meaning of the verb forms by reading the following pairs of sentences and then answering the question.

1. a. Dan was leaving the room when I walked in.
   b. Sam had left the room when I walked in.
   QUESTION: *Who did I run into when I walked into the room?*
   (ANSWER: Dan)

2. a. When the rain stopped, Gloria was riding her bicycle to work.
   b. When the rain stopped, Paul rode his bicycle to work.
   QUESTION: *Who got wet on the way to work?*

3. a. Dick went to the store because he was running out of food.
   b. Ann went to the store because she had run out of food.
   QUESTION: *Who is better at planning ahead?*

4. a. Ms. Lincoln taught at this school for nine years.
   b. Mr. Sanchez has taught at this school for nine years.
   QUESTION: *Who is teaching at this school now?*

5. a. Alice was walking to the door when the doorbell rang.
   b. George walked to the door when the doorbell rang.
   QUESTION: *Who expected the doorbell to ring?*

6. a. When I got there, Marie had eaten.
   b. When I got there, Joe ate.
   QUESTION: *Who was still hungry when I got there?*

7. a. Don lived in Chicago for five years.
   b. Carlos has been living in Chicago for five years.
   QUESTION: *Who still lives in Chicago?*

8. a. Jane put some lotion on her face because she had been lying in the sun.
   b. Sue put some lotion on her face because she was lying in the sun.
   QUESTION: *Who put lotion on her face after she stood up?*

9. a. I looked across the street. Mr. Fox was waving at me.
   b. I looked across the street. Mrs. Cook waved at me.
      QUESTION: *Who began to wave at me before I looked across the street?*

□ **EXERCISE 43—ORAL (BOOKS CLOSED):** From the given situation, make up a "chain story." One person begins the story; then others continue the story in turn using certain cue words.

Example: (Pierre) had a terrible day yesterday. The trouble began early in the morning. His alarm clock rang at 7:00.

Cue: *when*

Student A: When his alarm clock rang, he got out of bed and stepped on a snake. He was nearly frightened to death, but the snake slithered away without biting him.

Cue: *after*

Student B: After the snake left, Pierre got dressed in a hurry and ran downstairs to have breakfast.

Cue: *while*

Student C: While he was running downstairs, he fell and broke his arm.

etc.

Possible situations to begin chain stories.

1. (. . .) had a terrible day yesterday.
2. (. . .) had a great vacation last summer.
3. (. . .) got into a lot of trouble a couple of days ago.
4. (. . .) had a really interesting experience last week.
5. (*Make up the beginning of a story.*)

Cue words (which may be used in any order):

1. when
2. after
3. before
4. while
5. by the time
6. as soon as
7. already
8. never
9. then
10. next
11. after that
12. later
13. for (*a length of time*)
14. since
15. because

☐ **EXERCISE 44—WRITTEN:** Break into groups and sit in a circle. Take out a piece of paper and write the following sentence, using the name of the person sitting to your right in place of (. . .).

(. . .) *had a strange experience yesterday.*

Then write one or two additional sentences, and pass your paper to the person sitting to your left, who will continue the story. Continue to pass the papers to the left until everyone in the group has had a chance to write part of the story.

Then decide which of the stories in your group is the most entertaining or the most interesting. As a group, make any necessary corrections in grammar or spelling. Read it aloud to the rest of the class.

(Note: You may wish to establish a time limit for each contribution to the story. When the time limit is up, each person must pass his/her paper even if it contains an unfinished sentence. The next person will then have to finish the sentence and continue writing the story.)

1–19 SIMPLE FUTURE/*BE GOING TO*

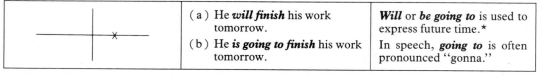

	(a) He *will finish* his work tomorrow.	*Will* or *be going to* is used to express future time.★
	(b) He *is going to finish* his work tomorrow.	In speech, *going to* is often pronounced "gonna."

★The use of *shall* with *I* or *we* to express future time is possible but uncommon in American English. *Shall* is used much more frequently in British than in American English.

☐ **EXERCISE 45—ORAL:** *Will* is usually contracted with personal pronouns in both speaking and informal writing. *Will* is often contracted with nouns and with other pronouns in speaking but not in writing. Practice pronouncing contracted *will* in the following sentences.

1. I'll come. He'll come. You'll come.
2. She'll help us. They'll help us too.
3. I'm sure we'll do well on the test.
4. It'll probably rain tomorrow.
5. Bob will (*Bob'll*) be here soon.
6. The weather will be hot in August.
7. Mary will come tomorrow.
8. Bill will be here too.
9. The children will be home at 3:00.
10. Who will be at the meeting?
11. Where will you be around five?
12. How long will Tom be here?
13. Nobody will recognize you in that wig.
14. That will be a lot of fun.
15. What will you do?

1–20 WILL VERSUS BE GOING TO

To express a PREDICTION—either *WILL* or *BE GOING TO* is used:	
(a) According to the weather report, it *will be* cloudy tomorrow. (b) According to the weather report, it *is going to be* cloudy tomorrow. (c) Be careful! You *'ll hurt* yourself! (d) Watch out! You *'re going to* hurt yourself!	When the speaker is making a prediction (a statement about something s/he thinks will be true or will occur in the future), either *will* or *be going to* is possible. There is no difference in meaning between (a) and (b). There is no difference in meaning between (c) and (d).

To express a PRIOR PLAN—only *BE GOING TO* is used:	
(e) A: Why did you buy this paint? B: I*'m going to paint* my bedroom tomorrow.	When the speaker is expressing a prior plan (something the speaker intends to do in the future because in the past s/he has made a plan or decision to do it), only *be going to* is used.* In (e): Speaker B has made a prior plan. She decided to paint her bedroom last week. She intends to paint her bedroom tomorrow.
(f) I talked to Bob yesterday. He is tired of taking the bus to work. He*'s going to buy* a car. That's what he told me.	In (f): The speaker knows Bob's intention to buy a car. Bob made the decision in the past and he intends to act on this decision in the future. *Will* is not appropriate in (e) and (f).

To express WILLINGNESS—only *WILL* is used:	
(g) A: The phone's ringing. B: I*'ll get* it.	In (g): Speaker B is saying: "I am willing, I am happy to get the phone." He is not making a prediction. He has made no prior plan to answer the phone. He is, instead, volunteering to answer the phone and uses *will* to show his willingness.
(h) A: I don't understand this problem. B: Ask your teacher about it. She*'ll help* you.	In (h): Speaker B feels sure about the teacher's willingness to help. *Be going to* is not appropriate in (g) and (h).

*COMPARE:

Situation 1: *A: Are you busy this evening?*
          *B: Yes. **I'm going to meet** Jack at the library at seven. We**'re going to study** together.*

In situation 1, only *be going to* is possible. The speaker has a prior plan, so he uses *be going to*.

Situation 2: *A: Are you busy this evening?*
          *B: Well, I really haven't made any plans. **I'll eat/I'm going to eat** dinner, of course. And then **I'll***
             ***probably watch/I'm probably going to watch** TV for a little while.*

In situation 2, either *will* or *be going to* is possible. Speaker B has not planned his evening. He is "predicting" his evening (rather than stating any prior plans), so he may use either *will* or *be going to*.

☒ **EXERCISE 46:** Use *WILL* and/or *BE GOING TO* with the verb in parentheses.

PART I: EXPRESSING PREDICTIONS

1. Sue (*graduate*) _will graduate/is going to graduate_ in June. After that, she (*begin*) _will begin/is going to begin_ work at an electronics firm.

2. Fred (*be*) _will be / is going to be_ at the meeting tomorrow. I think Jane (*come*) _will come / is gong to come_ too.

3. A: Can you give Ed a message for me?
   B: Sure. I (*see, probably*) _will probably see_ him at the meeting this evening.

4. The damage we do to our environment today (*affect*) _will be / is going to be_ the quality of life of future generations.

5. A: Mr. Swan (*be, not*) _will not be / is not going to be_ here next term. He has resigned. Who (*be*) _'ll be / is going to be_ the new teacher? Do you know?
   B: Yes. Mary Jefferson. Ms. Jefferson (*teach*) _is going to teach / will_ the same courses Mr. Swan taught: English, algebra, and geometry. I (*be*) _will be / am going to be_ in her algebra class. Do you know which algebra class you (*be*) _'ll / are going to be_ in next term?

PART II: EXPRESSING PRIOR PLAN VS. WILLINGNESS:
Use *be going to* if you think the speaker is expressing a prior plan. If you think there is no prior plan, use *will*.

6. A: This letter is in French, and I don't speak a word of French. Can you help me?
   B: Sure. I (*translate*) _will translate_ it for you.

7. A: Do you want to go shopping with me? I (*go*) _am going to go_ to the shopping mall downtown.
   B: Sure. What time do you want to leave?

8. A: This light doesn't work. The bulb is probably burned out. Where are the new light bulbs?

   B: I (*get*) _will get_ one for you.

9. A: It's cold in here.

   B: I agree. I (*turn*) _will turn_ the heater on.

   A: That's a good idea.

10. A: I (*enroll*) _am going to enroll_ in the community college next spring.

    B: Oh? I didn't know you wanted to go back to school.

    A: I need to sharpen my skills so I can get a better job. I (*take*) _am going to take_ a course in word processing.

11. A: Brrr. Who turned up the air conditioner? It's really cold in here. My nose is cold and my fingers are cold.

    B: I (*make*) _will make_ you a hot cup of tea.

    A: Thanks. That sounds good.

12. A: Oh, oh! I've spilled coffee on my shirt.

    B: Just a minute. I (*get*) _will get_ a damp cloth for you.

13. A: What do you want to be when you grow up?

    B: I (*be*) _am going to be_ an astronaut.

    A: Good for you!

14. A: Do you mind if I turn the TV off? I (*place*) _am going to place_ a long distance call, and it's hard to hear if the TV is on.

    B: No, that's fine. I wasn't watching it anyway.

15. A: Who wants to erase the board? Are there any volunteers?

    B: I (*do*) _will do_ it!

    C: I (*do*) _will do_ it!

    D: No, no! I (*do*) _will do_ it!

16. A: Why do you have an eraser in your hand?

    B: I (*erase*) _am going to erase_ the board.

1–21 EXPRESSING THE FUTURE IN TIME CLAUSES

(a) Bob will come soon. *When Bob comes*, we will see him. (b) Linda is going to leave soon. *Before she leaves*, she is going to finish her work. (c) I will get home at 5:30. *After I get home*, I will eat dinner. (d) The taxi will arrive soon. *As soon as it arrives*, we'll be able to leave for the airport. (e) They are going to come soon. I'll wait here *until they come*.	In (a): "When Bob comes" is a time clause.* ***when + subject + verb = a time clause*** ***Will*** or ***be going to*** is NOT used in a time clause. The meaning of the clause is future, but the simple present tense is used.

	A time clause begins with such words as ***when***, ***before***, ***after***, ***as soon as***, ***until*** and includes a subject and a verb. The time clause can come either at the beginning of the sentence or in the second part of the sentence:
	      When he comes, we'll see him.
	      OR:
	      We'll see him *when he comes*.

(f) I will go to bed *after I finish my work*. (g) I will go to bed *after I have finished my work*.	Occasionally, the present perfect is used in a time clause, as in (g). Examples (f) and (g) have the same meaning. The present perfect stresses the completion of the act in the time clause before the other act occurs in the future.

*A "time clause" is an adverb clause. See Chart 8-5 for more information.

☒ **EXERCISE 47:** Use *WILL/BE GOING TO* or the SIMPLE PRESENT. (In this exercise, both *will* and *be going to* are possible when a future tense is necessary, with little or no difference in meaning.)

1. Peter is going to leave in half an hour. He (*finish*) _____ *will finish /* _____ *is going to finish* _____ all of his work before he (*leave*) _____ *leaves* _____ .

2. I'm going to eat lunch at 12:30. After I (*eat*) _____ , I (*take, probably*) *will probably take / am probably* ~~going to take~~ a nap.

3. I'll get home around six. When I (*get*) _____ *get* _____ home, I (*call*) _____ *will* _____ Sharon.

4. I'm going to watch a TV program at nine. Before I (*watch*) _____ *watch* _____ that program, I (*write*) *'ll write / am going to write* a letter to my parents.

5. Gary will come soon. I (wait) *'ll wait / am going to wait*

   here until he (come) *come*.

6. I'm sure it will stop raining soon. As soon as the rain (stop) *stop (or has stopped)*

   _____, I (walk) *'ll walk / am going to walk* to the drugstore

   to get some film.

7. Right now I'm a junior in college. After I (graduate) *graduate*

   with a B.A., I (intend) *intend* to enter graduate school and

   work for an M.A. Perhaps I (go) *am going to go* on for a Ph.D. after I

   (get) *get* my Master's degree.

8. A: How long (stay, you) *will you stay / are going to stay* in this country?

   B: I (plan) *plan* to be here for about

   one more year. I (hope) *hope* to graduate a year from this

   June.

   A: What (do, you) *will you do* after you

   (leave) *leave*?

   B: I (return) *will return* home and (get)

   get a job. How about you?

   A: I (be) *will be* here for at least two more years

   before I (return) *return* home and (get) *get*

   a job.

☐ **EXERCISE 48—ORAL:** Complete the following with your own words. Use *WILL/BE
   GOING TO* and the SIMPLE PRESENT, as appropriate.

   on paper

   1. When I . . . this afternoon, I . . . .
      → *When I go downtown this afternoon, I'm going to go to the bank and the post
      office.*
   2. After I . . . tomorrow morning, I . . . .
   3. Tomorrow, I . . . before I . . . .
   4. I . . . when . . . next year.
   5. As soon as class . . . , I . . . .
   6. I . . . until my friend . . . .
   7. When I . . . tomorrow, I . . . .

1–22 USING THE PRESENT PROGRESSIVE AND THE SIMPLE PRESENT TO EXPRESS FUTURE TIME

PRESENT PROGRESSIVE	The present progressive may be used to express future time when the idea of the sentence concerns a planned event or definite intention. (COMPARE: A verb such as *rain* is not used in the present progressive to indicate future time because rain is not a planned event.)
(a) My wife has an appointment with a doctor. She *is seeing* Dr. North *next Tuesday*.	
(b) Sam has already made his plans. He *is leaving* *at noon tomorrow*.	
(c) A: What are you going to do this afternoon? B: *After lunch* I *am meeting* a friend of mine. We *are going* shopping. Would you like to come along?	A future meaning for the present progressive tense is indicated either by future time words in the sentence or by the context.
SIMPLE PRESENT	The simple present can also be used to express future time in sentences that concern events that are on a definite schedule or timetable. These sentences usually contain future time words. Only a few verbs are used in this way: e.g., *open, close, begin, end, start, finish, arrive, leave, come, return*.
(d) The museum *opens* at ten tomorrow morning.	
(e) Classes *begin* next week.	
(f) John's plane *arrives* at 6:05 P.M. next Monday.	

☒ **EXERCISE 49:** Indicate the meaning expressed by the italicized verbs by writing *in the future, now,* or *habitually* in the blanks.

1. I *am taking* four courses next semester.   *in the future*

2. I *am taking* four courses this semester.   *now*

3. Students usually *take* four courses every semester.   *habitually*

4. I'll mail this letter at the corner when I *take* Susan home.   F

5. My brother's birthday is next week. I *am giving* him a sweater.   F

6. Shhh. The broadcaster *is giving* the latest news about the crisis in England. I want to hear what she's saying. *big problem*   N

7. When I *graduate*, I'm going to return home.   F

8. When students *graduate*, they receive diplomas.   H

9. I'm tired. I *am going* to bed early tonight.   F

10. When I *am* in New York, I'm going to visit the Museum of Modern Art.   F

11. When I *am* home alone in the evening, I like to read or watch television.   _H_

12. A: Are you busy?
    B: Not really.
    A: What *are* you *doing*?   A: _N_

    B: I'*m writing* a letter to my folks.   B: _N_

    A: When you *finish* your letter, do you want to play a game of chess?   A: _F_

13. A: What *are* you *doing* after class?   A: _F_

    B: I'*m eating* at the cafeteria with Cindy. Do you want to join us?   B: _F_

14. Tony *will arrive* at eight tomorrow evening.   _F_

15. Tony *is going to arrive* at eight tomorrow evening.   _F_

16. Tony *is arriving* at eight tomorrow evening.   _F_

17. Tony *arrives* at eight tomorrow evening.   _F_

18. When Tony *arrives,* we'll have a party.   _F_

1–23 FUTURE PROGRESSIVE

	(a) I will begin to study at seven. You will come at eight. I **will be studying** when you come. (b) Right now I am sitting in class. At this same time tomorrow, I **will be sitting** in class.	The future progressive expresses an activity that will be *in progress at a time in the future*.
7 8	(c) Don't call me at nine because I won't be home. I **am going to be studying** at the library.	The progressive form of **be going to**: **be going to** + **be** + **-ing**
	(d) Don't get impatient. She **will be coming** soon. (e) Don't get impatient. She **will come** soon.	Sometimes there is little or no difference between the future progressive and the simple future, especially when the future event will occur at an indefinite time in the future, as in (d) and (e).

☒ **EXERCISE 50:** Use the FUTURE PROGRESSIVE or the SIMPLE PRESENT.

1. Right now I am attending class. Yesterday at this time, I was attending class. Tomorrow at this time, I (*attend*) _will be attending_ class.

2. Tomorrow I'm going to leave for home. When I (*arrive*) _____ _arrive_ _____ at the airport, my whole family (*wait*) _will be waiting_ _____ for me.

3. When I (*get*) _get_ _____ up tomorrow morning, the sun (*shine*) _will be shining_ _____, the birds (*sing*) _will be still singing_ _____, and my roommate (*lie, still*) _will be lying_ _____ in bed fast asleep.

4. A: When do you leave for Florida?

   B: Tomorrow. Just think. Two days from now I (*lie*) _will be lying_ _____ on the beach in the sun.

   A: Sounds great! I (*think*) _will be thinking_ _____ about you.

5. A: How can I get in touch with you while you're out of town?

   B: I (*stay*) _will be staying / stay_ _____ at the Pilgrim Hotel. You can reach me there.

6. Next year at this time, I (*do*) _will be doing_ _____ exactly what I am doing now. I (*attend*) _will be attending_ _____ school and (*study*) _will be studying_ _____ hard next year.

7. Look at those dark clouds. When class (*be*) _is_ _____ over, it (*rain, probably*) _will probably be raining_.

8. A: Are you going to be in town next Saturday?

   B: No. I (*visit*) _will be visiting_ _____ my aunt in Chicago.

1–24 FUTURE PERFECT

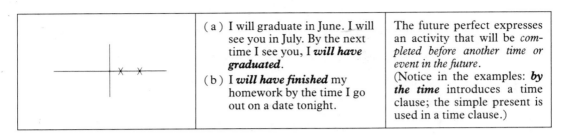

	(a) I will graduate in June. I will see you in July. By the next time I see you, I **will have graduated**. (b) I **will have finished** my homework by the time I go out on a date tonight.	The future perfect expresses an activity that will be *completed before another time or event in the future*. (Notice in the examples: **by the time** introduces a time clause; the simple present is used in a time clause.)

1–25 FUTURE PERFECT PROGRESSIVE *... by 2000. vào năm 2000,*

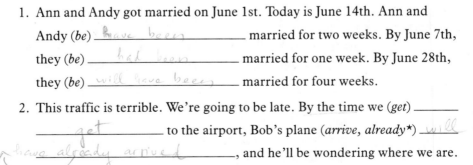

	(c) I will go to bed at ten P.M. He will get home at midnight. At midnight I will be sleeping. I **will have been sleeping** for two hours by the time he gets home.	The future perfect progressive emphasizes the *duration* of an activity that will be *in progress before another time or event in the future*.
	(d) When Professor Jones retires next month, he **will have taught** for 45 years. (e) When Professor Jones retires next month, he **will have been teaching** for 45 years.	Sometimes the future perfect and the future perfect progressive give the same meaning, as in (d) and (e). Also, notice that the activity expressed by either of these two tenses may begin in the past.

□ **EXERCISE 51:** Use any appropriate tense.

1. Ann and Andy got married on June 1st. Today is June 14th. Ann and
   Andy (*be*) _have been_ married for two weeks. By June 7th,
   they (*be*) _had been_ married for one week. By June 28th,
   they (*be*) _will have been_ married for four weeks.

2. This traffic is terrible. We're going to be late. By the time we (*get*) _____
   get to the airport, Bob's plane (*arrive, already*★) _will
   have already arrived_ , and he'll be wondering where we are.

★With the future perfect, **already** has two possible positions: *I will already have finished. I will have already finished.*

3. The traffic was very heavy. By the time we (*get*) _____ got _____ to the airport, Bob's plane (*arrive, already*) _____ had already arrived _____.

4. This morning I came to class at 9:00. Right now it is 10:00, and I am still in class. I (*sit*) _____ have been sitting _____ at this desk for an hour. By 9:30, I (*sit*) _____ had been sitting _____ here for a half an hour. By 11:00, I (*sit*) _____ will have been sitting _____ here for two hours.

5. I'm getting tired of sitting in the car. Do you realize that by the time we arrive in Phoenix, we (*drive*) _____ will have been driving / will have driven _____ for twenty straight hours?

6. Margaret was born in 1950. By the year 2000, she (*live*) _____ will have lived _____ on this earth for 50 years.

7. Go ahead and leave on your vacation. Don't worry about this work. By the time you (*get*) _____ get _____ back, we (*take*) _____ will have taken _____ care of everything.

8. I don't understand how those marathon runners do it! The race began over an hour ago. By the time they reach the finish line, they (*run*) _____ will have been running _____ steadily for more than two hours. I don't think I can run more than two minutes!

9. What? He got married again? At this rate, he (*have*) _____ will have had _____ a dozen wives by the time he (*die*) _____ dies _____.

10. We have been married for a long time. By our next anniversary, we (*be*) _____ will have been _____ married for 43 years.

□ **EXERCISE 52—ORAL/WRITTEN:** What do you think the world will be like a hundred years from now? What changes will have occurred between then and now? Use your imagination and make some predictions. Following are some topics to think about:

1. means of transportation
2. sources of energy
3. population growth
4. food sources
5. extinction of animal species
6. exploration of the oceans; of the earth's interior
7. space exploration; contact with beings from outer space
8. weapon technology
9. role of computers in daily life
10. long-term solutions to today's political crises
11. architecture

12. clothing styles
13. international language
14. international world government
15. international television; international communication via communication satellites

Note: You may wish to make comparisons among the past, the present, and the future. For example: *A hundred years ago, the automobile hadn't been invented. Today it is one of the most common means of transportation and has greatly changed the way people lead their lives. By the year _____, the automobile will have become obsolete. A hundred years from now, people will use small, jet-propelled, wingless flying machines in place of cars.*

☒ **EXERCISE 53:** Discuss the differences (if any) in meaning in the following groups of sentences. Some of the sentences need to be completed to make their meaning clear. *(Adverbial of time)*

1. a. He watches television.
   b. He is watching television.
2. a. I am sitting in class . *right now*
   b. I was sitting in class . . . .
   c. I will be sitting in class . . . .
3. a. I have finished my homework. *by now*
   b. I had finished my homework . *by yesterday .*
   c. I will have finished my homework . . . .
4. a. The students had left before the teacher arrived.
   b. The students left before the teacher arrived. *first activity* (when) *= immediately after*
   c. The students had left (when) the teacher arrived.
   d. The students left (when) the teacher arrived.
   e. The students were leaving (when) the teacher arrived. (when) *the same time*
5. a. I have been waiting for her for two hours.
   b. I had been waiting for her for two hours . . . .
   c. I will have been waiting for her for two hours . *by 8 o'clock today .*
6. a. Ali has been studying Chapter Three.
   b. He has studied Chapter Two.
   c. He studied Chapter Two . . . .
7. a. She has been doing a lot of research on that project.
   b. She has done a lot of research on that project.
8. a. I will study when you come. *(willing)*
   b. I am going to study when you come. *(plan)*
   c. I will be studying when you come.
   d. I am going to be studying when you come.
   e. I will have studied by the time you come.
   f. I will have been studying for two hours by the time you come.
9. a. He worked for that company for two years.
   b. He has been working for that company for two years.

10. a. The train will leave at 10:00 tomorrow morning.
    b. The train is going to leave at 10:00 tomorrow morning.
    c. The train leaves at 10:00 tomorrow morning.
    d. The train is leaving at 10:00 tomorrow morning.

☐ **EXERCISE 54—ORAL (BOOKS CLOSED):** In order to practice verb tenses, answer the questions in complete sentences.

1. What have we been studying? What is one tense we have studied since the beginning of the term? When, to the best of your recollection, did we study it?
2. What else will we have studied in this class by the time the term ends?
3. This class began on (*date*). Had you studied verb tenses before that?
4. We're going to finish studying Chapter 1 on (*day or date*). How long will we have been studying Chapter 1 by that time?
5. What were you doing at this time yesterday? What did you do after that?
6. What are you doing right now? How long have you been doing that?
7. What are you going to be doing at this time tomorrow?
8. What will you be doing tonight at midnight? What were you doing last night at midnight?
9. Where will you be living three years from now? Where were you living three years ago? Can you name one specific thing you did three years ago? Can you name one specific thing you will do three years from now?
10. What places have you been to since you came to (*this city*)? When?
11. Make some generalizations about things you do.
12. What are some things you have done many times since you came here?
13. What are some of the things you have done in your lifetime? When?
14. What have you done that no one else in this class (or in the world?) has ever done?
15. What is the exact place you are sitting right now?
    How long have you been sitting there today?
    How long will you have been sitting there by the time class is over?
    How often do you sit there during class?
    How many times have you sat there?
    Before today, when did you last sit there?
    Had you sat there before that?
    Where were you sitting at this time yesterday?
    Where are you going to be sitting at this time tomorrow?

☐ **EXERCISE 55:** Use any appropriate tense for the verbs in parentheses.

1. John is in my English class. He (*study*) ___is studying___
   English this semester. He (*take, also*) ___is also taking___ some other
   classes. His classes (*begin*) ___begin___ at 9:00 every day.

2. Yesterday John ate breakfast at 8:00. He (*eat, already*) *had already eaten* breakfast when he (*leave*) *left* for class at 8:45. He (*eat, always*) *always eats* breakfast before he (*go*) *goes* to class. I (*eat, not, usually*) *don't usually eat* breakfast before I (*go*) *go* to class. But I (*get, usually*) *usually get* hungry about midmorning. Tomorrow before I (*go*) *go* to class, I (*eat*) *am going to eat* breakfast.

3. John is in class every morning from 9:00 to 12:00. Two days ago, I (*call*) *called* him at 11:30, but I could not reach him because he (*attend*) *was attending* class at that time.

4. Don't try to call John at 11:30 tomorrow morning because he (*attend*) *will be attending* class at that time.

5. Yesterday John took a nap from 1:00 to 2:00. I came at 1:45. When I (*get*) *got* there, John (*sleep*) *was sleeping*. He (*sleep*) *had been sleeping* for 45 minutes by the time I came.

6. Right now John (*take*) *is taking* a nap. He (*fall*) *fell* asleep an hour ago. He (*sleep*) *has been sleeping* for an hour.

7. Three days ago, John (*start*) *started* to read *A Farewell to Arms*, a novel by Ernest Hemingway. It is a long novel. He (*finish, not*) *hasn't finished* reading it yet. He (*read*) *is reading* it because his English teacher assigned it.

8. Since the beginning of the semester, John (*read*) *has read* three novels. Right now he (*read*) *is reading* *A Farewell to Arms*. He (*read*) *has been reading* that novel for the past three days. He (*intend*) *intends* to finish it next week. In his lifetime, he (*read*) *has read* many novels, but this is the first Hemingway novel he (*read, ever*) *has ever read*.

9. Tomorrow, after he (*eat*) *eat* dinner, John (*go*) *will go* to a movie. In other words, he (*eat*) *will has eaten* dinner by the time he (*go*) *goes* to the movie.

□ **EXERCISE 56—ORAL:** Pair up with another student in the class.

STUDENT A:

(1) Use the questions in this exercise to initiate conversation with Student B.
(2) Do not simply read the questions. Look at the text briefly, then look directly at Student B each time you ask a question.
(3) If Student B does not answer fully or if you are interested in getting more information, ask your own questions in addition to those which are suggested.
(4) Pay special attention to verb tense usage in both the questions and the responses.

STUDENT B:

(1) Do not look at the written questions in this exercise. Only Student A should look at the text.
(2) Answer the questions fully. Often your response will consist of more than one sentence.
(3) Answer in complete sentences in order to practice using verb tenses.

1. What is happening in this room?
    What else is happening?
2. What was happening in this room when you walked in today?
    What else was happening?
3. What did you do yesterday? (*Student A: Listen carefully for past tense verbs*
    What else did you do?   *in the responses.*)
    And what else did you do?
4. How long have you been living in (*this city*)?
    How long will you have been living here by the end of (*the semester/term, etc.*)?
5. Where did you eat dinner last night?
    What did you have?
    How was it?
    What did you do after you had eaten?
6. What were you doing at 8 o'clock last night?
    What will you be doing at 8 o'clock tomorrow night?
7. Are you taking any classes besides English?
    How is everything going?
    What are you doing in one of your classes?
8. How long have we been talking to each other?
    What have we been talking about?
9. How do you like living here?
    Have you had any interesting experiences since you came here?
    Have you met any interesting people?
10. What do you think the world will be like when you are seventy years old?

□ **EXERCISE 57—ORAL:** Same as the preceding exercise.

1. What are you doing right now?
   What are you going to be doing for the next ten minutes or so?
2. What did you do last weekend? (*Student A: Listen carefully for past tense*
   What else did you do?   *verbs in the response.*)
   And what else did you do?
3. What is the teacher doing?
   How long has he/she been (*doing that*)?
4. What are you going to do for the rest of today?
   What will you be doing at midnight?
5. What will you have done by the time you go to bed tonight?
6. How long have you been studying English at this school?
   How long had you studied English before you came here?
   What have you been doing outside of class to improve your English?
7. What have we been doing for the past ten minutes or so?
   Why have we been (*doing that*)?
8. What are some of the things you have done since you came to (*this city*)?
9. Have you read a newspaper lately?
   What is happening in the world?
10. What countries have you visited?
    When did you visit (*a particular country*).
    Why did you go there?
    What did you like about that country?
    What did you dislike about that country?
    Are you planning to go back there again someday?

□ **EXERCISE 58—ORAL/WRITTEN:** Before you come to class, think of an interesting, dangerous, or amusing experience you have had. You will then tell that story to a classmate, who will report that experience in a composition.

□ **EXERCISE 59—ORAL:** In a short speech (two or three minutes), summarize an article in a recent newspaper. You may speak from notes if necessary, but your notes should contain no more than fifteen words. Use your notes only for a very brief outline of important information.

□ **EXERCISE 60:** Use any appropriate tense for the verbs in parentheses. In some instances, more than one tense is possible.★

1. A: There is something I have to tell you.

   B: Go ahead. I (*listen*) _am listening_ .

★Your teacher can tell you if one tense is more idiomatic, i.e., more likely to be used by a native speaker.

2. A: Hi, Ann. (*Meet, you*) _Have you met_ my friend, George Smith?

   B: No, I (*have, never*) _I have never had_ the pleasure.

   A: Then let me introduce you.

3. A: Stop! What (*you, do*) _are you doing_ ?

   B: I (*try*) _am trying_ to get this piece of toast out of the toaster. It's stuck.

   A: Well, don't use a knife. You (*electrocute*) _will electrocute_ yourself!

   B: What do you suggest I do?

   A: Unplug it first.

4. A: There's Jack.

   B: Where?

   A: He (*lie*) _is lying_ on the grass under that tree over there.

   B: Oh yes. I (*see*) _see_ him. He (*look, certainly*) _certainly looks_ comfortable. Let's go talk to him.

5. A: (*Take, you*) _Are you taking_ Econ 120 this semester?

   B: No, I _'m not_ .

   A: (*Take, you, ever*) _Have you ever taken_ it?

   B: Yes, I _have_ .

   A: When (*take, you*) _did you take_ it?

   B: Last semester.

   A: Who (*be*) _was_ your professor?

B: Dr. Lee.

A: Oh, I have the same professor. What (*be, he*) _____is he_____ like?

B: He (*be*) _____is_____ very good.

6. A: What's wrong with Chris?

B: While he (*yawn*) _____was yawning_____, a fly (*fly*) _____flew_____ into his mouth.

A: I (*believe, not*) _____don't believe_____ that! You (*kid*) _____are kidding_____ _____!

7. A: I (*go*) _____went_____ to a play last night.

B: (*Be, it*) _____Was it_____ any good?

A: I thought so. I (*enjoy*) _____enjoyed_____ it a lot.

B: What (*see, you*) _____did you see_____?

A: *Arsenic and Old Lace.* I (*see, never*) _____had never seen_____ it before.

B: Oh, I (*see*) _____have seen saw_____ that play too. I (*see*) _____saw_____ it a couple of years ago. It (*be*) _____is_____ good, (*be, not*) _____isn't_____ it?

8. A: I was in your hometown last month. It looked like a nice town. I (*be, never*) _____had never been_____ there before.

B: What (*do, you*) _____were you doing_____ in that part of the country?

A: My wife and I (*drive*) _____I drove_____ _____were driving_____ to Washington, D.C. to visit her family.

9. A: May I borrow some money? My check (*be*) _____was_____ supposed to arrive yesterday, but I still (*receive, not*) _____haven't received_____ it. I (*need*) _____needed_____ to buy a book for one of my classes, but I (*have, not*) _____don't have_____ any money.

B: Sure. I'd be happy to lend you some. How much (*need, you*) _____do you need_____?

A: How about five dollars? Thanks. I (*pay*) _____will pay_____ you back as soon as I (*get*) _____get_____ my check.

10. A: Hello?

   B: Hello. May I speak to Sue?

   A: She (*be, not*) __is not__ in right now. May I take a message?

   B: Yes. This is Art O'Brien. Would you please ask her to meet me at the library this afternoon? I (*sit*) ~~am going to sitting~~ __will be sitting__ at one of the study booths on the second floor.

☐ **EXERCISE 61:** Use any appropriate tense for the verbs in parentheses.

1. My grandfather (*fly, never*) __has never flown__ in an airplane, and he has no intention of ever doing so.

2. Jane isn't here yet. I (*wait*) __have been waiting__ for her since noon, but she still (*arrive, not*) __hasn't arrived__.

3. In all the world, there (*be*) __are__ only 14 mountains that (*reach*) __reach__ above 8,000 meters (26,247 feet).

4. I have a long trip ahead of me tomorrow, so I think I'd better go to bed. But let me say good-bye now because I won't see you in the morning. I (*leave, already*) __will already have left__ by the time you (*get*) __got__ up.

5. Right now we (*have*) __are having__ a heat wave. The temperature (*be*) __has been__ in the upper 90s for the last six days.

6. Last night I (*go*) __went__ to a party. When I (*get*) __got__ there, the room was full of people. Some of them (*dance*) __were dancing__ and others (*talk*) __were talking__. One young woman (*stand*) __was standing__ by herself. I (*meet, never*) __had never met__ her, so I (*introduce*) __introduced__ myself to her.

7. About three yesterday afternoon, Jessica (*lie*) __was lying__ in bed reading a book. Suddenly she (*hear*) __heard__ a

loud noise and (*get*) __got__ up to see what it was. She (*look*) __looked__ out the window. A truck (*back, just*) __had just backed__ into her new car!

8. Next month I have a week's vacation. I (*plan*) __am planning__ to take a trip. First, I (*go*) __am going to go/'ll__ to Madison, Wisconsin, to visit my brother. After I (*leave*) __leave__ Madison, I (*go*) __will go /am going to go__ to Chicago to see a friend who (*study*) __is studying__ at a university there. She (*live*) __has been living__ in Chicago for three years, so she (*know*) __knows__ her way around the city. She (*promise*) __has promised__ to take me to many interesting places. I (*be, never*) __have never been__ in Chicago, so I (*look*) __am looking__ forward to going there.

9. Yesterday while I (*sit*) __was sitting__ in class, I (*get*) __got__ the hiccups. The person who (*sit*) __was sitting__ next to me told me to hold my breath. I (*try*) __tried__ that, but it didn't work. The instructor (*lecture*) __was lecturing__, and I didn't want to interrupt him, so I just sat there trying to hiccup quietly. Finally, after I (*hiccup*) __had been hiccupped__ for almost five minutes, I (*raise*) __raised__ my hand and (*excuse*) __excused__ myself from the class to go get a drink of water.

10. The weather has been terrible lately. It (*rain*) __has been raining__ off and on for two days, and the temperature (*drop*) __has dropped__ at least twenty degrees. It (*be*) __isn't__ in the low 40s right now. Just three days ago, the sun (*shine*) __was shining__ and the weather was pleasant. The weather certainly (*change*) __changes__ quickly here. I never know what to expect. Who knows? When I (*wake*) __wake__ up tomorrow morning, maybe it (*snow*) __will be snowing__.

☐ **EXERCISE 62:** Use any appropriate tenses.

> *A:* Hi, my name is Jose.
> *B:* Hi, my name is Ali.

(1) JOSE: (*You, study*) _are you studying_ at this university?

(2) ALI: Yes, I _am_. _Are_ you?

(3) JOSE: Yes, I (*be*) _have been_ here since last September. Before that
I (*study*) _studied /was studying_ English at another school.

(4) ALI: What (*you, take*) _are you taking_ ?

(5) JOSE: I (*take*) _'m taking_ chemistry, math, psychology, and
American history. What (*take, you*) _are you taking_ ?

(6) ALI: I (*study*) _am studying_ English. I (*need*) _need_
to improve my English before I (*take*) _take_ regular
academic courses next semester.

(7) JOSE: How long (*you, be*) _have you been_ here?

(8) ALI: I (*be*) _have been_ here since the beginning of this semester.
Actually, I (*arrive*) _arrived_ in the United States six
months ago, but I (*study*) _have been studying_
English at this university only since January. Before that I (*live*) _lived/_
was living with my brother in Washington, D.C.

(9) JOSE: You (*speak*) _speak_ English very well. (*You, study*) _did_
you study a lot of English before you (*come*)
came to the United States?

(10) ALI: Yes. I (*study*) _studied_ English for ten years
in my own country. And also, I (*spend*) _spent_ some
time in Canada a couple of years ago. I (*pick*) _picked_ up
a lot of English while I (*live*) _was living_ there.

✗ (11) JOSE: You (*be*) _are_ lucky. When I (*come*) _came_
to the United States, I (*study, never*) _had never studied_
any English at all. So I had to spend a whole year studying nothing but
English before I (*start*) _started_ school.

(12) ALI: How long (*you, plan*) _*do you plan*_ to be in the U.S.?

(13) JOSE: I (*be, not*) _*am not*_ sure. Probably by the time I (*return*)
*return* home, I (*be*) _*will have been*_

here for at least five years. How about you?

(14) ALI: I (*hope*) _*hope*_ to be finished with all my work in two
and a half years.

□ **EXERCISE 63:** Use any appropriate tenses.

(1) Dear Ann,

(2)   I (*receive*) _*received*_ your letter about two weeks ago

(3) and (*try*) _*have tried*_ to find time to write you back ever

(4) since. I (*be*) _*have been*_ very busy lately. In the past two

(5) weeks, I (*have*) _*had*_ four tests, and I have another

(6) test next week. In addition, a friend (*stay*) _*has been staying*_ with

(7) me since last Thursday. She wanted to see the city, so we (*spend*) _*have spent*_ / *have been spent /*

(8) a lot of time visiting some of the interesting places here. We (*be*) _*have*_ *spent*

(9) _*been*_ to the zoo, the art museum, and the botanical gardens.

(10) Yesterday we (*go*) _*went*_ to the park and (*watch*) _*watched*_

(11) a balloon race. Between showing her the city and studying for my exams, I

(12) (*have, barely*) _*have barely had*_ enough time to breathe.

(13)   Right now it (*be*) _*is*_ 3 A.M. and I (*sit*) _*am sitting*_

(14) at my desk. I (*sit*) _*have been sitting*_ here five hours doing my

(15) studying. My friend's plane (*leave*) _*will leave // leave*_ at 6:05, so I *is leaving / is going to leave*

(16) (*decide*) _*have decided*_ not to go to bed. That's why I (*write*)

(17) _*am writing*_ to you at such an early hour in the day. I

(18) (*get*) _*am getting*_ a little sleepy, but I would rather stay up. I

(19) (*take*) _*will take /*_ *am going to take* a nap after I (*get*) _*get*_

(20) back from taking her to the airport.

(21)   How (*get, you*) _*are you getting*_ along? How (*go, your*

(22) *classes*) _*are your classes going*_? Please write soon.

☐ **EXERCISE 64—WRITTEN:** Write a letter to a friend or family member. Discuss your activities, thoughts, feelings, adventures in the present, past, and future. The purpose of this exercise is for you to use every possible tense.

Write about what you *do, are doing, have done, have been doing, did, were doing, had done, had been doing, will do, are going to do, will be doing, will have done,* and *will have been doing.* Include appropriate time expressions: *today, every day, right now, already, so far, since, next week,* etc.

Use the verb tenses in any order you wish and as many times as necessary. Try to write a natural-sounding letter.

☐ **EXERCISE 65—ERROR ANALYSIS:** All of the following sentences are adapted from student writing and contain typical errors. See how many of these errors you can find and correct.

Example: I visit my uncle home many time when I was a child.
Corrections: I *visited* my *uncle's* home many *times* when I was a child.

1. I am living at 3371 grand avenue since last september.
2. I have been in New York city two week ago.
3. My country have change its capital city five time.
4. Dormitory life is not quiet. Everyone shouted and make a lot of noise in the halls.
5. My friends will meet me when I will arrive at the airport.
6. Hasn't anyone ever tell you to knock on the door before you enter someone else's room? Didn't your parents taught you to do that?
7. When I was a child, I viewed thing from a much lower height. Many physical objects around me appear very large. When I want to move something such as a chair, I need help.
8. I will intend to go back home when I will finish my education.
9. The phone rung while I doing the dishes. I dry my hands and answer it. When I am hear my husband voice, I very happy.
10. I am in the United States for the last four months. During this time, I had done many thing and saw many place.
11. When the old man started to walk back to his cave, the sun has already hided itself behind the mountain.
12. While I am writing my composition last night, someone knocks on the door.

□ **EXERCISE 66—PREPOSITIONS:** Supply an appropriate preposition for each of the following expressions of time.

1. I'll meet you _____*in*_____ the morning.

2. I'll meet you _____in_____ the afternoon.

3. I'll meet you _____in_____ the evening.

4. I usually stay home _____at_____ night.

5. I get out of class _____at_____ noon.

6. I'll call you _____at_____ six o'clock.

7. She came _____on_____ Monday.*

8. She came _____in_____ March.

9. I was born _____in_____ 1970.

10. I was born _____on_____ March 15th.

11. I was born _____on_____ March 15th, 1970.

12. He played a trick on me _____on_____ April Fool's Day.

13. I'll help you _____in_____ a minute, just as soon as I finish this work.

14. I'll help you _____in_____ a moment, just as soon as I finish this work.**

15. _____at_____ the moment, I'm doing an exercise.

16. I'm living in the dorm _____at_____ present.

17. I like to go swimming _____in_____ the summer.

18. I like to go skiing _____in_____ the winter.

---

*___On___ is used for a particular day or date. ___In___ is used for a month or year.
**___In a moment___ means ___soon___. ___At the moment___ means ___at this time___ (or ___at that time___).

CHAPTER **2** *thinking verb*
helping verb

Modal Auxiliaries and Similar Expressions

2–1 INTRODUCTION

The modal auxiliaries in English are: ***can, could, had better, may, might, must, ought to, shall, should, will, would***. *have : Do (to) but be*

Modal auxiliaries generally express a speaker's attitudes, or "moods." For example, modals can express that a speaker feels something is necessary, advisable, permissible, possible, or probable; and, in addition, they can convey the strength of these attitudes.

Each modal has more than one meaning or use. (See Chart 2-23.)

(a) MODAL AUXILIARIES	Modals do not take a final **-s**, even when the subject is *he*, *she*, or *it*.
	    CORRECT: ***He can*** *do* it.
	    INCORRECT: He cans do it.

I
We
You
They
He
She
It   } + {   ***can*** *do* it.
could *do* it.
had better *do* it.
may *do* it.
might *do* it.
must *do* it.
ought to *do* it.
shall *do* it.
should *do* it.
will *do* it.
would *do* it.
	Modals are followed immediately by the simple form of a verb.
	    CORRECT: *He* ***can do*** *it.*
	INCORRECT: He can to do it./He can does it./He can did it.
	
	The only exception is ***ought***, which is followed by an infinitive (***to*** + the simple form of a verb).
	    CORRECT: *She* ***ought to go*** *to the meeting.*

(b) SIMILAR EXPRESSIONS
    be able to *do* it
    be going to *do* it
Should = ***be supposed to*** *do* it
Must = ***be to*** *do* it
    have to *do* it
    have got to *do* it
    used to *do* it
	In (b) is a list of some common expressions whose meanings are similar to those of some of the modal auxiliaries. For example, ***be able to*** is similar to ***can***; ***be going to*** is similar to ***will***.
	
	An infinitive (***to*** + the simple form of a verb) is used in these similar expressions.

How dare you do this?
He doesn't dare to do it.
He dare not do it

Dare Word

68

□ **EXERCISE 1—ERROR ANALYSIS:** All of the following contain errors in the forms of modals. Point out and correct the errors.

1. INCORRECT: *She can to see it.*
2. INCORRECT: *She cans see it.*
3. INCORRECT: *She can sees it.*
4. INCORRECT: *She can saw it.*
5. INCORRECT: *Can you please to pass the rice?*
6. INCORRECT: *Do you can see it?*★
7. INCORRECT: *They don't can go there.*★★

2–2 POLITE REQUESTS WITH "I" AS THE SUBJECT

MAY I COULD I	(a) *May I* (please) *borrow* your pen? (b) *Could I borrow* your pen (please)?	*May I* and *could I* are used to request permission. They are equally polite.★ Note in (b): In a polite request, *could* has a present or future meaning, not a past meaning.
CAN I	(c) *Can I borrow* your pen?	*Can I* is used informally to request permission, especially if the speaker is talking to someone s/he knows fairly well. *Can I* is usually not considered as polite as *may I* or *could I*.
	TYPICAL RESPONSES: Certainly. Yes, certainly. Of course. Yes, of course. Sure. (*informal*)	Often the response to a polite request consists of an action, a nod or shake of the head, or a simple "uh-huh."

★*Might* is also possible: *Might I borrow your pen. Might I* is quite formal and polite; it is used much less frequently than *may I* or *could I*.

★See Appendix 1, Chart B-1 for question forms with modals.
★★See Appendix 1, Chart C-1 for negative forms with modals.

2-3 POLITE REQUESTS WITH "YOU" AS THE SUBJECT

WOULD YOU WILL YOU	(a) **Would you pass** the salt (please)? (b) **Will you** (please) **pass** the salt?	The meaning of **would you** and **will you** in a polite request is the same. **Would you** is more common and is often considered more polite. The degree of politeness, however, is often determined by the speaker's tone of voice.
COULD YOU	(c) **Could you pass** the salt?	Basically, **could you** and **would you** have the same meaning. The difference is slight: **would you** = *Do you want to do this please?* **could you** = *Do you want to do this please, and is it possible for you to do this?* **Could you** and **would you** are equally polite.
CAN YOU	(d) **Can you pass** the salt?	**Can you** is often used informally. It usually sounds less polite than **could you** or **would you**.
	TYPICAL RESPONSES: Yes, I'd (I would) be happy to. Yes, I'd be glad to. Certainly. Sure. (*informal*)	A person usually responds in the affirmative to a polite request. If a negative response is necessary, a person might begin by saying, "I'd like to, but . . ." (e.g., "I'd like to pass the salt, but I can't reach it. I'll ask Tom to pass it to you.").

☒ **EXERCISE 2—ORAL (BOOKS CLOSED):** Ask and answer polite questions.

STUDENT A: Make a polite request for the given situation.
STUDENT B: Give a typical response.

1. You and (. . .) are sitting at the dinner table. You want the butter.
   → *Student A: (Anna), would you please pass me the butter?*
   Student B: Certainly, I'd be glad to. Here you are.
2. You want to ask your teacher a question.
3. You're at your friend's apartment. You want to use the phone.
4. You're speaking on the phone to your brother. You want him to pick you up at the airport when you arrive home.
5. You want to leave class early. You're speaking to your instructor.

6. You want (. . .) to meet you in front of the library at three this afternoon.

7. You knock on your professor's half-open door. He's sitting at his desk. You want to go in.

8. You want to make an appointment to see Dr. North. You're speaking to her secretary.

9. You are at a gas station. You want the attendant to check the oil.

10. You are in your chemistry class. You're looking at your textbook. On page 100 there is a formula which you do not understand. You want your professor to explain this formula to you.

11. You call your friend. Her name is (. . .). Someone else answers the phone.

12. You want to see (. . .)'s dictionary for a minute.

13. You want a stranger in an airport to keep her eye on your luggage while you get a drink of water.

14. You want (. . .) to tape something on the VCR tonight while you're away at a meeting.

2-4 POLITE REQUESTS WITH *WOULD YOU MIND*

ASKING PERMISSION (a) *Would you mind **if I closed** the window?* (b) *Would you mind **if I used** the phone?*	Notice in (a): ***would you mind if I*** is followed by the simple past.* The meaning in (a): *May I close the window? Is it all right if I close the window? Will it cause you any trouble or discomfort if I close the window?*
TYPICAL RESPONSES No. Not at all. No, of course not. No, that would be fine.	Another typical response might be "unh-unh," meaning *no.*
ASKING SOMEONE ELSE TO DO SOMETHING (c) *Would you mind **closing** the window?* (d) *Excuse me? Would you mind **repeating** that?*	Notice in (c): ***would you mind*** is followed by ***-ing*** (a gerund). The meaning in (c): *I don't want to cause you any trouble, but would you please close the window? Would that cause you any inconvenience?*
TYPICAL RESPONSES No. I'd be happy to. Not at all. I'd be glad to.	

*Sometimes in informal spoken English, the simple present is used: *Would you mind if I close the window?* (Note: The simple past does not refer to past time after *would you mind*; it refers to present or future time. See Chart 10-3 for more information.)

□ **EXERCISE 3:** Using the verb in parentheses, fill in the blank either with *if I* + *the past tense* or with *the -ing form of the verb*. In some of the sentences, either response is possible but the meaning is different.

1. I'm getting tired. I'd like to go home and go to bed. Would you mind (*leave*) _____*if I left*_____ early?

2. I'm sorry. I didn't understand what you said. Would you mind (*repeat*) _____*repeating*_____ that?

3. A: Are you going to the post office?

   B: Yes.

   A: Would you mind (*mail*) _____*mailing*_____ this letter for me?

   B: Not at all.

4. A: Are you coming with us?

   B: I know I promised to go with you, but I'm not feeling very good. Would you mind (*stay*) _____*if I stayed*_____ home?

   A: Of course not.

5. A: I still don't understand how to work this algebra problem. Would you mind (*explain*) _____*explaining*_____ it again?

   B: Not at all. I'd be happy to.

6. A: It's getting hot in here. Would you mind (*open*) _____*If I opened*_____ the window?

   B: No.

7. A: This is probably none of my business, but would you mind (*ask*) _____*If I asked*_____ you a personal question?

   B: It depends.

8. A: Would you mind (*smoke*) _____*If I smoked*_____?

   B: I'd really rather you didn't.

9. A: Excuse me. Would you mind (*speak*) _____*speaking*_____ a little more slowly? I didn't catch what you said.

   B: I'd be happy to.

10. A: I don't like this TV program. Would you mind (*change*) _____*If I changed*_____ the channel?

    B: Unh-unh.

2–5 USING IMPERATIVE SENTENCES TO MAKE POLITE REQUESTS

(a) **Shut** the door. (b) **Be** on time. (c) **Don't shut** the door. (d) **Don't be** late.	An imperative sentence has an understood subject (*you*), and the verb (e.g., *shut*) is in the simple form. *Shut the door. = (You) shut the door. Be on time. = (You) be on time.* In the negative, **don't** precedes the simple form of the verb.
(e) **Turn** right at the corner.	An imperative sentence can be used to give directions, as in (e).
(f) **Shut** the door.	An imperative sentence can be used to give an order, as in (f).
(g) **Please shut** the door. **Shut** the door, **please**.	It can also be used to make a polite request, as in (g), when the word **please** is added.*

*Sometimes **would you/could you** is added as a tag question (almost as an afterthought) to turn an imperative into a polite request; e.g., *Shut the door, would/could you?* Sometimes, usually in a formal situation, **won't you** is added to an imperative as a tag question to make a polite request; e.g., *Have a seat, won't you?* (See Appendix 1, Chart B-4 for information about tag questions.)

☐ **EXERCISE 4—ORAL (BOOKS CLOSED):** Turn the following imperative sentences into polite requests.

Example: Open the window.
Possible responses: Please open the window. Could you please open the window? Would you mind opening the window?

Example: Give me a cup of coffee.
Possible responses: May I please have a cup of coffee? Could you get me a cup of coffee?

1. Turn on the light.
2. Give me that book.
3. Sit down.
4. Say that again.
5. Give me your pen.
6. Pass me the butter.
7. Give me a ride home in your car.
8. Tell me what time it is.
9. Mail these letters if you go to the post office.
10. Close the window and turn on the air conditioner.
11. Let me out of the elevator.

☐ **EXERCISE 5—ORAL (BOOKS CLOSED):** Ask polite questions in the following situations. Use any appropriate modal (**may, could, would,** etc.) or polite imperative.

1. Your plane leaves at six P.M. tomorrow. You want your friend to take you to the airport.
2. You're sitting at your friend's house. A bowl of fruit is sitting on the table. You want an apple.
3. You're in class. You're hot. The window is closed.

4. You're in a car. Your friend's driving. You want her to stop at the next mailbox so you can mail a letter.

5. You're trying to study. Your roommate is playing his music tapes very loudly, and this is bothering you.

6. You call your friend. Someone else answers and tells you that he's out. You want to leave a message.

7. You want your pen. You can't reach it, but your friend can. You want her to hand it to you.

8. You're at a restaurant. You want some more coffee.

9. You're at your friend's house. You want to help her set the dinner table.

10. You're the teacher. You want a student to shut the door.

11. You want to make a telephone call. You're in a store and have to use a pay phone, but you don't have any change. All you have is (a one-dollar bill). You ask a clerk for change.

12. You're at a restaurant. You've finished your meal and are ready to leave. You ask the waiter for the check.

13. You call your boss's house. His name is Mr. Smith. You want to talk to him. His wife answers the phone.

14. You're giving a dinner party. Your guests have just arrived. You want to get them something to drink.

15. Your guests have arrived. You want them to sit down.

16. You're walking down the hall of the classroom building. You need to know what time it is. You ask a student you've never met.*

17. You're in the middle of the city. You're lost. You're trying to find the bus station. You stop someone on the street to ask for directions.

18. You call the airport. You want to know what time Flight 62 arrives.

19. You're in a department store. You find a sweater that you like, but you can't find the price tag. You ask the clerk to tell you how much it costs.

20. It's your first day on campus. You're supposed to be at the library for a meeting, but you can't find the library. You ask for information from another student you meet on the sidewalk.

□ **EXERCISE 6—ORAL/WRITTEN:** What are some common polite requests you have heard or have said in the following places?

1. in this classroom
2. at a restaurant
3. at a clothing store
4. at an airport
5. on the telephone
6. at a service station ➤

*The responses to 16 through 20 may include noun clauses. For word order in noun clauses, see Chapter 7.

Must = have to = have got to — no using in essay.

2-6 EXPRESSING NECESSITY: *MUST, HAVE TO, HAVE GOT TO*

Must > had to

(a) All applicants **must take** an entrance exam.	**Must** and **have to** both express necessity.
(b) All applicants **have to take** an entrance exam.	In (a) and (b): It is necessary for every applicant to take an entrance exam. There is no other choice. The exam is required.
(c) I'm looking for Sue. I **have to talk** to her about our lunch date tomorrow. I can't meet her for lunch because I **have to go** to a business meeting at 1:00.	In everyday statements of necessity, **have to** is used more commonly than **must**. **Must** is usually stronger than **have to** and can indicate urgency or stress importance. In (c): The speaker is simply saying, "I need to do this and I need to do that." In (d): The speaker is strongly saying, "This is very important!"
(d) Where's Sue? I **must talk** to her right away. I have an urgent message for her.	
(e) I **have to** ("hafta") be home by eight.	Note: **have to** is usually pronounced "hafta"; **has to** is usually pronounced "hasta."
(f) He **has to** ("hasta") go to a meeting tonight.	
(g) I **have got to go** now. I have a class in ten minutes.	**Have got to** also expresses the idea of necessity: (g) and (h) have the same meaning. **Have got to** is informal and is used primarily in spoken English. **Have to** is used in both formal and informal English.
(h) I **have to go** now. I have a class in ten minutes.	
(i) I **have got to go** ("I've gotta go/I gotta go") now.	Usual pronunciation of **got to** is "gotta." Sometimes **have** is dropped in speech: "I gotta do it."
(j) PRESENT or FUTURE I **have to/have got to/must study** tonight.	The idea of past necessity is expressed by **had to**. There is no other past form for **must** (when it means necessity) or **have got to**.
(k) PAST: I **had to study** last night.	

☐ **EXERCISE 7—ORAL (BOOKS CLOSED):** Answer the questions. Practice pronouncing the usual spoken forms of **have to** and **have got to**.

1. What are some of the things you have to do today or tomorrow?
2. What does (. . .) have to do today?
3. What have you got to do after class?
4. What has (. . .) got to do after class?
5. Can you think of something very important that you must do today or tomorrow?
6. What is something that you had to do yesterday?
7. Ask a classmate a question using **have to** and **what time/where/how often/why**.*

---

*A form of **do** is used with **have to** in questions: e.g., *When does he have to leave?*

You must not take the paper time.
(≠)
don't have to

2-7 LACK OF NECESSITY AND PROHIBITION: *HAVE TO* AND *MUST* IN THE NEGATIVE

LACK OF NECESSITY (a) Tomorrow is a holiday. We **don't have to go** to class. (b) I can hear you. You **don't have to shout**.*	When used in the negative, **must** and **have to** have different meanings.
	do not have to = *lack of necessity*. In (a): It is not necessary for us to go to class tomorrow because there is a holiday.
PROHIBITION (c) You **must not look** in the closet. Your birthday present is hidden there. (d) You **must not tell** anyone my secret. Do you promise?	**must not** = *prohibition* (DO NOT DO THIS!) In (c): Do not look in the closet. I forbid it. Looking in the closet is prohibited.
	Negative contraction: **mustn't**. (The first "t" is not pronounced: "muss-ənt.")

*Lack of necessity may also be expressed by **need not** + *the simple form of a verb*: *You **needn't shout***. The use of **needn't** as an auxiliary is chiefly British other than when it is used in certain common expressions such as "You needn't worry."

☐ **EXERCISE 8:** Use **must not** or **do not have to** in the following.

1. I've already finished all my work, so I ___don't have to___ study tonight. I think I'll read for a while.

2. I ___must not___ forget to take my key with me.

3. You ___don't have to___ introduce me to Dr. Gray. We've already met.

4. A person ___doesn't have to___ become rich and famous in order to live a successful life.

5. In order to be a good salesclerk, you ___must not___ be rude to a customer.

6. I ___don't have to___ go to the doctor. I'm feeling much better.

7. A person ___doesn't have to___ get married in order to lead a happy and fulfilling life.

8. Johnny! You ___must not___ play with sharp knives.

9. We ___don't have to___ go to the concert if you don't want to, but it might be good.

10. An entering freshman _doesn't have to_ declare a major immediately. The student may wait a few semesters before deciding upon a major.

11. Bats _don't have to_ see in order to avoid obstacles. They can navigate in complete darkness.

12. This is an opportunity that comes once in a lifetime. We _must not_ _____ let it pass. We must act.

13. If you encounter a growling dog, you _must not_ show any signs of fear. If a dog senses fear, it is more likely to bite a person.

14. Tigers are magnificent animals. We _must not_ allow them to become extinct.

15. The class trip to the art museum is optional. You _don't have to_ _____ go, but you might enjoy it.

□ **EXERCISE 9—ORAL (BOOKS CLOSED):** Complete the sentences with your own words.

Example: Students don't have to . . . .
Possible response: Students in elementary school don't have to pay tuition.
Example: Students must not . . . .
Possible response: Students must not cheat during tests.

1. Children must not . . . .
2. Children don't have to . . . .
3. Drivers must not . . . .
4. Drivers don't have to . . . .
5. We don't have to . . . .
6. We must not . . . .
7. (. . .) doesn't have to . . . .
8. (. . .) must not . . . .
9. Waiters must not . . . .
10. Waiters don't have to . . . .
11. I don't have to . . . .
12. I must not . . . .

had better > should, ought to

2–8 ADVISABILITY: *SHOULD, OUGHT TO, HAD BETTER*

(a) You **should study** harder. You **ought to study** harder. (b) Drivers **should obey** the speed limit. Drivers **ought to obey** the speed limit.	**Should** and **ought to** have the same meaning: they express advisability. The meaning ranges in strength from a suggestion ("This is a good idea.") to a statement about responsibility or duty ("This is a very important thing to do."). In (a): "This is a good idea. This is my advice." In (b): "This is an important responsibility."
(c) You **shouldn't leave** your keys in the car.	Negative contraction: **shouldn't**.★
(d) I **ought to** ("otta") **study** tonight, but I think I'll watch TV instead.	**Ought to** is sometimes pronounced "otta" in informal speaking.
(e) The gast tank is almost empty. We **had better stop** at the next service station. (f) You **had better take** care of that cut on your hand soon, or it will get infected.	In meaning, **had better** is close to **should/ought to**, but **had better** is usually stronger. Often **had better** implies a warning or a threat of possible bad consequences. In (e): If we don't stop at a service station, there will be a bad result. We will run out of gas. Notes: **Had better** has a present or future meaning. It is followed by the simple form of a verb. It is more common in speaking than writing.
(g) You**'d better** take care of it. (h) You **better** take care of it. (i) You**'d better not** be late.	Contraction: **'d better**, as in (g). Sometimes in speaking, **had** is dropped, as in (h). Negative form: **had better + not**.

★**Ought to** is not commonly used in the negative. If it is used in the negative, the **to** is often dropped: *You **oughtn't** (to) leave your keys in the car.*

☐ **EXERCISE 10—ORAL:** Complete the following sentences.

1. I should study tonight because . . . .
2. I ought to study tonight because . . . .
3. I had better study tonight. If I don't, ...
4. I should wash my clothes today, but . I can't do it .
5. I'd better wash my clothes today, or I don't wash my clothes today .
6. It's a beautiful day. We ought to . . . .
7. It looks like rain. If you're going out, you'd better . . . .
8. You'd better obey the speed limit. If . you get cught ,
9. You shouldn't stay up late tonight because . . . .
10. You'd better not stay up late tonight. If you do . . . .

⊠ **EXERCISE 11—ORAL (BOOKS CLOSED):** Give advice in the following situations by using *should, ought to,* or *had better*.

Example: I have a test tomorrow.
Response: You should (ought to, had better) study tonight. *you should look up it die*

1. I'm writing a composition, and there is a word I don't know how to spell.
2. I don't feel good. I think I'm catching a cold.
3. I can't see the blackboard when I sit in the back row.
4. I'm cold.

had better (BE)

Consequently (adv):
vậy thì, bởi thế, do vậy

chán g tô là tê

5. My <u>foot</u> is <u>asleep</u>.
6. I'm homesick.
7. I have a problem with my student visa.
8. My roommate snores and I can't get to sleep.
9. I need to improve my English.
10. I can't stop yawning.
11. My library book is due today.
12. There's no food in my house, and some guests are coming to dinner tonight.
13. I have only twenty-five cents in my pocket, but I need some money to go out tonight.
14. My apartment is a mess, and my mother is coming to visit me tomorrow.
15. I'm about to leave on a trip, but the gas gauge in my car is on empty.
16. I have a toothache.
17. I have the flu.
18. My friend is arriving at the airport this evening. I'm supposed to pick him up, but I've forgotten what time his plane gets in.
19. I have the hiccups.

□ **EXERCISE 12—ORAL:** Which sentence in the following pairs is stronger? Discuss situations in which a speaker might say these sentences.

1. a. You *should go* to a doctor.
   b. You'd *better go* to a doctor.
2. a. Mary *should go* to work today.
   b. Mary *must go* to work today.
3. a. We'*ve got to go* to class.
   b. We *ought to go* to class.

4. a. I *have to go* to the post office.
   b. I *should go* to the post office.
5. a. We *shouldn't go* into that room.
   b. We *must not go* into that room.
6. a. You'd *better not go* there alone.
   b. You *shouldn't go* there alone.

□ **EXERCISE 13:** Use either *should* or *must/have to* in the following. In some sentences either is possible, but the meaning is different.

1. A person ___have to___ eat in order to live.

2. A person ___should___ eat a balanced diet.

· have to 100%
→ don't have to 50-60%/80%
· must 95% {responsibility}
→ must not 100%
· should 70%
→ should not 90%

3. If you want to become a doctor, you ___must___ go to medical school for many years.

4. We ___should___ go to Colorado for our vacation.

5. According to my academic advisor, I ___have to___ take another English course.

6. I ___should___ write to my folks tonight, but I think I'll wait and do it tomorrow.

7. You ___must___ have a passport if you want to travel abroad.

8. Everyone ___should___ have certain goals in life.

9. Rice ___must___ have water in order to grow.

10. I ___should___ go to class, but I don't feel good. I think I'd better stay home.

11. If a door is locked, you ___have to___ use a key to open it.

12. I don't have enough money to take the bus, so I ___have to___ walk home.

13. If you don't know how to spell a word, you ___should___ look it up in the dictionary.

14. This pie is very good. You ____should____ try a piece.

15. This pie is excellent! You ____must____ try a piece.*

2–9   THE PAST FORM OF *SHOULD*

(a) I had a test this morning. I didn't do well on the test because I didn't study for it last night. **I should have studied** last night.	Past form: ***should have*** + *past participle*.*
(b) You were supposed to be here at 10 P.M., but you didn't come until midnight. We were worried about you. You **should have called** us. (You did not call.) *j'ai rien*	In (a): "I should have studied" means that studying was a good idea, but I didn't do it. I made a mistake.
	Usual pronunciation of **should have**: "should-of" or "shoulda."
(c) I hurt my back. **I should not have carried** that heavy box up two flights of stairs. (I carried the box and now I am sorry.)	In (c): "I should not have carried" means that I carried something, but it turned out to be a bad idea. I made a mistake.
(d) We went to the movie, but it was a bad movie. We wasted our time and money. We **should not have gone** to the movie.	Usual pronunciation of **should not have**: "shouldn't-of" or "shouldn't'a."

*The past form of ***ought to*** is ***ought to have*** + *past participle*. (*I ought to have studied.*) It has the same meaning as the past form of ***should***. In the past, ***should*** is used more commonly than ***ought to***. ***Had better*** is only rarely used in a past form (e.g., *He* ***had better have taken*** *care of it.*) and usually only in speaking, not writing.

☐ **EXERCISE 14—ORAL:** Make sentences based on the following situations. Use ***should have*** + *past participle*.

1. Tom made a mistake yesterday. He left the door to his house open, and a bird flew in. He had a terrible time catching the bird.
   → *Tom shouldn't have left the door open.*

2. There was an important meeting yesterday afternoon, but you decided not to go. That was a mistake.

3. Ann didn't feel good a couple of days ago. I told her to see a doctor, but she didn't. That was a mistake. Now she is very sick.

4. I didn't invite Sam to my party. That made him feel bad. I'm sorry I didn't invite him.

———

*Sometimes in speaking, ***must*** has the meaning of a very enthusiastic ***should***.

He should do ... (present)

He should have done this exercise yesterday. (past tense)

5. Mary sold her car. That was a mistake because now she can't take trips to see her friends and relatives.

6. Alex signed a contract to buy some furniture without reading it thoroughly. Now he has discovered that he is paying a lot more money than he expected. He made a mistake.

☑ **EXERCISE 15—ORAL (BOOKS CLOSED):** Use *should have* + *past participle* in your response.

Example: You failed the test because you didn't study.
Response: I should have studied.
Example: You didn't study because you went to a movie.
Response: I shouldn't have gone to a movie.

1. You are cold because you didn't wear a coat.
2. You misspelled a word because you didn't look it up in the dictionary.
3. Your friend is upset because you didn't write him a letter.
4. You are broke now because you spent all your money foolishly.
5. The room is full of flies because you opened the window.
6. You don't have any food for dinner because you didn't go to the grocery store.
7. You overslept this morning because you didn't set your alarm clock.
8. Your friends went to (*New Orleans*) over vacation. They had a good time. You didn't go with them, and now you are sorry.
9. John loved Mary, but he didn't marry her. Now he is unhappy.
10. John loved Mary, and he married her. But now he is unhappy.
11. You didn't have a cup of coffee. Now you are sleepy.
12. You didn't stop for gas, and then you ran out of gas on the highway.
13. You were sick yesterday, but you went to class anyway. Today you feel worse.
14. The weather was beautiful yesterday, but you stayed inside all day.
15. You bought your girlfriend a box of candy for her birthday, but she doesn't like candy.
16. The little girl told a lie. She got into a lot of trouble.
17. You have a stomach ache because you ate (*five hamburgers*).
18. You had to pay a fine because your library book was overdue.
19. You lent your car to (. . .), but s/he had an accident because s/he was driving on the wrong side of the road.
20. When (. . .) fell asleep on the overnight train from (*place name*) to (*place name*), her purse was stolen.

2–10 EXPECTATIONS: *BE SUPPOSED TO* AND *BE TO*

(a) The game *is supposed to begin* at 10:00. (b) The game *is to begin* at 10:00. (c) The committee *is supposed to meet* tomorrow. (d) The committee *is to meet* tomorrow.	*Be supposed to* and *be to* (a form of *be* followed immediately by an infinitive, e.g., *is to begin*) express the idea that someone (I, we, they, the teacher, lots of people, my father, etc.) expects something to happen. *Be supposed to* and *be to* often express expectations about scheduled events or correct procedures. In (a) and (b): The speaker expects the game to begin at 10:00 because that is the schedule. *Be to* is stronger, more definite, than *be supposed to*.
COMPARE: (e) I *should go* to the meeting. I can get some information if I go. Going to the meeting is a good idea.	*Be supposed to* and *be to* also express expectations about behavior; often they give the idea that someone expects a particular person to do something.
(f) I *am supposed to go* to the meeting. My boss told me that he wants me to attend.	*Be supposed to* is close in meaning to *should*, but *be supposed to*, as in (f), gives the idea that someone else expects (requests or requires) this behavior.
COMPARE: (g) I *must be* at the meeting. The meeting can't occur without me because I'm the only one who has certain information.	*Be to* is close in meaning to *must*, but *be to*, as in (h), includes the idea that someone else strongly expects (demands or orders) this behavior.
(h) I *am to be* at the meeting. My boss ordered me to be there. He will accept no excuses.	*Be to* is used to state strong expectations: e.g., rules, laws, instructions, demands, orders.

☐ **EXERCISE 16—ERROR ANALYSIS:** Find and correct the errors in the following sentences.

1. The building custodian supposed to unlock the classrooms every morning.

2. You're not suppose to open that door.

3. Where are we suppose to meet?

4. I have a meeting at seven tonight. I suppose to be there a little early to discuss the agenda.

5. When we go to the store, Annie, you do not suppose to handle the glassware. It might break, and then you'd have to pay for it out of your allowance.

□ **EXERCISE 17—ORAL:** Restate the following rules in sentences with *be to*.

1. NO SMOKING. → *You are not to smoke*.
2. KEEP OFF THE GRASS.
3. NO EATING OR DRINKING IN THIS ROOM.
4. MOVE TO THE REAR OF THE BUS.
5. DO NOT JOKE WITH AIRPORT PERSONNEL WHILE YOUR HAND LUGGAGE IS BEING INSPECTED.
6. USE THE STAIRS IN CASE OF FIRE. DO NOT USE THE ELEVATOR.
7. NO LITTERING.
8. SLOWER TRAFFIC KEEP RIGHT.

□ **EXERCISE 18—ORAL (BOOKS CLOSED):** Practice using *be to*. Make up several sentences using *be to* for each of the following situations.

Example:　　　　　The teacher gave the students a writing assignment. Tell us what the students are to do.

Possible response:　They are to write a composition./They are to write it about a person they admire./They are to hand it in next Tuesday./They are to write it in ink./They are not to write it in pencil.

1. Jack's back hurt, so he went to a doctor. She gave him some instructions. Tell us what he is to do and what he is not to do.
2. This is your assignment for the next class. (*Supply an assignment.*) Can you repeat to me what you are to do?
3. Your son has some jobs to do before he can go outside and play. What is he to do?
4. You have a new job as a cook. Your boss told you what she expects of you. Can you tell us what she expects of you?
5. You are on a committee to make rules for this school. The committee is writing a list of rules. What does this list include?
6. All of us use the library. What behavior is expected of us? ("*We are to . . . .*")
7. You are in charge of some children at a playground. You want to make sure they understand the rules you set. Tell them the rules. ("*Children, you are to . . . .*")
8. Who lives in an apartment building or dormitory? What is expected of its residents?

□ **EXERCISE 19—ORAL:** Which sentence in each pair is stronger?

1. a. You *have got to wear* your seatbelt.
   b. You *should wear* your seatbelt.
2. a. You *are to wear* your seatbelt.
   b. You *ought to wear* your seatbelt.
3. a. You *must wear* your seatbelt.
   b. You *had better wear* your seatbelt.
4. a. You *have to wear* your seatbelt.
   b. You *are supposed to wear* your seatbelt.
5. a. We *are to bring* our own pencils to the test.
   b. We *are supposed to bring* our own pencils.
6. a. We *are supposed to bring* our own pencils.
   b. We *have to bring* our own pencils.
7. a. We *ought to bring* our own pencils.
   b. We *have got to bring* our own pencils.
8. a. We *had better bring* our own pencils.
   b. We *should bring* our own pencils.

□ **EXERCISE 20—ORAL:** Complete the following and discuss the meaning you wish to express by giving reasons for your statement.

Example: I'd better . . . .
Possible response: I'd better write my mother a letter. (*Reason*: If I don't, there will be a bad result: she'll be angry or start worrying about me or feel hurt.)

1. I should . . . .
2. I'm supposed to . . . .
3. I ought to v
4. I'd better . . . . study
5. I have to . . . .
6. I've got to . . . .
7. I am to . . . .
8. I must . . . .
9. I shouldn't . . . .
10. I'm not supposed to . . . .
11. I'd better not . . . .
12. I don't have to . . . .
13. I am not to . . . .
14. I must not . . . .

2–11 MAKING SUGGESTIONS: *LET'S, WHY DON'T, SHALL I/WE*

(a) ***Let's go*** to a movie. (b) ***Let's not go*** to a movie. ***Let's stay*** home instead.	***Let's*** = ***let us***. ***Let's*** is followed by the simple form of a verb. Negative form: ***let's*** + ***not*** + *simple verb*. The meaning of ***let's***: "I have a suggestion for us."
(c) ***Why don't we go*** to a movie? (d) ***Why don't you come*** around seven? (e) ***Why don't I give*** Mary a call?	***Why don't*** is used primarily in spoken English to make a friendly suggestion. In (c): ***why don't we go*** = ***let's go***. In (d): I suggest that you come around seven. In (e): Should I give Mary a call? Do you agree with my suggestion?
(f) ***Shall I open*** the window? Is that okay with you? (g) ***Shall we leave*** at two? Is that okay? (h) Let's go, ***shall we***? (i) Let's go, ***okay***?	When ***shall*** is used with "I" or "we" in a question, the speaker is usually making a suggestion and asking another person if s/he agrees with this suggestion. Sometimes "shall we?" is used as a tag question after ***let's***. More informally, "okay?" is used as a tag question, as in (i).

□ **EXERCISE 21—ORAL:** Pair up with another student. Together make up a short dialogue (5 to 10 lines) that includes the given sentence(s) and ***why don't***. (Include ***let's***, too, if you wish.) Then present your dialogue to the class.

> *Example:* I don't feel very good.
> *Dialogue:* A: Is something the matter, Carlos?
> B: *I don't feel very good.*
> A: Oh? What's wrong?
> B: My stomach feels a little upset.
> A: Maybe it's something you ate. *Why don't you go home and rest for a while?*
> B: I think I will.

1. I don't feel good.
2. I'm hungry.
3. Where should we go for our vacation?
4. I'm sleepy.
5. What a beautiful day it is! We shouldn't stay inside all day.
6. It's hot in here.
7. I don't know what this word means.
8. There's a meeting tonight, but I really don't want to go.

9. I'd like to eat out tonight.
10. The children are bored.
11. I don't like my job.
12. What do you feel like doing tonight?

2–12 MAKING SUGGESTIONS: *COULD*

--What should we do tomorrow? (a) Why don't we go on a picnic? (b) We *could go* on a picnic.	*Could* can be used to make suggestions. (b) is similar to (a) in meaning; i.e., the speaker is suggesting a picnic.
--I'm having trouble in math class. (c) You *should talk* to your teacher.	*Should* gives definite advice. In (c), the speaker is saying: "I believe it is important for you to do this. This is what I recommend."
--I'm having trouble in math class. (d) You *could talk* to your teacher. Or you *could ask* Ann to help you with your math lessons. Or I *could try* to help you.	*Could* offers suggestions or possibilities. In (d), the speaker is saying: "I have some possible suggestions for you. It is possible to do this. Or it is possible to do that."★
--I failed my math class. (e) You *should have talked* to your teacher and gotten some help from her during the term.	*Should have* gives "hindsight advice."★★ In (e), the speaker is saying: "It was important for you to talk to the teacher, but you didn't do it. You made a mistake."
--I failed my math class. (f) You *could have talked* to your teacher. Or you *could have asked* Ann to help you with your math. Or I *could have tried* to help you.	*Could have* offers "hindsight possibilities."★★ In (f), the speaker is saying: "You had the chance to do this or that. It was possible for this or that to happen. You missed some good opportunities."

★*Might* (but not *may*) can also be used to make suggestions (*You might talk to your teacher.*), but the use of *could* is more common.
★★"Hindsight" refers to looking at something after it happens.

☐ **EXERCISE 22:** Discuss Speaker B's use of *should* and *could* in the following dialogues. In your own words, what is Speaker B saying?

1. A: Ted doesn't feel good. He has a bad stomach ache.
   B: He *should see* a doctor.
2. A: Ted doesn't feel good. He has a bad stomach ache. What do you think he should do?
   B: Well, I don't know. He *could see* a doctor. He *could see* Dr. Smith. Or he *could see* Dr. Jones. Or he *could* simply *stay* in bed for a day and hope he feels better tomorrow.

3. A: I need to get to the airport.
   B: You *should take* the airport bus. It's cheaper than a taxi.

4. A: I need to get to the airport.
   B: Well, you *could take* the airport bus. Or you *could take* a taxi. Maybe Fred *could take* you. He has a car.

5. A: I took a taxi to the airport, and it cost me a fortune.
   B: You *should have taken* the airport bus.

6. A: I took a taxi to the airport, and it cost me a fortune.
   B: You *could have taken* the airport bus. Or maybe Fred *could have taken* you.

☐ **EXERCISE 23—ORAL (BOOKS CLOSED):** Answer the questions. Use *could* to suggest possibilities. Use *should* only if you want to give strong, definite advice.

Example: I need to get to the airport. Any suggestions?
Possible response: You could take a taxi or the airport bus. Or I could take you if I can borrow my brother's car.
Possible response: In my opinion, you should take the airport bus.

1. I don't have any plans for this weekend. I need some suggestions.
2. (. . .) and I want to go to a nice restaurant for dinner tonight. Any suggestions? we could
3. I need to get from here to (*name of a place in this city/town*). Any suggestions?
4. (. . .) needs to buy an umbrella, but s/he doesn't know where to go. S/he needs some suggestions.
5. I'm hungry. I'm going to eat an egg. Give me some suggestions on how to cook it. What are the possibilities?
6. I need to get a car, but it can't be very expensive. Any suggestions?
7. I bought a (*name of a car*), but I'm unhappy with it. In hindsight, can you suggest other possibilities for a kind of car I could have bought?
8. I went to the food store yesterday and bought some bread. That's all. But then when it came time for me to fix myself some dinner, all I had was some bread and butter. Suggest some possibilities of other things I could have bought.
9. I went to (*name of a place*) for my vacation last summer, but I didn't enjoy it. In hindsight, can you suggest some other possibilities that I didn't think of? (I had only five days and a limited amount of money.)
10. (. . .) went to (*name of a restaurant*) for dinner last night, but the food was terrible. Do you have any hindsight suggestions?

2–13 EXPRESSING DEGREES OF CERTAINTY: PRESENT TIME

--Why isn't John in class? **100% sure**: He *is* sick. **95% sure**: He *must be* sick. **less than 50% sure**: { He *may be* sick. He *might be* sick. He *could be* sick.	"Degree of certainty" refers to how sure we are—what we think the chances are—that something is true. If we are sure something is true in the present, we don't need to use a modal. For example, if I say, "John is sick," I am sure; I am stating a fact that I am sure is true. My degree of certainty is 100%.
--Why isn't John in class? (a) He *must be* sick. (Usually he is in class every day, but when I saw him last night, he wasn't feeling good. So my best guess is that he is sick today. I can't think of another possibility.)	**Must** is used to express a strong degree of certainty about a present situation, but the degree of certainty is still less than 100%.
	In (a): The speaker is saying: "Probably John is sick. I have evidence to make me believe that he is sick. That is my logical conclusion, but I do not know for certain."
--Why isn't John in class? (b) He *may be* sick. (c) He *might be* sick. (d) He *could be* sick. (I don't really know. He may be at home watching TV. He might be at the library. He could be out of town.)	**May**, **might**, and **could** are used to express a weak degree of certainty.
	In (b), (c), and (d): The speaker is saying: "Perhaps, maybe,* possibly John is sick. I am only making a guess. I can think of other possibilities." (b), (c), and (d) have the same meaning.

*__Maybe__ (spelled as one word) is an adverb: __Maybe__ he is sick. __May be__ (spelled as two words) is a verb form: He __may be__ sick.

☐ **EXERCISE 24—ORAL (BOOKS CLOSED):** From the given information, make your "best guess" by using **must**.

Example: Alice always gets the best grades in the class. Why?
Response: She must study hard./She must be intelligent.

1. (. . .) is yawning. Why?
2. (. . .) is sneezing and coughing. Why?
3. (. . .) is wearing a wedding ring. Why?
4. (. . .) is shivering and has goose bumps. Why?
5. (. . .)'s stomach is growling. Why? *He must be hungry.*
6. (. . .) is scratching his arm. Why?
7. (. . .) is going to get married in five minutes. His/her hands are shaking. Why?

8. (. . .) has already had two glasses of water, but now he/she wants another. Why?

9. (. . .) is smiling. Why?

10. (. . .) is crying. Why?

11. You just picked up a telephone receiver, but there is no dial tone. Why?

12. There is a restaurant in town that is always packed (full). Why?

13. I am in my car. I am trying to start it, but the engine won't turn over. I left my lights on all day. What's wrong?

14. Every night there is a long line of people waiting to get into (*a particular movie*). I wonder why.

15. Don't look at your watch. What time is it?

☐ **EXERCISE 25—ORAL (BOOKS CLOSED):** Respond by using "I don't know" + *may/might/could*.

Example: (. . .)'s grammar book isn't on her desk. Where is it?
Response: I don't know. It may/might/could be in her book bag.

1. (. . .) isn't in class today. Where is s/he? (*I don't know. S/he . . . .*)

2. Where does (. . .) live? (*I don't know. S/he . . . .*)

3. What do you think I have in my briefcase/pocket/purse?

4. What kind of watch is (. . .) wearing?

5. I can't find my pen. Do you know where it is?

6. How old do you think (*someone famous*) is?

⊞ **EXERCISE 26:** Complete the sentences by using *must* or *may/might/could* with the expressions in the list or with your own words.

be about ten	be very proud	✔ like green
be at a meeting	feel terrible	miss them very much
be crazy	fit Jimmy	
be rich	have the wrong number	

1. A: Have you noticed that Professor Adams wears something green every day?

   B: I know. He _must like green._

2. A: Ed just bought his wife a diamond necklace with matching earrings.

   B: That's expensive! He ___must be crazy___

   A: He is.

3. A: Look at the man standing outside the window on the fifteenth floor of
   the building. *he could be crazy*
   B: He _____ *must be crazy* _____
   A: I agree. Only a nut would do something like that.

4. A: Where's Ms. Adams? She's not in her office.
   B: I don't know. She _____ *might be at a meeting* /*could, may*
   A: If you see her, would you tell her I'm looking for her?
   B: Certainly, Mr. French.

5. A: Hello?
   B: Hello. May I speak to Ron?
   A: I'm sorry. You _____ *must have the wrong number* _____
   There's no one here by that name.

6. A: I've heard that your daughter recently graduated from law school and
   that your son has gotten a scholarship to the state university. You _____
   _____ *must be very proud* _____
   B: We are.

7. A: You're coughing and sneezing, blowing your nose, and running a
   fever. You _____ *must feel terrible* _____
   B: I do.

8. A: This winter jacket is still in good shape, but Tommy has outgrown it. Do you think it would fit one of your sons?

B: Well, it's probably too small for Johnny, too, but it ___might___ ___fit jimmy___.

9. A: How long has it been since you last saw your family?

B: Over a year.

A: You ___must miss them very much___

B: I do.

10. A: How old is their daughter now?

B: Hmmm. I think she was born around the same time our daughter was born. She ___(must) might be about ten___

2–14 DEGREES OF CERTAINTY: PRESENT TIME NEGATIVE

100% sure:	Sam *isn't* hungry.
99% sure:	Sam *couldn't be* hungry. / Sam *can't be* hungry.
95% sure:	Sam *must not be* hungry.
less than 50% sure:	Sam *may not be* hungry. / Sam *might not be* hungry.

(a) Sam doesn't want anything to eat. He *isn't* hungry. He told me his stomach is full. He says he isn't hungry. I believe him.	In (a): The speaker is sure that Sam is not hungry.
(b) Sam *couldn't/can't be* hungry! That's impossible! I just saw him eat a huge meal. He has already eaten enough to fill two grown men. Did he really say he'd like something to eat? I don't believe it.	In (b): The speaker believes that there is no possibility that Sam is hungry (but the speaker is not 100% sure). Notice the negative use: *couldn't* and *can't* forcefully express the idea that the speaker believes something is impossible.
(c) Sam isn't eating his food. He *must not be* hungry. That's the only reason I can think of.	In (c): The speaker is expressing a logical conclusion, a "best guess."
(d) I don't know why Sam isn't eating his food. He *may/might not be* hungry right now. Or maybe he doesn't feel well. Or perhaps he ate just before he got here. Who knows?	In (d): The speaker uses *may not/might not* to mention a possibility.

☑ **EXERCISE 27—ORAL:** Complete the sentences by giving your "best guess."

1. A: Sally has flunked every test so far this semester.
   B: She must not . . . *study very hard.*
2. A: Who are you calling?
   B: Dick. The phone is ringing, but there's no answer.
   A: He must not . *be. home*
3. A: I'm trying to be a good host. I've offered Alice a glass of water, a cup of coffee or tea, a soft drink. She doesn't want anything.
   B: She must not . *be. thirsty*
4. A: I offered Mr. Chang some nuts, but he refused them. Then I offered him some candy, and he accepted.
   B: He must not . *like some things . . . .*
5. A: Jack seems very lonely to me.
   B: I agree. He must not . *have any friend .*
6. A: I've been trying to get Timmy into bed for the past hour, but he's still playing with his toys.
   B: He must not . . *be sleepy*

☐ **EXERCISE 28—ORAL:** Give possible reasons for Speaker B's conclusions.

1. A: Someone is knocking at the door. It might be Mary.
   B: It couldn't be Mary. (*Reason? Mary is in Moscow./Mary went to a movie tonight.*)
2. A: Someone left this wool hat here. I think it belongs to Alex.
   B: It couldn't belong to him. (*Reason?*)
3. A: Someone told me that Fred is in Norway.
   B: That can't be right. He couldn't be in Norway. (*Reason?*)
4. A: Look at that big bird. Is it an eagle?
   B: It couldn't be an eagle. (*Reason?*)
5. A: Someone told me that Jane quit school.
   B: You're kidding! That can't be true. (*Reason?*)

☐ **EXERCISE 29—ORAL:** Discuss the meaning of the italicized verbs in the following.

1. **SITUATION:** Anna looks at some figures in her business records:
   $3456 + $7843 = $11,389.
   a. At first glance, she says to herself, "Hmmm. That *may not be* right."
   b. Then she looks at it again and says, "That *must not be* right. 6 + 3 is 9, but 5 + 4 isn't 8."
   c. So she says to herself, "That *couldn't be* right!"
   d. Finally, she adds the figures herself and says, "That *isn't* right."

2. **SITUATION:** Some people are talking about Ed.

   a. Tim says, "Someone told me that Ed quit his job, sold his house, and moved to an island in the Pacific Ocean."

   b. Lucy says, "That *may not be* true."

   c. Linda says, "That *must not be* true."

   d. Frank says, "That *can't be* true."

   e. Don says, "That *isn't* true."

3. **SITUATION:** Tom and his young son hear a noise on the roof.

   a. Tom says, "I wonder what that noise is."

   b. His son says, "It *may be* a bird."

   c. Tom: "It *can't be* a bird. It's running across the roof. Birds don't run across roofs."

   d. His son: "Well, some birds do. It *could be* a big bird that's running fast."

   e. Tom: "No, I think it *must be* some kind of animal. It *might be* a mouse."

   f. His son: "It sounds much bigger than a mouse. It *may be* a dragon!"

   g. Tom: "Son, it *couldn't be* a dragon. We don't have any dragons around here. They exist only in story books."

   h. His son: "It *could be* a little dragon that you don't know about."

   i. Tom: "Well, I suppose it *might be* some kind of lizard."

   j. His son: "I'll go look."

   k. Tom: "That's a good idea."

   l. His son comes back and says, "Guess what, Dad. It's a rat."

4. Make up your own dialogue:

   SITUATION: You and your friend are at your home. You hear a noise. You discuss the noise: what *may/might/could/must/may not/couldn't/must not* be the cause. Then you finally find out what is going on.

2–15 DEGREES OF CERTAINTY: PAST TIME

PAST TIME: AFFIRMATIVE		In (a): The speaker is sure.
	--Why wasn't Mary in class?	In (b): The speaker is making a logical conclusion; e.g., "I saw Mary yesterday and found out that she was sick. I assume that is the reason why she was absent. I can't think of any other good reason."
(a)	100%: She *was* sick.	
(b)	95%: She *must have been* sick.	
(c) less than 50%:	She *may have been* sick. She *might have been* sick. She *could have been* sick.	In (c): The speaker is mentioning one possibility.
PAST TIME: NEGATIVE		
(d)	100%: Sam *wasn't* hungry.	In (d): The speaker is sure.
(e)	99%: Sam *couldn't have been* hungry. Sam *can't have been* hungry.	In (e): The speaker believes that it is impossible for Sam to have been hungry.
(f)	95%: Sam *must not have been* hungry.	In (f): The speaker is making a logical conclusion.
(g) less than 50%:	Sam *may not have been* hungry. Sam *might not have been* hungry.	In (g): The speaker is mentioning one possibility.

☐ **EXERCISE 30—ORAL (BOOKS CLOSED):** Respond first with *may have/might have/could have*. Then use *must have* after you get more information.

Example: Jack was absent yesterday afternoon. Where was he?

Possible response: *I don't know. He may have been at home. He might have gone to a movie. He could have decided to go to the zoo because the weather was so nice.*

Follow-up: What if you overhear him say, "My sister's plane was late yesterday afternoon. I had to wait almost three hours." Now what do you think?

Expected response: *He must have been at the airport to meet his sister's plane.*

1. Jack didn't stay home last night. Where did he go?
   --What if you overhear him say, "I usually go there to study in the evening because it's quiet, and if I need to use any reference books, they're right there."

2. How did Jack get to school today?
   --What if you see him pull some car keys out of his pocket?

3. Jack took a vacation in a warm sunny place. Where do you suppose he went?
   --What if you then overhear him say, "Honolulu is a nice city."

4. Jack visited a person in this class yesterday. Do you know who he visited?
   --What if I say this person (*supply a certain distinguishing characteristic*)?

5. Jack walked into class this morning with a broken arm. What happened?
   --Then you overhear him say, "After this I'm going to watch where I'm going when I'm riding my bicycle."

☐ **EXERCISE 31—ORAL:** Discuss the speakers' meanings in the following. Supply possible reasons for each speaker's conclusion.

1. **SITUATION:** Bob didn't come to the meeting.
   Speaker A: He might not have known about it.
   Speaker B: He must not have known about it.
   Speaker C: He couldn't have known about it.
   Speaker D: He didn't know about it.

2. **SITUATION:** Last night in an old mansion, someone killed Mrs. Peacock with a revolver in the dining room.
   Speaker A: The killer might have been Colonel Mustard.
   Speaker B: But it may not have been Colonel Mustard. It could have been Mrs. White, you know.
   Speaker C: It couldn't have been Mrs. White. It can't have been Colonel Mustard either.
   Speaker D: I think it must have been Miss Scarlet.
   Speaker E: No, it wasn't Miss Scarlet, Colonel Mustard, or Mrs. White.

☒ **EXERCISE 32:** Complete the dialogues. Use an appropriate form of *must* with the verbs in parentheses. Use the negative if necessary.

1. A: Paula fell asleep in class this morning.
   B: She (*stay up*) _____ **must have stayed up** _____ too late last night.

2. A: Jim is eating everything in the salad but the onions. He's pushed all of the onions over to the side of his plate with his fork.
   B: He (*like*) ____ must not like ____ onions.

3. A: George had to give a speech in front of 500 people.
   B: Whew! That's a big audience. He (*be*) __must have been__ *(felt)* nervous.
   A: He was, but nobody could tell.

4. A: What time is it?
   B: Well, we came at seven, and I'm sure we've been here for at least an hour. So it (*be*) ___must be___ around eight o'clock.

5. A: My favorite magazine doesn't come in the mail anymore. I wonder why.

B: Did your subscription run out?

A: That's probably the problem. I (*forget*) _must have forgotten_ to renew it.

6. A: I met Marie's husband at the reception and we said hello to each other, but when I asked him a question in English, he just smiled and nodded.

   B: He (*speak*) _must not speak_ much English.

7. A: Where's Dorothy? I've been looking all over for her.

   B: I saw her about ten minutes ago in the living room. Have you looked there?

   A: Yes, I've looked everywhere. She (*leave*) _must have left_.

8. A: Listen. Do you hear a noise downstairs?

   B: No, I don't hear a thing.

   A: You don't? Then something (*be*) _must be_ wrong with your hearing.

9. A: You have a black eye! What happened?

   B: I walked into a door.

   A: Ouch! That (*hurt*) _must have hurt_.

   B: It did.

10. A: Who is your teacher?

    B: I think his name is Mr. Rock, or something like that.

    A: Mr. Rock? Oh, you (*mean*) _must mean_ Mr. Stone.

11. A: I grew up in a small town.

    B: That (*be*) _must have been_ dull.

    A: It wasn't at all. You can't imagine the fun we had.

12. A: Why are you here so early?

    B: Sam told me that the party started at seven o'clock.

    A: No, it doesn't start until eight o'clock. You (*misunderstand*) _must have misunderstood_.

2–16 DEGREES OF CERTAINTY: FUTURE TIME

100% sure: Kay **will do** well on the test.	→ (*The speaker feels sure.*)
90% sure: { She **should do** well on the test. She **ought to do** well on the test. }	→ (*The speaker is almost sure.*)
less than 50% sure: { She **may do** well on the test. She **might do** well on the test. She **could do** well on the test. }	→ (*The speaker is guessing.*)

(a) Kay has been studying hard. She **should do/ought to do** well on the test tomorrow.	**Should/ought to** can be used to express expectations about future events. In (a): The speaker is saying, "Kay will probably do well on the test. I expect her to do well. That is what I think will happen."
(b) I wonder why Sue hasn't written us. We **should have heard/ought to have heard** from her last week.	The past form of **should/ought to** is used to mean that the speaker expected something that did not occur.

□ **EXERCISE 33:** Use **will, should/ought to,** or **must** in the following. In some, more than one of the modals is possible. Discuss the meanings that the modals convey.*

1. Look at all the people standing in line to get into that movie. It ___must___ be a good movie.

2. Let's go to the lecture tonight. It __should/ought to OR will__ be interesting.

3. Look. Jack's car is in front of his house. He ___must___ be at home. Let's stop and visit him.

4. A: Hello. May I speak to Jack?

   B: He isn't here right now.

   A: What time do you expect him?

   B: He ___should / will / ought to___ be home around nine or so.

5. A: Who do you think is going to win the game tomorrow?

   B: Well, our team has better players, so we ___should / ought to___ win, but you never know. Anything can happen in sports.

---

*COMPARE: **Must** expresses a strong degree of certainty about a *present* situation. (See Chart 2-13.) **Should** and **ought to** express a fairly strong degree of certainty about a *future* situation. **Will** indicates that there is no doubt in the speaker's mind about a future event.

6. A: It's very important for you to be there on time.

   B: I ___will___ be there at seven o'clock. I promise!

7. A: What time are you going to arrive?

   B: Well, the trip takes about four hours. I think I'll leave sometime around noon, so I ___should / ~~will~~ / ought to___ get there around four.

8. A: Here are your tickets, Mr. Anton. Your flight ___will___ depart from Gate 15 on the Blue Concourse at 6:27.

   B: Thank you. Could you tell me where the Blue Concourse is?

9. A: Susie is yawning and rubbing her eyes.

   B: She ___must___ be sleepy. Let's put her to bed early tonight.

10. A: Martha has been working hard all day. She left for work before dawn this morning.

    B: She ___will / should / ought to___ be really tired when she gets home this evening.

11. A: Where can I find the address for the University of Chicago?

    B: I'm not sure, but you ___should / will / ought to___ be able to find that information at the library. The library carries catalogues of most of the universities in the United States.

12. A: When's dinner?

    B: We're almost ready to eat. The rice ___ought to / should / will___ be done in five minutes.

13. A: Where's your dictionary?

    B: Isn't it on my desk?

    A: No.

    B: Then it must be in the bookcase. You ___should / ought to___ find it on the second shelf. Is it there?

14. Hmmm. I wonder what's causing the delay. Ellen's plane ___should / ought to___ have been here an hour ago.

15. I thought I had a dollar in my billfold, but I don't. I ___must___ have spent it.

16. Ed has been acting strangely lately. He ____must____ be in love.

2–17 PROGRESSIVE FORMS OF MODALS

(a) Let's just knock on the door lightly. Tom *may be sleeping*. (*right now*) (b) All of the lights in Ann's room are turned off. She *must be sleeping*. (*right now*)	Progressive form, present time: *modal* + *be* + *-ing*. Meaning: *in progress right now*.
(c) Sue wasn't at home last night when we went to visit her. She *might have been studying* at the library. (d) Al wasn't at home last night. He has a lot of exams coming up soon, and he is also working on a term paper. He *must have been studying* at the library.	Progressive form, past time: *modal* + *have been* + *-ing*. Meaning: *in progress at a time in the past*.

☐ **EXERCISE 34:** Complete the sentences with the verbs in parentheses. Use *must*, *should*, or *may/might/could*. Use the appropriate progressive forms.

1. Look. Those people who are coming in the door are carrying wet umbrellas. It (*rain*) ___must be raining___.

2. A: Why is Margaret in her room?

   B: I don't know. She (*do*) ___may be doing___ her homework.

3. A: Do you smell smoke?

   B: I sure do. Something (*burn*) ___must be burning___.

4. A: The line's been busy for over an hour. Who do you suppose Frank is talking to?

   B: I don't know. He (*talk*) ___may be talking___ to his parents. Or he (*talk*) ___may be talking___ to his sister in Chicago.

5. A: What's all that noise upstairs? It sounds like a herd of elephants.

   B: The children (*play*) ___must be playing___ some kind of game.

   A: That's what it sounds like to me, too. I'll go see.

6. A: I need to call Howard. Do you know which hotel he's staying at in Boston?

   B: Well, he (stay) _____may be staying_____ at the Hilton, but I'm not sure. He (stay) _____may be staying_____ at the Holiday Inn.

7. A: What are you doing?

   B: I'm writing a letter to a friend, but I (study) _____should be studying_____. I have a test tomorrow.

8. A: Did you know that Andy just quit school and started to hitchhike to Alaska?

   B: What? You (kid) _____must be kidding_____!

9. A: Did Ed mean what he said about Andy yesterday?

   B: I don't know. He (kid) _____may have been kidding_____ when he said that, but who knows?

10. A: Did Ed really mean what he said yesterday?

    B: No, I don't think so. I think he (kid) _____must have been kidding_____.

2-18 USING *USED TO* (HABITUAL PAST) AND *BE USED TO*

(a) Jack *used to live* in Chicago.	In (a): At a time in the past, Jack lived in Chicago, but he does not live in Chicago now. *Used to* expresses a habit, activity, or situation that existed in the past but which no longer exists.
(b) Mary *is used to* cold weather. (c) Mary *is accustomed to* cold weather.	*Be used to* means *be accustomed to*. (b) and (c) have the same meaning: Living in a cold climate is usual and normal to Mary. Cold weather, snow, and ice do not seem strange to her.
COMPARE: (d) Jack *used to live* in Chicago. (e) Mary *is used to living* in a cold climate. She *is accustomed to living* there.	To express habitual past, *used* is followed by an infinitive, e.g., *to live* as in (d). *Be used to* and *be accustomed to* are followed by an *-ing* verb form (a gerund*), as in (e).
(f) Bob moved to Alaska. After a while he *got used to/got accustomed to* living in a cold climate.	In the expressions *get used to* and *get accustomed to*, *get* means *become*.

*See Chart 4-2, *Using Gerunds as the Objects of Prepositions*.

□ **EXERCISE 35:** Add an appropriate form of *be* if necessary. If no form of *be* is necessary, write Ø in the blank. (The symbol Ø means: "nothing is needed here.")

1. I have lived in Malaysia for a long time. I __*am*__ used to consistently warm weather.

2. I __Ø__ used to live in Finland, but now I live in France.

3. I __am__ used to sitting at this desk. I sit here every day.

4. I __Ø__ used to sit in the back of the classroom, but now I prefer to sit in the front row.

5. When I was a child, I __Ø__ used to play games with my friends in a big field near my house after school every day.

6. It's hard for my children to stay inside on a cold, rainy day. They __are__ used to playing outside in the big field near our house. They play there almost every day.

7. A teacher __is__ used to answering questions. Students, especially good students, always have a lot of questions.

8. People __Ø__ used to believe the world was flat.

9. Mrs. Hansen __Ø__ used to do all of the laundry and cooking for her family. Now the children are older and Mrs. Hansen has gone back to teaching, so the whole family shares these household chores.

10. Trains __Ø__ used to be the main means of cross-continental travel. Today, most people take airplanes for long-distance travel.

11. Ms. Stanton's job requires her to travel extensively throughout the world. She __is__ used to traveling by plane.

12. You and I are from different cultures. You __are__ used to having fish for breakfast. I __am__ used to having cheese and bread for breakfast.

□ **EXERCISE 36—ORAL (BOOKS CLOSED):** Answer the questions in complete sentences.

I. *used to* (*habitual past*)

1. What did you use to do on summer days when you were a child?
2. . . . in class when you were in elementary school?

3. . . . for fun when you were younger?
4. . . . for exercise on weekends?
5. . . . after school was out when you were a teenager?
6. . . . with your family when you were growing up?
7. What was your daily routine when you were living (*in Bangkok*)?
8. How has your way of life changed in the last few years? What did you use to do that you don't do now?

II. *be used to/be accustomed to*

Example: You have to take a bus to school. Are you accustomed to that?

Response: No, I'm not accustomed to taking a bus to school. I'm accustomed to walking to school.

9. You have to get up at 6:30 every morning. Are you used to that? (*No . . . .*)
10. You have to eat your big meal at six o'clock. Are you accustomed to that?
11. Last night you went to bed at one A.M. Are you accustomed to that?
12. You are living (*in a dormitory*). Are you accustomed to that?
13. You have to speak English all the time. Are you used to that?
14. The weather is very cold. You have to wear heavy clothes. Are you used to that?
15. You borrowed your friend's car, so you have to drive a stick-shift car. Are you accustomed to that?
16. You have a roommate. You have to share your room with another person. Are you used to that?
17. Many people in the United States drink coffee with their meals. Are you accustomed to doing that?
18. You live in your own apartment now. You have to make your own breakfast. Are you used to that?

III. *get used to/get accustomed to*

19. What adjustments do young people have to make, what do they have to get used to or accustomed to when they move from their parents' houses into their own apartments?
20. . . . a person who moves from a warm to a cold climate?
21. . . . a student who moves into a dormitory?
22. . . . a woman when she gets married or a man when he gets married?
23. You are living in a new environment. You have had to make adjustments. What have you gotten used to? What haven't you gotten used to or can't you get used to?

2–19 USING *WOULD* TO EXPRESS A REPEATED ACTION IN THE PAST

(a) When I was a child, my father ***would read*** me a story at night before bed. (b) When I was a child, my father ***used to read*** me a story at night before bed.	***Would*** can be used to express *an action* that was repeated regularly in the past. When ***would*** is used to express this idea, it has the same meaning as ***used to*** (*habitual past*). (a) and (b) have the same meaning.
(c) I ***used to live*** in California. He ***used to be*** a Boy Scout. They ***used to have*** a Ford.	When ***used to*** expresses *a situation* that existed in the past, as in (c), ***would*** may not be used as an alternative. ***Would*** is used only for regularly repeated *actions* in the past.

☐ **EXERCISE 37:** In order to practice using ***would*** to express a repeated action in the past, use ***would*** whenever possible in the following sentences. Otherwise, use ***used to***.

1. I (*be*) _____ **used to be** _____ very shy. Whenever a stranger came to our house, I (*hide*) _____ **would hide** _____ in a closet.

2. I remember my Aunt Susan very well. Every time she came to our house, she (*give*) _____ would give _____ me a big kiss and pinch my cheek.

3. Illiteracy is still a problem in my country, but it (*be*) _____ used to be _____ _____ much worse.

4. I (*be*) _____ used to be _____ afraid of flying. My heart (*start*) _____ would start _____ pounding every time I stepped on a plane. But now I'm used to flying and enjoy it.

5. I (*be*) _____ used to be _____ an anthropology major. Once I was a member of an archaeological expedition. Every morning, we (*get*) _____ would get _____ up before dawn. After breakfast, we (*spend*) _____ would spend _____ our entire day in the field. Sometimes one of us (*find*) _____ would find _____ a particularly interesting item, perhaps an arrowhead or a piece of pottery. When that happened, other members of the group (*gather*) _____ would gather _____ around to see what had been unearthed.

6. I got a new bicycle when I was ten. My friends (*ask*) _would ask_
_____ to ride it, but for years I (*let, never*) _would never_
_____ let _____ anyone else use it.

7. When my grandfather was a boy and had a cold, his mother (*make*)
would make / used to him go to bed. Then she (*put*) _would_
_ put _ goose fat on his chest.

8. When I was a child, I (*take*) _____ would take _____ a flashlight to
bed with me so that I could read comic books without my parents'
knowing about it.

9. Last summer, my sister and I took a camping trip in the Rocky
Mountains. It was a wonderful experience. Every morning, we (*wake*)
would wake up to the sound of singing birds. During the
day, we (*hike*) _____ would hide _____ through woods and along
mountain streams. Often we (*see*) _____ would see _____ deer. On
one occasion we saw a bear and quickly ran in the opposite direction.

10. I can remember Mrs. Sawyer's fifth grade class well. When we arrived
each morning, she (*sit*) _would be sitting_ at her desk. She
(*smile, always*) _would always smile_ and (*say*) _____ say _____
_____ hello to each student as he or she entered.
When the bell rang, she (*stand*) _____ would stand _____ up and (*clear*)
_____ clear _____ her throat. That was our signal to be quiet.
Class was about to begin.

2–20 EXPRESSING PREFERENCE: *WOULD RATHER*

(a) I ***would rather go*** to a movie tonight *than* **study** grammar. (b) ***I'd rather study*** history *than* (**study**) biology.	***Would rather*** expresses preference. In (a): Notice that the simple form of a verb follows both ***would rather*** and ***than***. In (b): If the verb is the same, it does not have to be repeated after ***than***.
—How much do you weigh? (c) ***I'd rather not tell*** you.	Contraction: ***I would*** = ***I'd***. Negative form: ***would rather*** + ***not***.
(d) The movie was okay, but I ***would rather have gone*** to the concert last night.	The past form: ***would rather have*** + *past participle*. Usual pronunciation: "I'd rather-of."
(e) ***I'd rather be lying*** on a beach in Florida *than* (**be**) **sitting** in class right now.	Progressive form: ***would rather*** + ***be*** + ***-ing***.

□ **EXERCISE 38—ORAL:** Use ***would rather*** to complete the sentences.

1. A: Do you want to go to the concert tonight?
   B: Not really. I _____
2. A: Did you go to the concert last night?
   B: Yes, but I _____
3. A: What are you doing right now?
   B: I'm studying grammar, but I _____
4. A: Do you want to come with us to the museum tomorrow?
   B: Thanks, but I . . . .
5. A: I . . . than . . . .
   B: Not me. I . . . than . . . .

□ **EXERCISE 39—ORAL (BOOKS CLOSED):** Answer in complete sentences.

1. You are in (*name of place*) right now. Where would you rather be?
2. What would you rather do than go to class?
3. What did you do last night? What would you have rather done?
4. What are you doing right now? What would you rather be doing?

Begin your answer with "No, I'd rather . . . ."

5. Do you want to go to a movie tonight? (to a concert?) (to the zoo tomorrow?)
6. Do you want to play tennis this afternoon? (go bowling?) (shoot pool?)
7. Do you want to eat at the cafeteria? (at a Chinese restaurant?)
8. Would you like to live in (*name of a city*)?

106 □ CHAPTER 2

2–21 USING *CAN* AND *BE ABLE TO*

(a) Tom is strong. He *can lift* that heavy box.	*Can* usually expresses the idea that something is possible because certain characteristics or conditions exist. *Can* combines the ideas of *possibility* and *ability*.
(b) I *can play* the piano. I've taken lessons for many years.	
(c) You *can see* fish at an aquarium.	In (a): It is possible for Tom to lift that box because he is strong.
(d) That race car *can go* very fast.	In (b): It is possible for me to play the piano because I have acquired that ability.
	In (c): It is possible to see fish at an aquarium because an aquarium has fish.
	In (d): It is possible for that car to go fast because of its special characteristics.
(e) Dogs can bark, but they *cannot/can't talk*.	Negative form: *cannot* or *can't*. (Also possible, but not as common: *can not*, written as two words.)
COMPARE:	In (f): I can walk to school because certain conditions exist.
(f) I *can walk* to school. It's not far.	In (g): I am less than 50% certain that I will walk to school.
(g) I *may walk* to school. Or I may take the bus.	
COMPARE:	*Can* is also used to give permission. In giving permission, *can* is usually used in informal situations, as in (h); *may* is usually used in formal situations, as in (i).
(h) I'm not quite ready to go, but you *can leave* if you're in a hurry. I'll meet you later.	
(i) When you finish the test, you *may leave*.	
COMPARE:	The use of *be able to* in the simple present (*am/is/are able to*) is uncommon (but possible).
(j) Tom *can lift* that box.	
(k) *Uncommon*: Tom *is able to lift* that box.	
(l) Ann *will be able to lift* that box. Bob *may be able to lift* that box. Sue *should be able to lift* that box. Jim *used to be able to lift* that box.	*Be able to* is more commonly used in combination with other auxiliaries, as in (l).

☐ **EXERCISE 40:** *Can* is usually pronounced /kən/. *Can't* is usually pronounced /kænt/. Try to determine whether the teacher is saying *can* or *can't* in the following sentences.*

    1. The secretary *can/can't* help you.

    2. My mother *can/can't* speak English.

    3. My friend *can/can't* meet you at the airport.

    4. Mr. Smith *can/can't* answer your question.

---

*Sometimes even native speakers have a little difficulty distinguishing between *can* and *can't*.

5. We *can/can't* come to the meeting.
6. *Can/can't* you come?
7. You *can/can't* take that course.
8. I *can/can't* cook.
9. Our son *can/can't* count to ten.
10. I *can/can't* drive a stick-shift car.

☐ **EXERCISE 41—ORAL:** Make sentences, answer questions, discuss meanings as suggested in the following.

1. Name a physical ability that you have and a physical ability you don't have.
2. Name an acquired ability that you have and an acquired ability you don't have.
3. There's no class tomorrow.
   a. What can you do tomorrow?
   b. What may (might) you do tomorrow?
   c. What are you going to do tomorrow?
4. a. What are the possible ways you can get to school?
   b. What are the possible ways you may get to school tomorrow?
5. What is the difference in use of **can** and **may** in the following?
   a. Sure! You can borrow five dollars from me. You *can pay* me back later.
   b. You *may pay* the bill either in person or by mail.
6. Compare the following, using **can** and **can't**:
   a. people and animals

      (*Example: Birds can fly, but people can't.*)

   b. adults and children
   c. women and men
7. Plan your next vacation and describe what you:
   a. may do on your vacation.
   b. can do on your vacation.
   c. will do on your vacation.
8. Make sentences that include the following verb phrases:
   a. might be able to
   b. will be able to
   c. should be able to
   d. may not be able to
   e. must not be able to
   f. should have been able to
   g. might not have been able to
   h. used to be able to

2-22 PAST ABILITY: *COULD*

(a) When I was younger, I *could run* fast. (*Probable meaning*: I used to be able to run fast, but now I can't run fast.)	In affirmative sentences about past ability, *could* usually means "used to be able to." The use of *could* usually indicates that the ability existed in the past but does not exist now.
(b) Tom has started an exercise program. He *was able to run* two miles yesterday without stopping or slowing down.	If the speaker is talking about an ability to perform an act at one particular time in the past, *was/were able to* can be used in affirmative sentences but not *could*. *Could* is not appropriate in (b).
--*Did you read the news about the mountain climbers?* (c) INCORRECT: *They **could reach** the top of Mt. Everest yesterday.* (d) CORRECT: They *were able to reach* the top yesterday. They *managed to reach* the top yesterday. They *reached* the top yesterday.	Note that (c) is incorrect. Instead of *could*, the speaker needs to use *were able to*, *managed to*, or *the simple past*.
(e) They *couldn't reach/weren't able to reach* the top yesterday. (f) Tom *couldn't run/wasn't able to run* five miles yesterday.	In negative sentences, there is no difference between using *could* and *was/were able to*.

☐ **EXERCISE 42—ORAL:** Substitute *could* for the italicized verbs if possible.

1. We had a good time yesterday. We *went* to the zoo. The children *enjoyed* themselves very much. They *saw* polar bears and elephants. (*No substitution of "could" is possible.*)

2. When I lived in St. Louis, I *went* to the zoo whenever I wanted to, but now I live in a small town and the nearest zoo is a long way away. ("*I could go*" *can be used instead of* "*I went*" *to give the idea of* "*used to be able to.*")

3. Usually I don't have time to watch TV, but last night I *watched* the news while I was eating dinner. I *heard* the news about the political situation in my country.

4. When I lived at home with my parents, I *watched* TV every day if I wanted to, but now while I'm going to school, I live in a small apartment and don't have a television set.

5. When I worked as a secretary, I *was able to type* 60 words a minute without making a mistake. My typing skills aren't nearly as good now.

6. Yesterday I *typed* these reports for my boss. I don't type very well, but I *was able to finish* the reports without making too many mistakes.

7. When I went to my favorite fishing hole last Sunday, I *caught* two fish. I *brought* them home and *fixed* them for dinner.

8. When I was a child, the river that flows through our town had plenty of fish. My mother used to go fishing two or three times a week. Usually she *caught* enough for our dinner within an hour or so. ~~could catch~~

9. Last night Mark and I had an argument about politics. Finally, I *managed to convince* him that I was right. ~~could convince~~

10. My grandfather was a merchant all his life. He knew how to make a sale by using psychology. He *was able to convince* anyone to buy anything, whether they needed it or not.

11. The game we went to yesterday was exciting. The other team *played* good defense, but my favorite player *managed to score* two goals.

12. At the sale yesterday, I *got* this new hat for half price. Quite a bargain, don't you think?

13. When I ran into Mrs. Forks yesterday, I *recognized* her even though I hadn't seen her for years.

14. The students are finished with this exercise. They *did* it without much trouble.

2–23 SUMMARY CHART OF MODALS AND SIMILAR EXPRESSIONS

AUXILIARY	USES	PRESENT/FUTURE	PAST
may	(1) polite request	*May* I *borrow* your pen?	
	(2) formal permission	You *may leave* the room.	
	(3) less than 50% certainty	--Where's John? He *may be* at the library.	He *may have been* at the library.
might	(1) less than 50% certainty	--Where's John? He *might be* at the library.	He *might have been* at the library.
	(2) polite request (*rare*)	*Might* I *borrow* your pen?	
should	(1) advisability	I *should study* tonight.	I *should have studied* last night
	(2) 90% certainty	She *should do* well on the test. (*future only, not present*)	She *should have done* well on the test.
ought to	(1) advisability	I *ought to study* tonight.	I *ought to have studied* last night.
	(2) 90% certainty	She *ought to do* well on the test. (*future only, not present*)	She *ought to have done* well on the test.

AUXILIARY	USES	PRESENT/FUTURE	PAST
had better	(1) advisability with threat of bad result	You **had better be** on time, or we will leave without you.	*(past form uncommon)*
be supposed to	(1) expectation	Class **is supposed to begin** at 10.	Class **was supposed to begin** at 10.
be to	(1) strong expectation	You **are to be** here at 9:00.	You **were to be** here at 9:00.
must	(1) strong necessity	I **must go** to class today.	I **had to go** to class yesterday.
	(2) prohibition *(negative)*	You **must not** open that door.	
	(3) 95% certainty	Mary isn't in class. She **must be** sick. *(present only)*	Mary **must have been** sick yesterday.
have to	(1) necessity	I **have to go** to class today.	I **had to go** to class yesterday.
	(2) lack of necessity *(negative)*	I **don't have to go** to class today.	I **didn't have to go** to class yesterday.
have got to	(1) necessity	I **have got to go** to class today.	I **had to go** to class yesterday.
will	(1) 100% certainty	He **will be** here at 6:00. *(future only)*	
	(2) willingness	--The phone's ringing. I**'ll get** it.	
	(3) polite request	**Will** you please **pass** the salt?	
be going to	(1) 100% certainty	He **is going to be** here at 6:00. *(future only)*	
	(2) definite plan	I**'m going to paint** my bedroom. *(future only)*	I **was going to paint** my room, but I didn't have time.
can	(1) ability/possibility	I **can run** fast.	I **could run** fast when I was a child, but now I can't.
	(2) informal permission	You **can use** my car tomorrow.	
	(3) informal polite request	**Can** I **borrow** your pen?	
	(4) impossibility *(negative only)*	That **can't be** true!	That **can't have been** true!

(continued)

AUXILIARY	USES	PRESENT/FUTURE	PAST
could	(1) past ability		I *could run* fast when I was a child.
	(2) polite request	*Could* I *borrow* your pen? *Could* you *help* me?	
	(3) suggestion	--I need help in math. You *could talk* to your teacher.	You *could have talked* to your teacher.
	(4) less than 50% certainty	--Where's John? He *could be* at home.	He *could have been* at home.
	(5) impossibility (*negative only*)	That *couldn't be* true!	That *couldn't have been* true!
be able to	(1) ability	I *am able to help* you. I *will be able to help* you.	I *was able to help* him.
would	(1) polite request	*Would* you please *pass* the salt? *Would* you *mind* if I left early?	
	(2) preference	I *would rather go* to the park than *stay* home.	I *would rather have gone* to the park.
	(3) repeated action in the past		When I was a child, I *would visit* my grandparents every weekend.
used to	(1) repeated action in the past		I *used to* visit my grandparents every weekend.
shall	(1) polite question to make a suggestion	*Shall* I *open* the window?	
	(2) future with "I" or "we" as subject	I *shall* arrive at nine. (*will = more common*)	

Note: Use of modals in reported speech is discussed in Chapter 7. Use of modals in conditional sentences is discussed in Chapter 10.

□ **EXERCISE 43—ORAL:** Discuss the differences in meaning, if any, in the following groups of sentences.

1. a. May I use your phone?
   b. Could I use your phone?
   c. Can I use your phone?

2. a. You should take an English course.
   b. You ought to take an English course.
   c. You're supposed to take an English course.
   d. You must take an English course.
3. a. You should see a doctor about that cut on your arm.
   b. You had better see a doctor about that cut on your arm.
   c. You have to see a doctor about that cut on your arm.
4. a. You must not use that door.
   b. You don't have to use that door.
5. a. I will be at your house by six o'clock.
   b. I should be at your house by six o'clock.
6. --*There is a knock at the door. Who do you suppose it is?*
   a. It might be Sally.
   b. It may be Sally.
   c. It could be Sally.
   d. It must be Sally.
7. --*There's a knock at the door. I think it's Mike.*
   a. It may not be Mike.
   b. It couldn't be Mike.
   c. It can't be Mike.
8. --*Where's Jack?*
   a. He might have gone home.
   b. He must have gone home.
   c. He had to go home.
9. a. Each student should have a health certificate.
   b. Each student is to have a health certificate.
   c. Each student must have a health certificate.
10. a. If you're having a problem, you could talk to Mrs. Anderson.
    b. If you're having a problem, you should talk to Mrs. Anderson.
11. a. I've got to go.
    b. I have to go.
    c. I should go.
    d. I'm supposed to go.
    e. I'd better go.
    f. I'd rather go.
12. --*I needed some help.*
    a. You should have asked Tom.
    b. You could have asked Tom.
13. a. When I was living at home, I would go to the beach every weekend with my friends.
    b. When I was living at home, I used to go the beach every weekend with my friends.

□ **EXERCISE 44:** Use a modal or similar expression with each verb in parentheses. More than one auxiliary may be possible. Use the one that seems most appropriate to you.

(had better, ought to, have to, must)

1. It looks like rain. We (*shut*) __Should shut__ the windows.

2. Ann, (*hand, you*) __Could you hand__ me that dish? Thanks.
   (would (can, will))

3. I returned a book to the library yesterday. It was two weeks overdue, so I (*pay*) __had to pay__ a fine of $1.40. I (*return*) __Should have returned__ the book when it was due.

4. Spring break starts on the thirteenth. We (*go, not*) __don't have to go__ to classes again until the twenty-second. *(won't)*

5. (*Make, I*) __May/I make__ an appointment to see Dean Witherspoon? *(could)*

6. Neither of us knows the way to their house. We (*take*) __Should/May take__ a map with us or we'll probably get lost. *(can)*

7. The baby is only a year old, but she (*say, already*) __can already say__ a few words. *(is already able to say)*

8. You (*tell, not*) __must not tell__ Jack about the party. It's a surprise birthday party for him. *(shouldn't; had better not; can't tell)*

9. Excuse me. I didn't understand. (*Repeat, you*) __Would you V repeat__ what you said? *(please)*

10. In the United States, elementary education is compulsory. All children (*attend*) __must attend__ six years of elementary school. *(have to)*

11. When I was younger, I (*run*) _____Could run_____ ten miles without stopping. But now I (*run, not*) _____can't run_____ more than a mile or two.

12. There was a long line in front of the theater. We (*wait*) _____had to wait_____ almost an hour to buy our tickets.

13. A: I'd like to go to a warm, sunny place next winter. Any suggestions?

    B: You (*go*) _____Could go_____ to Hawaii or Mexico. Or how about Spain?

14. I don't feel like going to the library to study this afternoon. I (*go*) _____Would rather go_____ to the shopping mall than to the library.

15. A: Mrs. Wilson got a traffic ticket. She didn't stop at a stop sign.

    B: That's surprising. Usually she's a very cautious driver and obeys all the traffic laws. She (*see, not*) _____must not have seen_____ the sign.

16. Microwave ovens make cooking fast and easy. If you have a microwave, you (*cook*) _____can cook_____ this frozen dinner in five minutes.

17. Annie, you (*clean*) (had better, ought to, should, have to) _____must clean_____ this mess before Dad gets home. He'll be mad if he sees all this stuff all over the living room floor.

18. A: This is Steve's tape recorder, isn't it?

    B: It (*be, not*) _____Could not be_____ his. He doesn't have a tape recorder, at least not that I know of. It (*belong*) _____might / must / may belong_____ to Lucy or to Linda. They sometimes bring their tape recorders to class.

19. I had a good time when I was a teenager. When my friends and I got together, we (*do*) _____would / used to do_____ anything and everything that sounded like fun.

20. A: You're always too tense. It's not good for you. You (*learn*) (must, ought to, had better, have to) _____should learn_____ to relax.

    B: How?

    A: Pay attention to your muscles. When they're tight, take a few long, deep breaths. Deep breaths (*be*) _____can be_____ very relaxing.

☐ **EXERCISE 45:** Use a modal or similar expression with each verb in parentheses. More than one auxiliary may be possible. Use the one that seems most appropriate to you.

1. Don is putting on a little weight around his middle. He (*get*) _Should_ _get_ more exercise.

2. I'm sleepy. I (*keep, not*) _can't keep_ my eyes open. I (*go*) _had better go_ to bed before I fall asleep right here.

   Should, ought to, have to / had

3. In my country, a girl and boy (*go, not*) _I can not go / must not_ out on a date unless they are accompanied by a chaperone.

   must not

4. Jimmy was serious when he said he wanted to be a cowboy when he grew up. We (*laugh, not*) _should not have laughed_ at him. We hurt his feelings.

5. (*Cash, you*) _Would / you cash_ this check for me?

   can / could

6. This is none of his business. He (*stick, not*) _should not stick_ his nose into other people's business.

   oughtn't

7. My wife and ten children are coming to join me here. They (*live, not*) _can't live_ in my dormitory room. I (*find*) _must (have to) find / had better_ an apartment.

8. A: (*Speak, I*) _May I speak_ to Peggy?

   I can, could

   B: She (*come, not*) _can't come_ to the phone right now. (*Take, I*) _May I take_ message?

   can

9. A: Where are you going?

   B: I (*go*) _have to go / have got to go_ to the library. I have to do some research for my term paper.

10. A: How are you planning to get to the airport?

    B: By taxi.

    A: You (*take*) _should take_ a shuttle bus instead. It's cheaper than a taxi. You (*get*) _can get_ one in front of the hotel. It picks up passengers there on a regular schedule.

    could, ought to / may

11. A: Why didn't you come to the party last night?

    B: I (*study*) _had to study_.

A: You (*come*) *should have come*. We had a good time.

12. A: Should I go to the University of Iowa or Iowa State University?

B: Think it over for a few days. You (*make, not*) *don't have to make*
_____ up your mind right now. There's no hurry.

13. A: The phone's ringing again. Let's not answer it. Just let it ring.

B: No, we (*answer*) *(had better, ought to, have to) I should answer* it. It (*be*) *could be /might,*
_____ important. *may*

14. Jane's looking at the test paper the teacher just returned. She's smiling.
She (*pass*) *must have passed* the test. 95%

15. It's not like Tony to be late. He (*be*) *should have been* here an hour ago. I hope nothing bad happened.

16. A: This is a great open-air market. Look at all this wonderful fresh fish.
What kind of fish is this?

B: I'm not sure. It (*be*) *may /might, could be* ocean perch. Let's ask.

17. The teacher called on Sam in class yesterday, but he kept looking out the window and didn't respond. He (*daydream*) *must have been*.

18. When I arrived home last night, I discovered that I had forgotten my key.
My roommate was asleep, but I (*wake*) *was able to wake* him
(had to wake)
by knocking loudly on the door.

19. A: Did you enjoy the movie last night?

B: It was okay, but I (*stay*) *would rather have √ stayed* home and (*watch*)
watched or (should have stayed) TV. There was a good program on that I
wanted to catch. I only went because my wife wanted to see the movie.

20. A: Somebody called you while you were out, but she didn't leave her name.

B: Who did it sound like? Anybody you know?

A: Well, it (*be*) *may /could, might have been* Phyllis, but that's just a
guess. I (*ask*) *could I might I should have asked* who was
calling, but I didn't.

B: That's okay.

※ EXERCISE 46—ERROR ANALYSIS: Find and correct the errors in the following.

1. If you have a car, you can traveled around the United States.

2. During class the students must to sit quietly. When the students have questions, they must to raise their hands.

3. When you send for the brochure, you should included a self-addressed, stamped envelope.

4. A film director must has control over every aspect of a movie.

5. When I was a child, I can went to the roof of my house and saw all the other houses and streets.

6. While I was working in the fields, my son would brought me oranges or candy.

7. I used to break my leg in a soccer game three months ago.

8. May you please help me with this?

9. Many students would rather to study on their own than going to classes.

10. We supposed to bring our books to class every day.

□ EXERCISE 47—PREPOSITIONS: Supply appropriate prepositions.

1. I am not familiar __with__ that author's works.

2. He doesn't approve _____ smoking.

3. I subscribe __to__ several magazines.

4. Water consists __of__ oxygen and hydrogen.

5. I became uncomfortable because she was staring __at__ me.

6. She hid the candy __from__ the children.

7. He never argues __with__ his wife.

8. I arrived __in__ this country two weeks ago.

9. We arrived __at__ the airport ten minutes late.

10. Has Mary recovered __from__ her illness?

11. I pray __for__ peace.

12. I am envious __of / of__ people who can speak three or four languages fluently.

13. Why are you angry __at / with__ me? Did I do something wrong?

14. They are very patient ___with___ their children.

15. The students responded ___to___ the questions.

☐ **EXERCISE 48—PHRASAL VERBS:** Supply appropriate prepositions for the following two-word or three-word verbs.

1. A: Where did you grow ___up___?
   B: In Seattle, Washington.

2. A: I'm trying to find yesterday's newspaper. Have you seen it?
   B: I'm afraid I threw it ___away___. I thought you had finished reading it.

3. A: Don't forget to turn the lights ___off___ before you go to bed.
   B: I won't.

4. A: I have a car, so I can drive us to the festival.
   B: Good.
   A: What time should I pick you ___up___?
   B: Any time after five would be fine.

5. A: We couldn't see the show at the outdoor theater last night.
   B: Why not?
   A: It was called ___off___ on account of rain.
   B: Did you get a raincheck?

6. A: Thomas looks sad.
   B: I think he misses his girlfriend. Let's try to cheer him ___up___.

7. A: I would like to check this book ___out___. What should I do?
   B: Take the book to the circulation desk and give the librarian your student I.D.

8. A: What brought ___up___ your decision to quit your present job?
   B: I was offered a better job.

9. A: How many people showed ___up___ for the meeting yesterday?
   B: About twenty.

10. A: How was your vacation?
    B: I had a great time.
    A: When did you get ___back___ home?
    B: A couple of days ago. I had planned to stay a little longer, but I ran ___out___ ___of___ money.

CHAPTER **3**

The Passive

3-1   FORMING THE PASSIVE

ACTIVE: (a) Mary **helped** the boy. S V O PASSIVE: (b) The boy **was helped** by Mary. S V	Form of the passive: **be** + *past participle*.
	In the passive, *the object* of an active verb *becomes the subject* of the passive verb: ''the boy'' in (a) becomes the subject of the passive verb in (b). (a) and (b) have the same meaning.
ACTIVE: (c) An accident **happened**. PASSIVE: (d) *(none)*	Only transitive verbs (verbs that are followed by an object) are used in the passive. It is not possible to use verbs such as **happen**, **sleep**, **come**, and **seem** (intransitive verbs) in the passive. (See Appendix 1, Chart A-1.)

	ACTIVE			PASSIVE		
simple present	Mary	*helps*	John.	John	*is helped*	by Mary.
present progressive	Mary	*is helping*	John.	John	*is being helped*	by Mary.
present perfect	Mary	*has helped*	John.	John	*has been helped*	by Mary.
simple past	Mary	*helped*	John.	John	*was helped*	by Mary.
past progressive	Mary	*was helping*	John.	John	*was being helped*	by Mary.
past perfect	Mary	*had helped*	John.	John	*had been helped*	by Mary.
simple future	Mary	*will help*	John.	John	*will be helped*	by Mary.
be going to	Mary	*is going to help*	John.	John	*is going to be helped*	by Mary.
future perfect*	Mary	*will have helped*	John.	John	*will have been helped*	by Mary.

*The progressive forms of the present perfect, past perfect, future, and future perfect are very rarely used in the passive.

☐ **EXERCISE 1:** Change the active to the passive by supplying the correct form of **be**.

1. Tom *opens* the door. → The door _____*is*_____ *opened* by Tom.
2. Tom *is opening* the door. → The door _*is being*_ *opened* by Tom.
3. Tom *has opened* the door. → The door _*has been*_ *opened* by Tom.
4. Tom *opened* the door. → The door _*was*_ *opened* by Tom.
5. Tom *was opening* the door. → The door _*was being*_ *opened* by Tom.
6. Tom *had opened* the door. → The door _*had been*_ *opened* by Tom.
7. Tom *will open* the door. → The door _*will be*_ *opened* by Tom.
8. Tom *is going to open* the door. → The door _*is going to be*_ *opened* by Tom.
9. Tom *will have opened* the door. → The door _*will have been*_ *opened* by Tom.

☐ **EXERCISE 2:** Change the active to the passive.

1. Shakespeare *wrote* that play. → *That play was written by Shakespeare.*
2. Bill *will invite* Ann to the party. → Ann will be invited to the party by Bill.
3. Alex *is preparing* that report. → That report is being prepared by Alex.
4. Waitresses and waiters *serve* customers. Customers are served by waitresses and waiters.
5. The teacher *is going to explain* the lesson. The lesson is going to be explained by the teacher.
6. Shirley *has suggested* a new idea. A new idea has been suggested by Shirley.
7. Two horses *were pulling* the farmer's wagon. The farmer's wagon was being pulled by two horses.

8. Kathy *had returned* the book to the library. *The book had been returned to the library by Kathy.*

9. By this time tomorrow, the president *will have made* the announcement. *will have been made*

10. I *didn't write* that note. Jim *wrote* it. *That note wasn't written by me. It was written by Jim*

11. Alice *didn't make* that pie. *Did* Mrs. French *make* it? *That pie wasn't made by Alice. Was it made by Mrs French*

12. *Does* Prof. Jackson *teach* that course? I know that Prof. Adams *doesn't teach* it. *Is that course taught by Prof. J? & I know that it isn't taught by Prof ?*

13. Mrs. Andrews *hasn't signed* those papers yet. *Has* Mr. Andrews *signed* them yet? *Prof ? These papers haven't been signed by Mrs yet. Has them been signed by*

14. *Is* Mr. Brown *painting* your house? *Is your house being painted by Mr. Brown?*

15. His tricks *won't fool* me. *I won't be fooled by his tricks.*

☐ **EXERCISE 3:** Change the active to passive if possible. Some verbs are intransitive and cannot be changed.

1. A strange thing happened yesterday. (*no change*)

2. Jackie scored the winning goal. → *The winning goal was scored by Jackie.*

3. My cat died. *(no change)*

4. I agree with Dr. Ikeda's theory.

5. Dr. Ikeda developed that theory. *That theory was developed by Dr. Ikeda.*

6. Timmy dropped the cup. *The cup was dropped by timmy.*

7. The cup fell to the floor.

8. The assistant manager interviewed me. *I was interviewed by —*

9. It rained hard yesterday.

10. A hurricane destroyed the small fishing village. *The small — was destroyed by A*

11. Dinosaurs existed millions of years ago.

12. A large vase stands in the corner of our front hallway.

13. The children seemed happy when they went to the zoo.

14. After class, one of the students always erases the chalkboard. *After class, the chalkboard is erased always by one of the students*

15. The solution to my problem appeared to me in a dream.

3-2 USING THE PASSIVE

(a) Rice **is grown** in India. (b) Our house **was built** in 1890. (c) This olive oil **was imported** from Spain.	Usually the passive is used without a "**by** phrase." The passive is most frequently used when it is not known or not important to know exactly who performs an action. In (a): Rice is grown in India by people, by farmers, by someone. In sentence (a), it is not known or important to know exactly who grows rice in India. (a), (b), and (c) illustrate the most common use of the passive, i.e., without the "**by** phrase."
(d) *Life on the Mississippi* **was written** by Mark Twain.	The "**by** phrase" is included only if it is important to know who performs an action. In (d), *by Mark Twain* is important information.
(e) My aunt **made** this rug. (*active*) (f) This rug **was made** by my aunt. That rug **was made** by my mother.	If the speaker/writer knows who performs an action, usually the active is used, as in (e).
	The passive may be used with the "**by** phrase" instead of the active when the speaker/writer wants to focus attention on the subject of a sentence. In (f) the focus of attention is on two rugs.

☐ **EXERCISE 4:** Why is the use of the passive appropriate in the following sentences? What would be the active equivalents of the passive sentences?

1. My sweater was made in England.

2. The new highway will be completed sometime next month.

3. Language skills are taught in every school in the country.

4. Beethoven's Seventh Symphony was performed at the concert last night.

5. The World Cup soccer games are being televised all over the world.

6. This composition was written by Ali. That one was written by Yoko.

7. The Washington Monument is visited by hundreds of people every day.

8. The chief writing material of ancient times was papyrus. It was used in Egypt, Greece, and other Mediterranean lands.

9. Parchment, another writing material that was widely used in ancient times, was made from the skins of animals such as sheep and goats. After the hair had been removed, the skins were stretched and rubbed smooth.

10. Paper, the main writing material today, was invented by the Chinese.

□ **EXERCISE 5:** Change the following active sentences to passive sentences if possible. (Some of the verbs are intransitive and cannot be changed.) Keep the same tense. Include the "*by* phrase" only if necessary.

1. People grow corn in Iowa. → *Corn is grown in Iowa.*

2. Peter came here two months ago. (*no change*)

3. Someone made this antique table in 1734. *This antique was made in 1734*

4. An accident happened at the corner of Fifth and Main. (*no change*) *intransitive*

5. Someone stole my purse. *My purse was stole*

6. Someone was making the coffee when I walked into the kitchen.

7. Translators have translated that book into many languages.

8. Jim's daughter drew that picture. My son drew this picture.

9. The judges will judge the applicants on the basis of their originality.

10. My sister's plane will arrive at 10:35.

11. Is Professor Rivers teaching that course this semester?

12. When did someone invent the radio? *When was the radio invented?*

13. The mail carrier had already delivered the mail by the time I left for school this morning.

14. When is someone going to announce the results of the contest?

15. After the concert was over, hundreds of fans mobbed the rock music star outside the theater.

16. Ever since I arrived here, I have been living in the dormitory because someone told me that it was cheaper to live there than in an apartment. *I was told that it was*

17. They* are going to build the new hospital next year. They have already built the new elementary school.

18. If you* expose a film to light while you are developing it, you will ruin the negatives.

---

*In #17, *they* is an impersonal pronoun; it refers to "some people" but to no people in particular. In #18, *you* is an impersonal pronoun; it refers to any person or people in general.

3-3 INDIRECT OBJECTS AS PASSIVE SUBJECTS

I.O. **D.O.** (a) Someone gave **Mrs. Lee** an award. (b) **Mrs. Lee** was given an award.	**I.O.** = indirect object. **D.O.** = direct object. Either an indirect object or a direct object may become the subject of a passive sentence.
(c) Someone gave **an award** to Mrs. Lee. (d) **An award** was given to Mrs. Lee.	(a), (b), (c), and (d) have the same meaning. Note in (d): When the direct object becomes the subject, **to** is usually used in front of the indirect object.*

*The omission of **to** is more common in British English than American English: *An award was given Mrs. Lee.*

☐ **EXERCISE 6:** Find the INDIRECT OBJECT in each sentence, and make it the focus of attention by using it as the subject of a passive sentence. Use the "**by** phrase" only if necessary.

1. Someone handed Ann a menu at the restaurant.
   (*indirect object = Ann*) → *Ann was handed a menu at the restaurant.*
2. Indiana University has awarded Peggy a scholarship.
3. Some company paid Fred three hundred dollars in consulting fees.
4. A local advertising company has offered Maria a good job.
5. They will send you a bill at the end of the month.
6. Someone will give the starving people a week's supply of rice as soon as the food supplies arrive in the famine-stricken area.

☐ **EXERCISE 7—ORAL (BOOKS CLOSED):** Change active to passive.

Example: Someone built that house ten years ago.
Response: That house was built ten years ago.

1. Someone invited you to a party.
2. Someone wrote that book in 1987.
3. (. . .) wrote that book in 1987.
4. People grow rice in many countries.
5. The secretary is typing the letter.
6. Someone is televising the game.
7. Teachers teach reading in the first grade.
8. Someone has offered (. . .) a good job.
9. Someone told you to be here at ten.
10. Someone published that book in 1985.
11. Someone has sent (. . .) an invitation to a wedding.
12. Someone made that hat in Mexico.

13. Someone will serve dinner at six.
14. Someone is going to serve dinner at six.
15. Someone will announce the news tomorrow.
16. Someone will give the exam next week.
17. Someone has paid the bill.
18. Someone has made a mistake.
19. Someone has watered the plants.
20. The teacher is giving a test in the next room right now.
21. The teacher is asking you to use the passive.

□ **EXERCISE 8—ORAL (BOOKS CLOSED):** Use the passive in your response.

Example: **Teacher to A:** Someone stole your watch.
　　　　　　　　A: My watch was stolen.
　　　　　　Teacher to B: What happened to (. . .)'s watch?
　　　　　　　　B: It was stolen.
Example: **Teacher to A:** People speak Arabic in many countries.
　　　　　　　　A: Arabic is spoken in many countries.
　　　　　　Teacher to B: Is Arabic a common language?
　　　　　　　　B: Yes. It is spoken in many countries.

1. **A:** Someone stole your pen.
　　B: What happened to (. . .)'s pen?
2. **A:** People speak Spanish in many countries.
　　B: Is Spanish a common language?
3. **A:** People play soccer in many countries.
　　B: Is soccer a popular sport?
4. **A:** Mark Twain wrote that book.
　　B: Who is the author of that book?
5. **A:** You went to a movie last night, but it bored you.
　　B: Why did (. . .) leave the movie before it ended?
6. **A:** Someone returned your letter.
　　B: (. . .) sent a letter last week, but s/he put the wrong address on it. What happened to the letter?
7. **A:** Someone robbed the bank.
　　B: What happened to the bank?
8. **A:** The police caught the bank robber.
　　B: Did the bank robber get away?
9. **A:** A judge sent the bank robber to jail.
　　B: What happened to the bank robber?
10. **A:** The government requires each international student to have a visa.
　　B: Is it necessary for international students to have visas?
11. **A:** Someone established this school in 1900.
　　B: How long has this school been in existence?

12. A: There is a party tomorrow night. Someone has invited you to go to that party.

   B: Is (. . .) going to the party?

13. A: Something confused you.

   B: Why did (. . .) ask you a question?

14. A: Someone discovered gold in California in 1848.

   B: What happened in California in 1848?

15. A: I read about a village in the newspaper. Terrorists attacked the village.

   B: What happened to the village?

16. A: People used candles for light in the seventeenth century.

   B: Was electricity used for light in the seventeenth century?

17. A: The pilot flew the hijacked plane to another country.

   B: What happened to the hijacked plane?

18. A: When you had car trouble, a passing motorist helped you.

   B: Yesterday (. . .) was driving down (*Highway 40*) when suddenly his/her car started to make a terrible noise. So s/he pulled over to the side of the road. Did anyone help him/her?

19. A: Someone had already made the coffee by the time you got up this morning.

   B: Did (. . .) have to make the coffee when s/he got up?

20. A: Someone had already sold the chair by the time you returned to the store.

   B: Did (. . .) buy the chair?

□ **EXERCISE 9:** Use the words in the following list to complete the sentences. All of the sentences are passive. Use any appropriate tense.

build	frighten	report
cause	✔ invent	spell
confuse	kill	surprise
divide	offer	surround
expect	order	wear

1. The electric light bulb ___ *was invented* ___ by Thomas Edison.

2. An island ___ *is surrounded* ___ by water.

3. The -*ing* form of "sit" ___ *is spelled* ___ with a double *t*.

4. Even though construction costs are high, a new dormitory ___ *will be* ___ ___ *built* ___ next year.

5. The class was too large, so it _was divided_ into two sections.

6. A bracelet _is worn_ around the wrist.

7. The Johnson's house burned down. According to the inspector, the fire _was caused_ by lightning.

8. Al got a ticket for reckless driving. When he went to traffic court, he _was ordered_ to pay a fine of $100.

9. I read about a hunter who _was killed_ by a wild animal.

10. The hunter's fatal accident _was reported_ in the newspaper yesterday.

11. I didn't expect Lisa to come to the meeting last night, but she was there. I _was surprised_ to see her there.

12. Last week I _was offered_ a job at a local bank, but I didn't accept.

13. The children _are frightened_ in the middle of the night when they heard strange noises in the house.

14. Could you try to explain this math problem to me again? Yesterday in class I _was confused_ by the teacher's explanation.

15. A: Is the plane going to be late?
    B: No. It _is being ordered_ to be on time.
    was

□ **EXERCISE 10:** Use active or passive, in any appropriate tense, for the verbs in parentheses.

1. The Amazon valley is extremely important to the ecology of the earth. Forty percent of the world's oxygen (*produce*) _is produced_ there.

2. The game (*win, probably*) _probably will be won_ by the other team tomorrow. They're a lot better than we are.

3. There was a terrible accident on a busy downtown street yesterday. Dozens of people (*see*) _saw_ it, including my friend, who (*interview*) _was interviewed_ by the police.

4. In my country, certain prices (*control*) _are controled_ by the government, such as the prices of medical supplies. However, other prices (*determine*) _are determined_ by how much people are willing to pay for a product.

5. Yesterday the wind (*blow*) _blew_ my hat off my head. I had to chase it down the street. I (*want, not*) _don't want_ to lose it because it's my favorite hat and it (*cost*) _cost_ a lot.

6. Right now Alex is in the hospital. He (*treat*) _was treated_ _is being treated_ for a bad burn on his hand and arm.

7. Yesterday a purse-snatcher (*catch*) _was caught_ by a dog. While the thief (*chase*) _was chased_ by the police, he (*jump*) _jumped_ over a fence into someone's yard, where he encountered a ferocious dog. The dog (*keep*) _kept_ the thief from escaping.

8. Frostbite may occur when the skin (*expose*) _is exposed_ to extreme cold. It most frequently (*affect*) _affects_ the skin of the cheeks, chin, ears, fingers, nose, and toes.

9. The first fish (*appear*) _appears_ on the earth about 500 million years ago. Up to now, over 20,000 kinds of fish (*name*) _have been named_ and (*describe*) _described_ by scientists. New species (*discover*) _____ every year, so the total increases continually.

10. Proper first aid can save a victim's life, especially if the victim is bleeding heavily, has stopped breathing, or (*poison*) _is poisoned_ _has been_ .

11. The government used to support the school. Today it (*support*) _is_ _supported_ by private funds as well as by the tuition the students pay.

12. Richard Anderson is a former astronaut. Several years ago, at age 52, Anderson (*inform*) _was informed_ by his superior at the aircraft corporation that he could no longer be a test pilot. He (*tell*) _tell (told)_ _____ that he was being relieved of his duties because of his age. Claiming age discrimination, he took the corporation to court.

13. In the early 80s, photographs of Mars (*send*) _were sent_ back to earth by unmanned space probes. From these photographs, scientists have been able to make detailed maps of the surface of Mars.

14. A network of lines (*discover*) _was discovered_ on Mars' surface by an Italian astronomer around the turn of the century. The astronomer (*call*) _called_ these lines "channels," but when the Italian word (*translate*) _was translated_ into English, it became "canals." As a result, some people thought the lines were waterways that (*build*) _were built_ by some unknown living creatures. We now know that the lines are not really canals. Canals (*exist, not*) _don't exist_ on Mars.

3-4 THE PASSIVE FORM OF MODALS AND SIMILAR EXPRESSIONS*

		THE PASSIVE FORM: *modal* + *be* + *past participle*	
(a)	Tom	*will*	*be invited*	to the picnic.
(b)	The window	*can't*	*be opened*.	
(c)	Children	*should*	*be taught*	to respect their elders.
(d)		*May I*	*be excused*	from class?
(e)	This book	*had better*	*be returned*	to the library before Friday.
(f)	This letter	*ought to*	*be sent*	before June 1st.
(g)	Mary	*has to*	*be told*	about our change in plans.
(h)	Fred	*is supposed to*	*be told*	about the meeting.

		THE PAST-PASSIVE FORM: *modal* + *have been* + *past participle*	
(i)	The letter	*should*	*have been sent*	last week.
(j)	This house	*must*	*have been built*	over 200 years ago.
(k)	Jack	*ought to*	*have been invited*	to the party.

*See Chapter 2 for a discussion of the form, meaning, and use of modals and similar expressions.

→ active : John should have sent the letter last week

☐ **EXERCISE 11:** Complete the sentences with the given words, active or passive.

1. James _should be told_ the news as soon as possible.

(*should* + *tell*)

2. Someone _____ *should tell* _____ James the news immediately.

(*should + tell*)

3. James _*should have been told*_ the news a long time ago.

(*should + tell*)

4. Meat _____ in a refrigerator or it will spoil.

(*must + keep*)

5. You _____ meat in a refrigerator or it will spoil.

(*must + keep*)

6. We tried, but the window _____. It was painted shut.

(*couldn't + open*)

7. I tried, but I _____ the window.

(*couldn't + open*)

8. Good news! I _____ a job soon. I had an interview at an engineering firm yesterday.

(*may + offer*)

9. Chris has good news. The engineering firm where she had an interview yesterday _*may offer*_ her a job soon.

(*may + offer*)

10. I hope Chris accepts our job offer, but I know she's been having interviews with several companies. She _____ _____ a job by a competing firm before we made our offer.

(*may + already + offer*)

11. A competing firm _*may already have offered*_ Chris a job before we made our offer.

(*may + already + offer*)

---

*A midsentence adverb such as **already** may be placed after the first auxiliary (e.g., *might already have come*) or after the second auxiliary (e.g., *might have already come*).

12. The class for next semester is too large. It _ought to be_
divided in half, but there's not enough money in
the budget to hire another teacher.

(*ought to + divide*)

13. Last semester's class was too large. It _ought to have_
been divided in half.

(*ought to + divide*)

14. These books _have to be returned_ to the library
by tomorrow.

(*have to + return*)

15. Polly _have to return_ these books by next Friday.

(*have to + return*)

16. A: Andy, your chores _had better be finished_
by the time I get home, including taking out the garbage.

B: Don't worry, Mom. I'll do everything you told me to do.

(*had better + finish*)

17. A: Andy, you _had better finished_ your chores before
Mom gets home.

B: I know. I'll do them in a minute. I'm busy right now.

(*had better + finish*)

18. This application _is supposed to be sent_ to the
personnel department soon.

(*be supposed to + send*)

19. Ann's birthday was on the 5th, and now it's already the 8th. Her birthday
card _should have been sent_ a week ago. Maybe we'd
better give her a call to wish her a belated happy birthday.

(*should + send*)

20. A: Ann didn't expect to see her boss at the labor union meeting.

B: She _must have been surprised_ when she saw him.

A: She was.

(*must + surprise*)

□ **EXERCISE 12:** Use the verb in parentheses with any appropriate modal or similar expression. All of the sentences are passive. In many sentences, more than one modal is possible. Use the modal that sounds best to you.

1. The entire valley (*see*) _____ *can be seen* _____ from their mountain home.

2. He is wearing a gold band on his fourth finger. He (*marry*) ___ must be ___ _____.

3. According to our teacher, all of our compositions (*write*) ___ must be ___ _____ in ink. He won't accept papers written in pencil.

4. I found this book on my desk when I came to class. It (*leave*) _____ _____ by one of the students in the earlier class.

5. Five of the committee members will be unable to attend the next meeting. In my opinion, the meeting (*postpone*) _____ _____.

6. A child (*give, not*) ___ should not given ___ ____ everything he or she wants.

7. Your daughter has a good voice. Her interest in singing (*encourage*) _____ ___ should be ___ _____.

8. Try to speak slowly when you give your speech. If you don't, some of your words (*misunderstand*) ___ should be ___ _____.

9. Some UFO sightings (*explain, not*) ___ can't be ___ _____ easily. No one is able to explain them easily.

10. What? You tripped over a chair at the party and dropped your plate of food into a woman's lap? You (*embarrass*) _____must have been_____ _____!

11. She is very lazy. If you want her to do anything, she (*push*) _____ _____.

12. The hospital in that small town is very old and can no longer serve the needs of the community. A new hospital (*built*) _____should have been_____ _____ years ago.

13. Whales (*save*) _____must be_____ _____ from extinction.

14. We can't wait any longer! Something (*do*) _____must be_____ _____ immediately!

15. In my opinion, she (*elect*) _____will be_____ _____ because she is honest, knowledgeable, and competent.

☐ **EXERCISE 13—ORAL/WRITTEN:** Create sentences from the given subjects and verbs. Use the passive if possible, with or without a "*by* phrase." Use the active only if the verb is intransitive. Make the subject singular or plural as you wish. Use modals as you wish.

Example: tape recorder/make
Possible responses: This tape recorder was made in Korea.
My tape recorder was made in Japan.
The tape recorders we use in lab class were made in the United States.

Example: automobile accident/happen
Possible responses: An automobile accident happened near my apartment building a few days ago.
The automobile accident I read about in the newspaper happened on Highway 5 during rush hour.
The automobile accident Tom told me about must have happened not far from my uncle's house.

1. (*name of a language*)/speak
2. (*kind of game*)/play
3. earthquake/occur
4. news/report
5. steel/produce
6. food/serve
7. dark cloud/appear
8. jeans/wear
9. gold/mine
10. bill/pay

11. (*name of a thing*)/invent
12. (*name of a place/thing*)/discover
13. (*kind of car*)/manufacture
14. computer/cost
15. newspaper/sell
16. I/bite
17. (*name of a person*)/respect

18. friend/agree
19. bride/kiss
20. I/influence
21. movie/show
22. rice/cook
23. rule/obey
24. damage/cause

3-5 STATIVE PASSIVE

(a) The door *is old*. (b) The door *is green*. (c) The door *is locked*. = adj paticiple verb	In (a) and (b): *old* and *green* are adjectives. They describe the door. In (c): *locked* is a past participle. It is used as an adjective. It describes the door.
(d) I locked the door five minutes ago. (e) The door was locked by me five minutes ago. (f) Now the door *is locked*.	The passive form may be used to describe an existing situation or state, as in (f) and (i). No action is taking place. The action happened before. There is no "*by* phrase." The past participle functions as an adjective.
(g) Ann broke the window. (h) The window was broken by Ann. (i) Now the window *is broken*.	When the passive form expresses an existing state rather than an action, it is called the "stative passive."
(j) I **am interested** *in* Chinese art. (k) He **is satisfied** *with* his job. (l) Ann **is married** *to* Alex.	Often stative passive verbs are followed by a preposition other than *by*. (See Appendix 2.)
(m) I don't know where I am. I **am lost**. (n) I can't find my purse. It **is gone**. (o) I **am finished** *with* my work. (p) I **am done** *with* my work.	(m) through (p) are examples of idiomatic usage of the passive form. These sentences have no equivalent active sentences. (tình trạng)

☑ **EXERCISE 14:** Supply the stative passive of the given verbs. Use the SIMPLE PRESENT or the SIMPLE PAST.

1. It is hot in this room because the window (*close*) _____*is closed*_____.

2. Yesterday it was hot in this room because the window (*close*) ___was closed___
   _____.

tear : tire (n)
tear (v)

3. Sarah is wearing a blouse. It (*make*) _is made_ of cotton.

4. The door to this room (*shut*) _was shut_ .

5. Jim is sitting quietly. His elbows (*bend*) _are bent_ and his hands (*fold*) _____ in front of him.

6. We can leave now because class (*finish*) _is finished_ .

7. The lights in this room (*turn*) _are turned_ on.

8. This room (*crowd, not*) _isn't crowded_ .

9. We can't go any farther. The car (*stick*) _is stuck_ in the mud.

10. We couldn't go any farther. The car (*stick*) _was stuck_ in the mud.

11. My room is very neat right now. The bed (*make*) _is made_ , the floor (*sweep*) _is swept_ , and the dishes (*wash*) _are washed_ _____ .

12. We are ready to sit down and eat dinner. The table (*set*) _is set_ , the meat and rice (*do*) _are done_ , and the candles (*light*) _are lighted_ .

13. Where's my wallet? It (*go*) _is gone_ ! Did you take it?

14. Hmmm. My dress (*tear*) _is torn_ . I wonder how that happened.

15. Don't look in the hall closet. Your birthday present (*hide*) _is hidden_ _____ there.

☑ **EXERCISE 15:** Use an appropriate form of the words in the following list to complete the sentences.

bear (born)*	exhaust *tired*	plug in
block	go	qualify
confuse	insure	schedule
crowd	locate	spoil
divorce	✔ lose	stick
do	marry	turn off

_____

*In the passive, **born** is used as the past participle of **bear** to express "given birth to."

136 □ CHAPTER 3

1. Excuse me, sir. Could you give me some directions? I ___am lost___ .

2. Let's find another restaurant. This one __is__ too __crowded__ . We would have to wait at least an hour for a table.

3. The meeting __is scheduled__ for tomorrow at nine.

4. That's hard work! I __am exhausted__ . I need to rest for a while.

5. You told me one thing and John told me another. I don't know what to think. I __am confused__ .

6. Louise is probably sleeping. The lights in her room __are turned off__

7. Mrs. Wentworth's jewelry __is insured__ for $50,000.

8. I can't open the window. It __is stuck__ .

9. Carolyn and Joe were married to each other for five years, but now they __are divorced__ Divorce (n) + (v) by di.

10. I thought I had left my book on this desk, but it isn't here. It __was lost__ . I wonder where it is.

11. I'm sorry. You __are__ not _____ for the job. We need someone with a degree in electrical engineering.

12. I love my wife. I __am married__ to a wonderful woman.

13. We can't eat this fruit. It __is spoiled__ . We'll have to throw it away.

14. We'd better call a plumber. The water won't go down the drain. The drain __is blocked__ .

15. Vietnam __is located__ in Southeast Asia.

16. A: How old is Jack?

    B: He ___was born___ in 1970.

17. A: The TV set doesn't work.

    B: Are you sure? ___Is___ it ___plugged in___?

18. A: Is dinner ready?

    B: Not yet. The potatoes ___are___ not ___done___. They need another ten minutes.

□ **EXERCISE 16:** Supply the correct form of the verb in parentheses and an appropriate preposition. Use the SIMPLE PRESENT.

1. (*interest*)   Carol ___is interested in___ ancient history.

2. (*compose*)   of   Water _____ hydrogen and oxygen.

3. (*accustom*)   to   I _____ living here.

4. (*terrify*)   of   Our son _____ dogs.

5. (*finish*)   with   Pat _____ her composition.

6. (*oppose*)   to   I _____ that suggestion.

7. (*cover*)   with   It's winter, and the ground _____ snow.

8. (*satisfy*)   with   I _____ the progress I have made.

9. (*marry*)   to   Jack _____ Ruth.

10. (*divorce*)   from   Elaine _____ Ed.

11. (*acquaint*)   with   I _____ not _____ that author's work.

12. (*tire*)   of   I _____ sitting here.

13. (*relate*)   to   Your name is Mary Smith. _____ you _____ John Smith?

14. (*dedicate*)   to   Mrs. Robinson works in an orphanage. She _____ her work.

15. (*disappoint*) *in* ~~at~~ Jim got a bad grade because he didn't study. He _____

_____ himself.

16. (*scare*) *by* ~~of~~ Bobby is not very brave. He _____

_____ his own shadow.

17. (*commit*) *to* The administration _____

improving the quality of education at our school.

18. (*devote*) *to* Mr. and Mrs. Miller _____

each other.

19. (*dress*) *in* Walter _____ his best suit for his

wedding today.

20. (*do*) *with* We _____ this exercise.

3–6   THE PASSIVE WITH *GET*

(a) I**'m getting hungry**. Let's eat soon. (b) You shouldn't eat so much. You**'ll get fat**. (c) I stopped working because I **got sleepy**.	**Get** may be followed by certain adjectives.*
(d) I stopped working because I **got tired**. (e) They **are getting married** next month. (f) I **got worried** because he was two hours late.	**Get** may also be followed by a past participle. The past participle functions as an adjective; it describes the subject. The passive with **get** is common in spoken English but is often not appropriate in formal writing.

*Some of the common adjectives that follow **get** are: *angry, anxious, bald, better, big, busy, chilly, cold, dark, dizzy, empty, fat, full, good, heavy, hot, hungry, late, light, mad, nervous, old, rich, sick, sleepy, tall, thirsty, warm, well, wet, worse.*

☐ **EXERCISE 17:** Use any appropriate tense of **get** and an adjective from the following list to complete the sentences.

better	*hot*	*nervous*
busy	✔ *hungry*	*sleepy*
dark	*late*	*well*
full	*light*	*wet*

1. What time are we going to eat? I ____*am getting hungry*____ .

2. A: I *'m getting sleepy* .

   B: Why don't you take a nap? A couple of hours of sleep will do you good.

3. A: What time is it?

   B: Almost ten.

   A: I'd better leave soon. It *'s getting late* . I have to be at the airport by eleven.

4. I didn't have an umbrella, so I *got wet* while I was waiting for the bus yesterday.

5. Let's turn on the air conditioner. It *'s getting hot* in here.

6. Every time I have to give a speech, I *'m getting nervous* .

7. Would you mind turning on the light? It *'s getting dark* in here.

8. A: It's a long drive from Denver to here. I'm glad you finally arrived. What time did you leave this morning?

   B: At sunrise. We left as soon as it *'s getting light* outside.

9. A: Won't you have another helping?

   B: All of the food is delicious, but I really can't eat much more. I *am getting full* .

10. Maria's English is improving. It *'s getting better* .

11. Shake a leg! We don't have all day to finish this work! Get moving! Let's step on it! _____ and finish your work. There's no time to waste.

12. My friend was sick, so I sent him a card. It said, " *you are getting well* soon."

□ **EXERCISE 18:** Complete the sentences by using an appropriate form of **get** and the given verbs.

1. (*tire*)   I think I'll stop working. I *am getting tired* .

2. (*hurt*)   There was an accident, but nobody *is getting hurt* .

3. (*lose*)   We didn't have a map, so we *got lost* .

4. (*dress*)   We can leave as soon as you *get dressed*.

5. (*marry*)   When *was* you *get married*?

6. (*accustom*)   How long did it take you to *get accustomed* to living here?

7. (*worry*)   Sam was supposed to be home an hour ago, but he still isn't here. I *'m getting worry*.

8. (*upset*)   Just try to take it easy. Don't *get upset*.

9. (*confuse*)   I *got confused* because everybody gave me different advice.

10. (*do*)   We can leave as soon as I *get done* with this work.

11. (*depress*)   Chris *got depress* when she lost her job, so I tried to cheer her up.

12. (*invite*)   *Did* you *get invite* to the party?

13. (*bore*)   I *got bored*, so I didn't stay for the end of the movie.

14. (*pack*)   I'll be ready to leave as soon as I *get packed*.

15. (*pay*)   I *get paid* on Fridays. I'll give you the money I owe you next Friday. Okay?

16. (*hire*)   After Ed graduated, he *got hired* by an engineering firm.

17. (*fire*)   But later he *got fired* because he didn't do his work.

18. (*finish, not*)   Last night I *didn't get finished* with my homework until after midnight.

19. (*disgust*)   I *got disgusted* and left because the things they were saying at the meeting were ridiculous.

20. (*engage*)   First, they *got engaged*.

    (*marry*)   Then, they *got married*.

    (*divorce*)   Later, they *got divorced*.

(*remarry*)   Finally, they ___*got remarried*___. Today they are very happy.

☐ **EXERCISE 19—ORAL (BOOKS CLOSED):** Create sentences with *get* and the given words.

Example: dizzy
Possible response: I went on a really neat ride at the carnival last summer. It was a lot of fun even though I got dizzy.

1. sleepy
2. confused
3. married
4. wet
5. done
6. full
7. mad
8. nervous
9. excited
10. scared
11. dressed
12. rich
13. finished
14. lost
15. hurt
16. cheated
17. bored
18. elected
19. older
20. worried
21. worse
22. prepared
23. wrinkled
24. better and better

☒ **EXERCISE 20:** Use active or passive, in any appropriate tense, for the verbs in parentheses.

1. It's noon. The mail should be here soon. It (*deliver, usually*) _____ _____ sometime between noon and one o'clock.

2. Only five of us (*work*) _____ in the laboratory yesterday when the explosion (*occur*) _____. Luckily, no one (*hurt*) _____.

3. I was supposed to take a test yesterday, but I (*admit, not*) _____ _____ into the testing room because the examination (*begin, already*) _____.

4. According to a recent survey, out of every dollar an American spends on food, thirty-six cents (*spend*) _____ at restaurants.

5. I'm sorry I'm late. I (*hold up*) _____ by the rush hour traffic. It (*take*) _____ thirty minutes for me to get here instead of fifteen.

6. Before she graduated last May, Susan (*offer, already*) _____ _____ a position with a law firm.

7. According to many scientists, solar energy (*use*) _____ _____ extensively in the twenty-first century.

8. I (*study*) _____ English here for the last two months. My English (*get*) _____ better, but I still find it difficult to understand lectures.

9. Right now a student trip to the planetarium (*organize*) _____ _____ by Mrs. Hunt. You can sign up for it at her office.

10. He is a man whose name will go down in history. He (*forget, never*) _____ _____.

11. When you (*arrive*) _____ at the airport tomorrow, you (*meet*) _____ by a friend of mine. He (*wear*) _____ a red shirt and blue jeans. He (*be*) _____ fairly tall and (*have*) _____ dark hair. He (*stand*) _____ _____ near the main entrance. I'm sure you will be able to find him.

12. A: Yesterday (*be*) _____ a terrible day.

    B: What (*happen*) _____?

    A: First, I (*flunk*) _____ a test, or at least I think I did. Then I (*drop*) _____ my books while I (*walk*) _____ across campus and they (*fall*) _____ into a mud puddle. And finally, my bicycle (*steal*) _____ _____.

    B: You should have stayed in bed.

3–7 PARTICIPIAL ADJECTIVES

--The problem confuses the students. (a) It is a **confusing** problem.	The present participle conveys an active meaning. The noun it modifies does something. In (a): The noun "problem" does something; it "confuses." Thus, it is described as a "confusing problem."
--The students are confused by the problem. (b) They are **confused** students.	The past participle conveys a passive meaning. In (b): The students are confused by something. Thus, they are described as "confused students."
--The story amuses the children. (c) It is an **amusing** story.	In (c): The noun "story" performs the action.
--The children are amused by the story. (d) They are **amused** children.	In (d): The noun "children" receives the action.

☐ **EXERCISE 21:** Complete the sentences with the present or past participle of the verbs in italics.

1. The class *bores* the students. It is a _____*boring*_____ class.

2. The students *are bored by* the class. They are _____*bored*_____ students.

3. The game *excites* the people. It is an _____*exciting*_____ game.

4. The people *are excited by* the game. They are _____*excited*_____ people.

5. The news *surprised* the man. It was _____*surprising*_____ news.

6. The man *was surprised by* the news. He was a _____*surprised*_____ man.

7. The child *was frightened by* the strange noise. The _____*frightened*_____ child sought comfort from her father.

8. The strange noise *frightened* the child. It was a _____*frightening*_____ sound.

9. The work *exhausted* the men. It was _____*exhausting*_____ work.

10. The men *were exhausted*. The _____*exhausted*_____ men sat down to rest under the shade of a tree.

☐ **EXERCISE 22—ORAL (BOOKS CLOSED):** Respond with a present or past participle.

Example: If a book confuses you, how would you describe the book?
Response: confusing

Example: If a book confuses you, how would you describe yourself?
Response: confused

1. If a story amazes you, how would you describe the story?
   How would you describe yourself?
2. If a story depresses you, how would you describe the story?
   How would you describe yourself?
3. If some work tires you, how would you describe yourself?
   How would you describe the work?
4. If a movie bores you, how would you describe the movie?
   How would you describe yourself?
5. If a painting interests you, how would you describe yourself?
   How would you describe the painting?
6. If a situation embarrasses you . . . .
7. If a book disappoints you . . . .
8. If a person fascinates you . . . .
9. If a situation frustrates you . . . .
10. If a noise annoys you . . . .
11. If an event shocks you . . . .
12. If an experience thrills you . . . .

☐ **EXERCISE 23:** Complete the sentences with the present or past participle of the verbs in parentheses.

1. The (*steal*) _____ *stolen* _____ jewelry was recovered.

2. Success in one's work is a (*satisfy*) _____ experience.

3. The dragon was a (*terrify*) _____ sight for the villagers.

4. The (*terrify*) _____ villagers ran for their lives.

5. I found myself in an (*embarrass*) _____ situation last night.

6. A kid accidentally threw a ball at one of the school windows. Someone needs to repair the (*break*) _____ window.

7. A (*damage*) _____ earthquake occurred recently.

8. People are still in the process of repairing the many (*damage*) _____ buildings and streets.

9. I elbowed my way through the (*crowd*) _____ room.

10. The value endures. A gift given in love has (*endure*) _____ value.

11. No one lives in that (*desert*) _____ house except a few ghosts.

12. The thief tried to pry open the (*lock*) _____ cabinet.

13. Parents have a (*last*) _____ effect on their children.

14. The (*injure*) _____ woman was put into an ambulance.

15. I bought some (*freeze*) _____ vegetables at the supermarket.

☒ **EXERCISE 24:** Complete the sentences with the present or past participle of the verbs in parentheses.

1. I like to talk with her. I think she is an (*interest*) _____*interesting*_____ person.

2. That (*annoy*) _____ buzz is coming from the fluorescent light.

3. Use the (*give*) _____ words in the (*follow*) _____ _____ sentences.

4. The teacher gave us a (*challenge*) _____ assignment, but we all enjoyed doing it.

5. The (*expect*) _____ event did not occur.

6. A (*grow*) _____ child needs a (*balance*) _____ _____ diet.

7. There is an old saying: Let (*sleep*) _____ dogs lie.

8. No one appreciates a (*spoil*) _____ child.

9. At present, the (lead) _____ candidate in the senatorial race is Henry Moore.

10. It is sad. She led a (waste) _____ life.

11. We had a (thrill) _____ but hair-raising experience on our back-packing trip into the wilderness.

12. Last night while we were walking home, we saw an unidentified (fly) _____ object.

13. The (abandon) _____ car was towed away by a tow truck.

14. Any (think) _____ person knows that smoking is a destructive habit.

15. I still have five more (require) _____ courses to take.

16. The streets bustled with activity. We made our way through the (bustle) _____ streets.

☑ **EXERCISE 25—ERROR ANALYSIS:** Find and correct the errors in the following.

Example: I dressed my clothes.
Correction: I got dressed.

1. I am interesting in his ideas. *I get interested in his ideas.*

2. How many peoples have you been invited to the party?

3. When I returned home, everything is quite. I walk to my room, get undress, and going to bed.

4. I didn't go to dinner with them because I had already (been) eaten.

5. In class yesterday, I was confusing. I didn't understand the lesson.

6. I couldn't move. I was very frighten.

7. When we were children, we are very afraid of caterpillars. Whenever we saw one of these monsters, we run to our house before the caterpillars could attack us. I am still scare when I saw a caterpillar close to me.

8. One day, while the old man was cutting down a big tree near the stream, his axe was fallen into the water. He sat down and begin to cry because he does not have enough money to buy another axe.

□ **EXERCISE 26—WRITTEN:** Write a brief biography of someone you know well and admire—perhaps a parent, spouse, brother or sister, friend, colleague, or neighbor.

□ **EXERCISE 27—PHRASAL VERBS:** Supply appropriate prepositions. All of the following contain two-word or three-word verbs.

1. A: When do we have to turn ___in___ our assignments?

   B: They're due next Tuesday.

2. A: How does this tape recorder work?

   B: Push this button to turn it _____ and push that button to shut it _____.

3. A: May I borrow your dictionary?

   B: Sure. But please be sure to put it _____ on the shelf when you're finished.

4. A: I'm going to be in your neighborhood tomorrow.

   B: Oh? If you have time, why don't you drop ___by___ to see us?

   A: Thanks. That sounds like a good idea. Should I call first?

5. A: Look ___up___! A car is coming!

6. A: I got very irritated at one of my dinner guests last night.

   B: Why?

   A: There was an ashtray on the table, but she put her cigarette ___out___ on one of my good plates!

7. A: I need to talk to Karen.

   B: Why don't you call her _____? She's probably at home now.

8. A: Oh-oh. I made a mistake on the check I just wrote.

   B: Don't try to correct the mistake. Just tear _____ the check and throw it _____.

9. A: Are you here to apply for a job?

   B: Yes.

   A: Here is an application form. Fill it ___out___ and then give it ___back___ to me when you are finished.

10. A: Look. There's Mike.

   B: Where?

   A: At the other end of the block, walking toward the administration building. If we run, we can catch ___up___ with him.

11. A: Is your roommate here?

   B: Yes. She decided to come to the party after all. Have you ever met her?

   A: No, but I'd like to.

   B: She's the one standing over there by the far window. She has a blue dress ___on___. Come on. I'll introduce you.

12. A: Do you have a date for Saturday night?

   B: Yes. Jim Brock asked me ___out___. We're going bowling.

CHAPTER 4
Gerunds and Infinitives

A gerund = *the **-ing** form of a verb* (e.g., talking, playing, understanding).

An infinitive = ***to** + the simple form of a verb* (e.g., to talk, to play, to understand).

4–1 GERUNDS: INTRODUCTION

S   **V**
(a) ***Playing*** tennis is fun.
 	
    S   **V**   **O**
(b) We enjoy ***playing*** tennis.
 	
                 PREP   **O**
(c) He's excited about ***playing*** tennis.
	A gerund is the ***-ing*** form of a verb used as a noun.* A gerund is used in the same ways as a noun, i.e., as a subject or an object.
	
	In (a): ***playing*** is a gerund. It is used as the subject of the sentence. ***Playing tennis*** is a gerund phrase.
	
	In (b): ***playing*** is used as the object of the verb *enjoy*.
	
	In (c): ***playing*** is used as the object of the preposition ***about***.

*COMPARE the uses of the **-ing** form of verbs:
    (1) ***Walking*** is good exercise. → ***walking*** = a gerund, used as the subject of the sentence.
    (2) Bob and Ann are ***playing*** tennis. → ***playing*** = a present participle, used in the present progressive tense.
    (3) I heard some ***surprising*** news. → ***surprising*** = a present participle, used as an adjective.

4–2 USING GERUNDS AS THE OBJECTS OF PREPOSITIONS

(a) We talked **about going** to Canada for our vacation. (b) Sue is in charge **of organizing** the meeting. (c) I'm interested **in learning** more about your work.	A gerund is frequently used as the object of a preposition.
(d) I**'m used to sleeping** with the window open. (e) I**'m accustomed to sleeping*** with the window open. (f) I **look forward to going** home next month. (g) They **object to changing** their plans at this late date.	In (d) through (g): **to** is a preposition, not part of an infinitive form, so a gerund follows.
(h) We **talked about not going** to the meeting, but finally decided we should go.	Negative form: **not** precedes a gerund.

*Possible in British English: *I'm accustomed to sleep with the window open.*

⊠ **EXERCISE 1:** Supply an appropriate preposition and verb form.

1. Alice isn't interested ___*in*___ (look) ___looking___ for a new job.

2. Henry is excited ___about___ (leave) ___leaving___ for India.

3. You are capable ___of___ (do) ___doing___ better work.

4. I have no excuse ___for___ (be) ___being___ late.

5. I'm accustomed ___to___ (have) ___having___ a big breakfast.

6. The rain prevented us ___from___ (complete) ___completing___ the work.

7. Fred is always complaining ___about___ (have) ___having___ a headache.

8. Instead ___of___ (study) ___studying___, Margaret went to a ball game with some of her friends.

9. Thank you ___for___ (help) ___helping___ me carry the packages to the post office.

10. Mrs. Grant insisted ___on___ (know) ___knowing___ the whole truth.

11. He showed us how to get to his house ___to___ (draw) ___drawing___ a map.

12. You should take advantage ___of___ (live) ___living___ here.

13. Laura had a good reason ___for___ (go, not) ___not going___ to class yesterday.

14. Everyone in the neighborhood participated ___in___ (*search*) _____ searching_ for the lost child.

15. I apologized to Diane ___for___ (*make*) _making_ her wait for me.

16. The weather is terrible tonight. I don't blame you _for not_ (*want, not*) ___wanting_____ to go to the meeting.

17. Who is responsible ___for___ (*wash*) _washing_ and (*dry*) _drying_ _____ the dishes after dinner?

18. In addition ___to___ (*go*) _going_ to school full-time, Sam has a part-time job.

19. The angry look on his face stopped me _from_ (*speak*) _speaking_ _____ my mind.

20. Where should we go for dinner tonight? Would you object ___to___ (*go*) _going_ to an Italian restaurant?

21. The mayor made another public statement for the purpose ___of___ (*clarify*) _clarifying_ the new tax proposal.

22. The thief was accused ___about___ (*steal*) _stealing_ a woman's purse.

23. The jury found Mr. Adams guilty ___of___ (*take*) _taking_ money from the company he worked for and (*keep*) _keeping_ it for himself.

24. Bill isn't used ___to___ (*wear*) _wearing_ a suit and tie every day.

25. I'm going to visit my family during the school vacation. I'm looking forward ___to___ (*eat*) _eating_ my mother's cooking and (*sleep*) _sleeping_ in my own bed.

☐ **EXERCISE 2—ORAL (BOOKS CLOSED):** To practice using gerunds following prepositions, answer the questions in complete sentences. Answer either yes or no.

Example: Your friend was late. Did she apologize?
Response: Yes, she apologized/No, she didn't apologize *for being* late.

1. You were late for class yesterday. Did you have a good excuse?

2. You are going to (*Baltimore*) to visit your friends this weekend. Are you looking forward to that?
3. (. . .) picked up your pen when you dropped it. Did you thank him/her?
4. You're living in a cold/warm climate. Are you accustomed to that?
5. You're going to (*Hawaii*) for a vacation. Are you excited?
6. You interrupted (. . .) while s/he was speaking. Did you apologize?
7. The students in the class did pantomimes. Did all of them participate?
8. Someone broke the window. Do you know who is responsible?
9. Americans usually have their biggest meal in the evening. Are you used to doing that?
10. The weather is hot/cold. What does that prevent you from doing?
11. (. . .) has to do a lot of homework. Does s/he complain?
12. (. . .) was sick last week, so s/he stayed home in bed. Do you blame him/her?
13. (. . .) didn't study last night. What did s/he do instead?
14. You studied grammar last night. What did you do in addition?

□ **EXERCISE 3:** Using the words in parentheses and any other necessary words, complete the sentences.

1. Ken went to bed instead ____*of finishing his work.*____ (*finish*)
2. I thanked her __*for lending*__ (*lend*)
3. I'm excited __*about going to*__ (*go*)
4. I'm not accustomed __*to living in*__ (*live*)
5. He didn't feel good. He complained __*about having a*__ (*have*)
6. I don't blame you __*for not wanting to*__ (*want, not*)
7. I have a good reason __*for be late*__ (*be*)
8. It's getting late. I'm worried __*about missing my class*__ (*miss*)
9. I'm interested __*in finding out about*__ (*find out about*)
10. I'm thinking __*about going to*__ (*go*)
11. I apologized to my friend __*for being*__ (*be*)
12. I am/am not used __*to driving fast or slow*__ (*drive*)
13. Nothing can stop me __*from going*__ (*go*)
14. In that office, who is responsible __*for taking care of*__ (*take care of*)

☐ **EXERCISE 4:** *By + a gerund or gerund phrase* is used to express how something is done. Complete the following by using *by + a gerund or gerund phrase.*

1. Pat turned off the tape recorder ___ *by pushing the stop button.*

2. We show people we are happy ___ *by smiling.*

3. We decided who should get the last piece of pie ___ *by flipping a coin.*

4. We satisfy our hunger *by getting a good dinner*

5. We quench our thirst *by drinking cup of cake*

6. I found out what "quench" means *by looking up from the dictionary*

7. Tony improved his listening comprehension *by doing a lot of hw*

8. Alex caught my attention *by calling my name.*

9. They got rid of the rats in the building *by poisoning them*

10. My dog shows me she is happy *by jumping*

11. He accidentally electrocuted himself *by*

12. Sometimes teenagers get into trouble with their parents *by getting the separation from their divorce*

4–3 COMMON VERBS FOLLOWED BY GERUNDS

VERB + GERUND (a) I *enjoy playing* tennis.	Gerunds are used as the objects of certain verbs. In (a), *enjoy* is followed by a gerund (*playing*). *Enjoy* is not followed by an infinitive. *INCORRECT: I enjoy to play tennis.* Common verbs that are followed by gerunds are given in the list below.
(b) Joe *quit smoking.* (c) Joe *gave up smoking.*	(b) and (c) have the same meaning. Some two-word verbs, e.g., *give up*, are followed by gerunds. These two-word verbs are given in parentheses in the list below.

VERB + GERUND

enjoy	quit (give up)	avoid	consider (think about)
appreciate	finish (get through)	postpone (put off)	discuss (talk about)
mind	stop★	delay	mention
		keep (keep on)	suggest

★*Stop* can also be followed immediately by an infinitive of purpose (*in order to*). See Chart 4-11.
COMPARE the following:
  (1) *stop + gerund*: When the professor entered the room, the students *stopped talking*. The room became quiet.
  (2) *stop + infinitive of purpose*: While I was walking down the street, I ran into an old friend. I *stopped to talk* to him. (I stopped walking *in order to talk* to him.)

□ **EXERCISE 5—ORAL:** Make sentences from the given words. Use any tense. Use any subject.

Example: enjoy + read the newspaper
Possible response: I enjoy reading the newspaper every morning while I'm having my first cup of coffee.

1. enjoy + watch TV
2. mind + open the window
3. quit + eat desserts
4. give up + eat desserts
5. finish + eat dinner
6. get through + eat dinner
7. stop + rain
8. avoid + answer my question
9. postpone + do my work
10. put off + do my work

11. delay + leave on vacation
12. keep + work
13. keep on + work
14. consider + get a job
15. think about + get a job
16. discuss + go to a movie
17. talk about + go to a movie
18. mention + go to a concert
19. suggest + go on a picnic*
20. enjoy + listen to music

□ **EXERCISE 6:** By using a gerund, supply any appropriate completion for each of the following.

1. When Beth got tired, she stopped _working/studying_.

2. Would you mind ___opening___ the door? Thanks.

3. The weather will get better soon. We can leave as soon as it quits _____
   _____.

4. The police officer told him to stop, but the thief kept _____.

5. I enjoy ___having___ a long walk every morning.

6. I have a lot of homework tonight, but I'd still like to go with you later on.
   I'll call you when I get through ___doing my homework___,

7. I would like to have some friends over. I'm thinking about ___having___
   _____ a dinner party.

8. He told a really funny joke. We couldn't stop ___laughing___!

9. Jack almost had an automobile accident. He barely avoided ___hitting___
   ___doing___ another car at the intersection of 4th and Elm.

_____
*For other ways of expressing ideas with *suggest*, see Chart 7-8.

10. Where are you considering ___spending___ for vacation?

11. Sometimes I put off ___doing___ my homework.

12. You have to decide where you want to go to school next year. You can't postpone ___making___ that decision much longer.

13. I wanted to go to Mexico. Sally suggested ___flying (going)___ to Hawaii.

14. Tony mentioned ___talking___ the bus to school instead of walking.

15. I appreciate ___being___ able to study in peace and quiet.

4–4 *GO* + GERUND

(a) Did you **go shopping**? (b) We **went fishing** yesterday.	**Go** is followed by a gerund in certain idiomatic expressions to express, for the most part, recreational activities.

GO + GERUND

go birdwatching	*go hiking*	*go sightseeing*
go boating	*go hunting*	*go skating*
go bowling	*go jogging*	*go skiing*
go camping	*go mountain climbing*	*go sledding*
go canoeing	*go running*	*go swimming*
go dancing	*go sailing*	*go tobogganing*
go fishing	*go shopping*	*go window shopping*

☐ **EXERCISE 7—ORAL (BOOKS CLOSED):** Make up sentences using the given words. Use any subject. Use any tense.

Example: enjoy + go
Possible responses: I enjoy going to the zoo./My friend and I enjoyed going to a rock concert last weekend./Where do you enjoy going in (*this city*) when you have some free time?

1. finish + study
2. go + dance
3. keep + work
4. go + bowl
5. think about + wear
6. enjoy + play
7. go + fish
8. talk about + go + swim
9. stop + fight
10. postpone + go + camp
11. quit + rain
12. avoid + go + shop
13. give up + ask
14. discuss + go + birdwatch
15. appreciate + hear
16. mind + wait
17. think about + not go
18. suggest + go + window shop

4–5 COMMON VERBS FOLLOWED BY INFINITIVES

VERB + INFINITIVE (a) I *hope to see* you again soon. (b) He *promised to be* here by ten. (c) He *promised not to be* late.	Some verbs are followed immediately by an infinitive, as in (a) and (b). See Group A below. Negative form: *not* precedes the infinitive.
VERB + (PRO)NOUN + INFINITIVE (d) Mr. Lee *told me to be* here at ten o'clock. (e) The police *ordered the driver to stop*.	Some verbs are followed by a (pro)noun and then an infinitive, as in (d) and (e). See Group B below.
(f) I *was told to be* here at ten o'clock. (g) The driver *was ordered to stop*.	These verbs are followed immediately by an infinitive when they are used in the passive, as in (f) and (g).
(h) I *expect to pass* the test. (i) I *expect Mary to pass* the test.	*Ask, expect, would like, want,* and *need* may or may not be followed by a (pro)noun object. COMPARE: In (h): I think I will pass the test. In (i): I think Mary will pass the test.

GROUP A: VERB + INFINITIVE

hope to	*promise* to	*seem* to	*ask* to
plan to	*agree* to	*appear* to	*expect* to
intend to*	*offer* to	*pretend* to	*would like* to
decide to	*refuse* to		*want* to
			need to

GROUP B: VERB + (PRO)NOUN + INFINITIVE

tell someone to	*invite* someone to	*require* someone to	*ask* someone to
advise someone to**	*permit* someone to	*order* someone to	*expect* someone to
encourage someone to	*allow* someone to	*force* someone to	*would like* someone to
remind someone to	*warn* someone to		*want* someone to
			need someone to

*__Intend__ is usually followed by an infinitive (*I intend to go to the meeting*) but sometimes may be followed by a gerund (*I intend going to the meeting*) with no change in meaning.
A gerund is used after **advise (active) if there is no (pro)noun object. COMPARE:
    (1) He **advised buying** a Fiat.
    (2) He **advised me to buy** a Fiat. I **was advised to buy** a Fiat.

□ **EXERCISE 8:** Supply any appropriate completion for each sentence. Use either a gerund or an infinitive.

1. We're going out for dinner. Would you like _____*to join*_____ us?

2. Jack avoided _____*looking at*_____ me.

3. Fred didn't have any money, so he decided _____to get_____ a job.

4. The teacher reminded the students _____to do_____ their assignments.

5. Do you enjoy _____playing_____ soccer?

6. I was broke, so Jenny offered ___*to give*___ me a little money.

7. Mrs. Allen promised ___*to come*___ tomorrow.

8. My boss expects me ___*to do*___ this work ASAP.*

9. Jane had to go out again because she had forgotten ___*taking*___ some bread at the market.

10. Even though I asked the people in front of me at the movie ___*to be*___ _____ quiet, they kept ___*talking*___.

11. Joan and David were considering ___*to get*___ married in June, but they finally decided ___*to marry*___ until August.

12. Our teacher encourages us ___*to use*___ a dictionary whenever we are uncertain of the spelling of a word.

13. Before I left home to go away to college, my mother reminded me _____ ___*to write*___ her a letter at least once a week.

14. Mrs. Jackson warned her young son ___*to avoid*___ the hot stove. She was afraid he would burn his fingers.

15. I don't mind ___*feeling*___ alone.

16. The teacher seems ___*to be*___ in a good mood today, don't you think?

17. Lucy pretended ___*to understand*___ the answer to my question.

18. Dick intends ___*to write*___ his friend a letter.

_____
*ASAP = as soon as possible.

19. Residents are not allowed _to feed_ pets in my apartment building.

20. All applicants are required _to have_ an entrance examination.

21. Someone asked me _to buy_ this package.

22. I was asked _to buy_ this package.

23. Jack advised me _to rent_ a new apartment.

24. I was advised _to rent_ a new apartment.

25. Jack advised _renting_ a new apartment.

26. Jack suggested _coming_ a new apartment.

27. Ann advised her sister _to take_ the plane instead of driving to Oregon.

28. Ann advised _taking_ the plane instead of driving to Oregon.

EXERCISE 9: Using the given ideas and the verb in parentheses, make sentences, both active and passive, by using an infinitive phrase. (Omit the "**by** phrase" in the passive sentences.)

(19 Homework)

1. The teacher said to me, "You may leave early."

(_permit_)   ___The teacher permitted me to leave early.___   (active)

___I was permitted to leave early.___   (passive)

2. The secretary said to me, "Please give this note to Sue."

(_ask_)   The secretary asked me to give this note to (active)

I was asked the secretary to give this (passive)

3. My advisor said to me, "You should take Biology 109."

(_advise_)   My advisor advised me to take Biology 109

I was advised taking biology 109

4. When I went to traffic court, the judge said to me, "You must pay a thirty-dollar fine."

(_order_)   When I went to traffic court, the judge ordered me to pay a thirty-dollar fine

I was ordered to pay thirty-dollar fine

5. During the test, the teacher said to Greg, "Keep your eyes on your own paper."

   (warn) _____

   _____

6. During the test, the teacher said to Greg, "Don't look at your neighbor's paper."

   (warn) _____

   _____

7. At the meeting, the head of the department said to the faculty, "Don't forget to turn in your grade reports by the 15th."

   (remind) _____

   _____

8. Mr. Lee said to the children, "Be quiet."

   (tell) _____

   _____

9. The hijacker said to the pilot, "You must land the plane."

   (force) _____

   _____

10. When I was growing up, my parents said to me, "You may stay up late on Saturday night."

    (allow) _____

    _____

11. The teacher said to the students, "Speak slowly and clearly."

    (encourage) _____

    _____

12. The teacher always says to the students, "You are supposed to come to class on time."

    (expect) _____

    _____

□ **EXERCISE 10—ORAL:** In each of the following, report what someone said by using one of the verbs in the given list to introduce an infinitive phrase.

advise	*expect*	*remind*
allow	*force*	*require*
ask	*order*	*tell*
encourage	*permit*	*warn*

1. The professor said to Alan, "You may leave early."
   → *The professor allowed Alan to leave early.*
     Alan was allowed to leave early.
2. The general said to the soldiers, "Surround the enemy!"
3. Nancy said to me, "Would you please open the window?"
4. Bob said to me, "Don't forget to take your book back to the library."
5. Paul thinks I have a good voice, so he said to me, "You should take singing lessons."
6. Mrs. Anderson was very stern and a little angry. She shook her finger at the children and said to them, "Don't play with matches!"
7. I am very relieved because the Dean of Admissions said to me, "You may register for school late."
8. The law says, "Every driver must have a valid driver's license."
9. My friend said to me, "You should get some automobile insurance."
10. The robber had a gun. He said to me, "Give me all of your money."
11. Before the examination began, the teacher said to the students, "Work quickly."
12. My boss said to me, "Come to the meeting ten minutes early."

□ **EXERCISE 11—ORAL (BOOKS CLOSED): STUDENT A:** Make an active sentence from the given verbs. **STUDENT B:** Change the sentence to the passive; omit the "*by* phrase."

Example: allow me + leave
Student A: The teacher allowed me to leave class early last Friday because I had an appointment with my doctor.
Student B: (. . .) was allowed to leave class early last Friday because s/he had an appointment with his/her doctor.

1. remind me + finish
2. ask me + go
3. permit me + have
4. expect me + be
5. allow me + leave

6. warn me + not go
7. advise me + take
8. tell me + open
9. encourage me + visit
10. require us + take

4-6 COMMON VERBS FOLLOWED BY EITHER INFINITIVES OR GERUNDS

Some verbs can be followed by either an infinitive or a gerund, sometimes with no difference in meaning, as in Group A below, and sometimes with a difference in meaning, as in Group B below.	

GROUP A: VERB + INFINITIVE OR GERUND (WITH NO DIFFERENCE IN MEANING)

begin *like* *hate* *start* *love* *can't stand* *continue* *prefer*★ *can't bear*	The verbs in Group A may be followed by either an infinitive or a gerund with little or no difference in meaning.
(a) It ***began to rain***. / It ***began raining***. (b) I ***started to work***. / I ***started working***.	In (a): There is no difference between "began to rain" and "began raining."
(c) It ***was beginning to rain***.	If the main verb is progressive, an infinitive (not a gerund) is usually used.

GROUP B: VERB + INFINITIVE OR GERUND (WITH A DIFFERENCE IN MEANING)

remember *regret* lấy làm tiếc *forget* *try*	The verbs in Group B may be followed by either an infinitive or a gerund, but the meaning is different.
(d) Judy always ***remembers to lock*** the door.	***Remember*** + *infinitive* = remember to perform responsibility, duty, or task, as in (d).
(e) Sam often ***forgets to lock*** the door.	***Forget*** + *infinitive* = forget to perform a responsibility, duty, or task, as in (e).
(f) I ***remember seeing*** the Alps for the first time. The sight was impressive.	***Remember*** + *gerund* = remember (recall) something that happened in the past, as in (f).
(g) I'***ll never forget seeing*** the Alps for the first time.	***Forget*** + *gerund* = forget something that happened in the past, as in (g).★★
(h) I ***regret to tell*** you that you failed the test.	***Regret*** + *infinitive* = regret to say, to tell someone, to inform someone of some bad news, as in (h).
(i) I ***regret lending*** him some money. He never paid me back.	***Regret*** + *gerund* = regret something that happened in the past, as in (i).
(j) I'***m trying to learn*** English.	***Try*** + *infinitive* = make an effort, as in (j).
(k) The room was hot. I ***tried opening*** the window, but that didn't help. So I ***tried turning*** on the fan, but I was still hot. Finally, I turned on the air conditioner.	***Try*** + *gerund* = experiment with a new or different approach to see if it works, as in (k).

★Notice the patterns with ***prefer***:
   prefer + *gerund*: I ***prefer staying*** home ***to going*** to the concert.
   prefer + *infinitive*: I ***prefer to stay*** home ***than (to) go*** to the concert.

★★F_____ved by a gerund usually occurs in a negative sentence or a question: e.g., *I'll never forget, I can't _____ ever forgotten,* and *Can you ever forget* can be followed by a gerund phrase.

☐ **EXERCISE 12:** Complete the sentences with the correct form(s) of the verbs in parentheses.

1. I like (go) ___to go/going___ to the zoo.

2. The play wasn't very good. The audience started (leave) _to leave/leaving_ _____ before it was over.

3. After a brief interruption, the professor continued (lecture) _to lecture/_ _lecturing_.

4. The children love (swim) _swim/swimming_ in the ocean.

5. I hate (see) _to see/seeing_ any living being suffer. I can't bear it.

6. I'm afraid of flying. When a plane begins (move) _to move/moving_ down the runway, my heart starts (race) _to race/racing_. Oh-oh! The plane is beginning (move) _to move/moving_ and my heart is starting (race) _to race/racing_

7. When I travel, I prefer (drive) _driving_ to (take) _taking_ _____ a plane.

8. I prefer (drive) _to drive_ rather than (take) _to take_ a plane.

9. I always remember (turn) _to turn_ off all the lights before I leave my house.

10. I can remember (be) _being_ very proud and happy when I graduated.

11. Did you remember (give) _to give_ Jake my message?

12. I remember (play) _playing_ with dolls when I was a child.

13. What do you remember (do) _doing_ when you were a child?

14. What do you remember (do) _to do_ before you leave for class every day?

15. What did you forget (do) _to do_ before you left for class this morning?

16. I'll never forget (carry) _carrying_ my wife over the threshold when we moved into our first home.

17. I can't ever forget (watch) _watching_ our team score the winning goal in the last seconds of the game to capture the national championship.

18. Don't forget (do) _to do_ your homework tonight!

19. I regret (inform) _informing_ you that your loan application has not been approved.

20. I regret (listen, not) _not listening_ to my father's advice. He was right.

21. When a student asks a question, the teacher always tries (explain) _to explain_ the problem as clearly as possible.

22. I tried everything, but the baby still wouldn't stop crying. I tried (hold) _holding_ him. I tried (feed) _feeding_ him. I tried (burp) _burping_ him. I tried (change) _changing_ his diapers. Nothing worked.

☐ **EXERCISE 13:** Supply an appropriate form, gerund or infinitive, of the verbs in parentheses.

1. Mary reminded me (be, not) _not to be_ late for the meeting.

2. We went for a walk after we finished (*clean*) _cleaning_ up the kitchen.

3. I forgot (*take*) _to take_ a book back to the library, so I had to pay a fine.

4. When do you expect (*leave*) _to leave_ on your trip?

5. The baby started (*talk*) _talking/to talk_ when she was about eighteen months old.

6. I don't mind (*wait*) _to waiting_ for you. Go ahead and finish (*do*) _doing_ your work.

7. I've decided (*stay*) _to stay_ here over vacation and (*paint*) _to paint_ my room.

8. We discussed (*quit*) _quiting_ our jobs and (*open*) _openning_ our own business.

9. I'm getting tired. I need (*take*) _to take_ a break.

10. Sometimes students avoid (*look*) _loking_ at the teacher if they don't want (*answer*) _to answer_ a question.

11. The club members discussed (*postpone*) _to postponing_ the next meeting until March.

12. Most children prefer (*watch*) _to watch/watching_ television to (*listen*) _to listen_ to the radio.

13. My grandfather prefers (*read*) _to read / reading._

14. Did Carol agree (*go*) _to go_ (*camp*) _to camp_ with you?

15. As the storm approached, the birds quit (*sing*) _singing_.

16. The taxi driver refused (*take*) _to take_ a check. He wanted the passenger (*pay*) _to pay_ in cash.

17. The soldiers were ordered (*stand*) _to stand_ at attention.

18. The travel agent advised us (*wait, not*) _not to wait_ until August.

□ **EXERCISE 14—ORAL (BOOKS CLOSED):** Make sentences from the following verb combinations. Use "I" or the name of another person in the room. Use any appropriate tense or modal.

> *Example:*   like + go
> *Possible response:* I like to go (OR: going) to the park.
>
> *Example:*   ask + open
> *Possible response:* (. . .) asked me to open the window.

1. enjoy + listen
2. offer + lend
3. start + laugh
4. remind + take
5. postpone + go
6. look forward to + see
7. forget + bring
8. remember + go
9. prefer + live
10. finish + do
11. encourage + go
12. can't stand + have to wait
13. continue + walk
14. stop + walk
15. be interested in + learn
16. be used to + speak
17. consider + not go
18. suggest + go
19. advise + go
20. be allowed + have
21. order + stay
22. regret + take
23. want + go + shop
24. like + go + swim
25. keep + put off + do
26. decide + ask + come

□ **EXERCISE 15:** Supply an appropriate form, gerund or infinitive, of the verbs in parentheses.

1. Keep (*talk*) _____talking_____. I'm listening to you.

2. The children promised (*play*) ___to play____ more quietly. They promised (*make, not*) __not to make___ so much noise.

3. Linda offered (*look after*) __to look after__ my cat while I was out of town.

4. You shouldn't put off (*pay*) _____to pay_____ your bills.

5. Alex's dog loves (*chase*) ____chasing____ sticks.

6. Mark mentioned (*go*) _____going_____ to the market later today. I wonder if he's still planning (*go*) _____to go_____.

7. Fred suggested (*go*) _____going_____ (*ski*) _____skiing_____ in the mountains this weekend. How does that sound to you?

8. The doctor ordered Mr. Gray (*smoke, not*) _____not to smoke_____.

9. Don't tell me his secret. I prefer (*know, not*) _____not to know_____.

10. Could you please stop (*whistle*) _____whistling_____? I'm trying (*concentrate*) _____to concentrate_____ on my work.

11. She finally decided (*quit*) _____to quit_____ her present job and (*look for*) _____to look for_____ another one.

12. Did you remember (*turn off*) _____to turn off_____ the stove?

13. Jack was allowed (*renew*) _____to renew_____ his student visa.

14. Pat told us (*wait, not*) _____not to wait_____ for her.

15. Mr. Buck warned his daughter (*play, not*) _____not to play_____ with matches.

16. Would you please remind me (*call*) _____to call_____ Alice tomorrow?

17. Liz encouraged me (*throw away*) _____to throw away_____ my old running shoes and (*buy*) _____to buy_____ a new pair without holes in the toes.

18. I'm considering (*drop out of*) _____dropping out of_____ school, (*hitchhike*) _____hitchhiking_____ to New York, and (*try*) _____trying_____ (*find*) _____ a job.

19. Don't forget (*tell*) _____telling_____ Jane (*call*) _____to call_____ me about (*go*) _____going_____ (*swim*) _____swimming_____ tomorrow.

20. Sally reminded me (*ask*) _____to ask_____ you (*tell*) _____to tell_____ Bob (*remember*) _____to remember_____ (*bring*) _____bringing_____ his soccer ball to the picnic.

17, 23, 24

4–7   REFERENCE LIST OF VERBS FOLLOWED BY GERUNDS

1.	*admit*	He *admitted stealing* the money.
2.	*advise*	She *advised waiting* until tomorrow.
3.	*anticipate*	I *anticipate having* a good time on vacation.
4.	*appreciate*	I *appreciated hearing* from them.
5.	*avoid*	He *avoided answering* my question.
6.	*complete*	I finally *completed writing* my term paper.
7.	*consider*	I *will consider going* with you.
8.	*delay*	He *delayed leaving* for school.
9.	*deny*	She *denied committing* the crime.
10.	*discuss*	They *discussed opening* a new business.
11.	*dislike*	I *dislike driving* long distances.
12.	*enjoy*	We *enjoyed visiting* them.
13.	*finish*	She *finished studying* about ten.
14.	*forget*	I'*ll never forget visiting* Napoleon's tomb.
15.	*can't help*	I *can't help worrying* about it.
16.	*keep*	I *keep hoping* he will come.
17.	*mention*	She *mentioned going* to a movie.
18.	*mind*	*Would* you *mind helping* me with this?
19.	*miss*	I *miss being* with my family.
20.	*postpone*	Let's *postpone leaving* until tomorrow.
21.	*practice*	The athlete *practiced throwing* the ball.
22.	*quit*	He *quit trying* to solve the problem.
23.	*recall*	I *don't recall meeting* him before.
24.	*recollect*	I *don't recollect meeting* him before.
25.	*recommend*	She *recommended seeing* the show.
26.	*regret*	I *regret telling* him my secret.
27.	*remember*	I *can remember meeting* him when I was a child.
28.	*resent*	I *resent her interfering* in my business.
29.	*resist*	I *couldn't resist eating* the dessert.
30.	*risk*	She *risks losing* all of her money.
31.	*stop*	She *stopped going* to classes when she got sick.
32.	*suggest*	She *suggested going* to a movie.
33.	*tolerate*	She *won't tolerate cheating* during an examination.
34.	*understand*	I *don't understand his leaving* school.

4–8   REFERENCE LIST OF VERBS FOLLOWED BY INFINITIVES

A.   VERBS FOLLOWED IMMEDIATELY BY AN INFINITIVE

1.	*afford*	I *can't afford to buy* it.
2.	*agree*	They *agreed to help* us.
3.	*appear*	She *appears to be* tired.
4.	*arrange*	I'll *arrange to meet* you at the airport.
5.	*ask*	He *asked to come* with us.
6.	*beg*	He *begged to come* with us.
7.	*care*	I *don't care to see* that show.
8.	*claim*	She *claims to know* a famous movie star.
9.	*consent*	She finally *consented to marry* him.

(continued)

command : ra lệnh

	10. *decide*	I **have decided to leave** on Monday.
	11. *demand* đòi hỏi	I **demand to know** who is responsible.
xứng đáng	12. *deserve* Tự đế	She **deserves to win** the prize.
	13. *expect*	I **expect to enter** graduate school in the fall.
	14. *fail*	She **failed to return** the book to the library on time.
	15. *forget*	I **forgot to mail** the letter.
	16. *hesitate* ngần ngại	**Don't hesitate to ask** for my help.
	17. *hope*	Jack **hopes to arrive** next week.
	18. *learn*	He **learned to play** the piano.
	19. *manage* xoay sở	She **managed to finish** her work early.
	20. *mean*	I **didn't mean to hurt** your feelings.
	21. *need*	I **need to have** your opinion.
	22. *offer* đề nghị	They **offered to help** us.
	23. *plan*	I **am planning to have** a party.
	24. *prepare*	We **prepared to welcome** them.
	25. *pretend* giả vờ	He **pretends not to understand**.
	26. *promise* hứa	I **promise not to be** late.
	27. *refuse* từ chối	I **refuse to believe** his story.
	28. *regret*	I **regret to tell** you that you failed.
	29. *remember*	I **remembered to lock** the door.
	30. *seem*	That cat **seems to be** friendly.
	31. *struggle*	I **struggled to stay** awake.
	32. *swear*	She **swore to tell** the truth.
đe dọa	33. *threaten* đe dọa	She **threatened to tell** my parents.
tình nguyện	34. *volunteer* tình nguyện	He **volunteered to help** us.
	35. *wait*	I **will wait to hear** from you.
	36. *want*	I **want to tell** you something.
	37. *wish*	She **wishes to come** with us.

B. VERBS FOLLOWED BY A (PRO)NOUN + AN INFINITIVE

	38. *advise*	She **advised me to wait** until tomorrow.
	39. *allow*	She **allowed me to use** her car.
	40. *ask*	I **asked John to help** us.
	41. *beg* cầu xin	They **begged us to come**.
	42. *cause*	Her laziness **caused her to fail**.
	43. *challenge* thách thức	She **challenged me to race** her to the corner.
	44. *convince*	I couldn't **convince him to accept** our help.
	45. *dare*	He **dared me to do** better than he had done.
	46. *encourage*	He **encouraged me to try** again.
	47. *expect*	I **expect you to be** on time.
	48. *forbid* cấm, cẩm đoán	I **forbid you to tell** him.
	49. *force*	They **forced him to tell** the truth.
	50. *hire* thuê, mướn	She **hired a boy to mow** the lawn.
	51. *instruct* dạy nghề	He **instructed them to be careful.**
	52. *invite*	Harry **invited the Johnsons to come** to his party.
	53. *need*	We **needed Chris to help** us figure out the solution.
	54. *order* ra lệnh, đặt hàng	The judge **ordered me to pay** a fine.
	55. *permit* cho phép	He **permitted the children to stay** up late.
Convince	56. *persuade*	I **persuaded him to come** for a visit.
	57. *remind*	She **reminded me to lock** the door.
	58. *require*	Our teacher **requires us to be** on time.
	59. *teach*	My brother **taught me to swim**.
	60. *tell*	The doctor **told me to take** these pills.
khổ giục	61. *urge* thúc giục	I **urged her to apply** for the job.
	62. *want*	I **want you to be** happy.
	63. *warn*	I **warned you not to drive** too fast.

God bless you

Complete the sentence with *doing it* or *to do it*.

Example: I promise . . . .
Response: . . . to do it.

Can't stand = can't help + Grew
She can't help worrying

1. I enjoyed . *doing it*
2. I can't afford . *to do it*
3. She didn't allow me . *to do it* .
4. We plan . *to do it* .
5. Please remind me . *to do it* ,
6. I am considering . *doing it* ,
7. They postponed . *doing it* ,
8. He persuaded me . *to do it* .
9. I don't mind . . *doing it*
10. He avoided . . *doing it* .
11. I refused . *to do it* ,
12. I hope . *to do it* .
13. She convinced me . *to do it* ,
14. He mentioned . . *doing it* ,
15. I expect . *to do it* '
16. I encouraged him . *to do it* ,
17. I warned him not . *to do it* ,
18. We prepared . *to do it* ,
19. I don't recall . . *doing it* ,
20. We decided . . *to do it* ,

21. They offered . *to do it* ,
22. When will you finish . *doing it* .
23. Did you practice . *doing it* ,
24. She agreed . . . .
25. Keep . . . .
26. Stop . . . .
27. I didn't force him . . . .
28. I couldn't resist . . . .
29. How did he manage . . . .
30. He admitted . . . .
31. He denied . . . .
32. I didn't mean . . . .
33. She swore . . . .
34. I volunteered . . . .
35. He suggested . . . .
36. He advised me . . . .
37. He struggled . . . .
38. I don't want to risk . . . .
39. He recommended . . . .
40. I miss . . . .

(To the teacher: Repeat the exercise by having the students complete the sentences with their own words.)

□ **EXERCISE 17:** Complete the sentences with the correct form, gerund or infinitive, of the words in parentheses.

1. Margaret challenged me (*race*) __to race__ her across the pool.

2. David volunteered (*bring*) __to bring__ some food to the reception.

3. The students practiced (*pronounce*) __pronouncing__ the "th" sound in the phrase "these thirty-three dirty trees."

4. In the fairy tale, the wolf threatened (*eat*) __to eat__ a girl named Little Red Riding Hood.

5. Susie! How many times do I have to remind you (*hang up*) _to hang_ _up_ your coat when you get home from school?

6. The horses struggled (*pull*) _to pull_ the wagon out of the mud.

7. Janice demanded (*know*) _to know_ why she had been fired.

8. My skin can't tolerate (*be*) _being_ in the sun all day long. I get sunburned easily.

9. I avoided (*tell*) _telling_ Mary the truth because I knew she would be angry.

10. Fred Washington claims (*be*) _being_ (be) a descendant of George Washington.

11. Alex broke the antique vase. I'm sure he didn't mean (*do*) _to do_ it.

12. I urged Al (*return*) _to return_ to school and (*finish*) _to finish_ his education.

13. Mrs. Freeman can't help (*worry*) _worrying_ about her children.

14. Children, I forbid you (*play*) _to play_ in the street. There's too much traffic.

15. My little cousin is a blabbermouth! He can't resist (*tell*) _telling_ everyone my secrets!

16. I appreciate your (*take*) _taking_ the time to help me.

17. I can't afford (*buy*) _to buy_ a new car.

18. Ted managed (*change*) _to change_ my mind.

19. I think Sam deserves (*have*) _to have_ another chance.

20. Julie finally admitted (*be*) _being_ responsible for the problem.

21. I don't recall ever (*hear*) _hearing_ you mention his name before.

22. She keeps (*promise*) _promising_ (*visit*) _to visit_ us, but she never does.

23. He keeps (*hope*) _____hoping_____ and (*pray*) _____praying_____
    that things will get better.

24. I finally managed (*persuade*) __to persuade__ Jane (*stay*)
    __to stay__ in school and (*finish*) __to finish__ her
    degree.

4–9 USING GERUNDS AS SUBJECTS; USING *IT* + INFINITIVE

(a) ***Riding*** *with a drunk driver is dangerous.*	A gerund is frequently used as the subject of a sentence, as in (a).
(b) ***To ride*** *with a drunk driver is dangerous.* (c) ***It*** *is dangerous **to ride** with a drunk driver.*	Sometimes an infinitive is used as the subject of a sentence, as in (b). However, an infinitive is more commonly used with ***it***, as in (c). The word ***it*** refers to and has the same meaning as the infinitive phrase at the end of the sentence.*

*Sometimes a gerund is used with ***it*** when the speaker is talking about a particular situation and wants to give the idea of "while": *Tom was drunk. It was dangerous **riding** with him.* = *We were in danger while we were riding with him.*

☐ **EXERCISE 18—ORAL:** Complete the sentences. Use gerund phrases as subjects.

1. . . . isn't easy. → *Climbing to the top of a mountain isn't easy.*
2. . . . is hard.
3. . . . is usually a lot of fun.
4. . . . is boring.
5. . . . can be interesting.
6. . . . was a good experience.
7. Does . . . sound like fun to you?
8. . . . is considered impolite in my country.

☐ **EXERCISE 19—ORAL:** Restate the sentences by changing a sentence with a gerund as the subject to a sentence with ***it*** + *an infinitive phrase*, and vice-versa.

1. Teasing animals is cruel. → *It is cruel to tease animals.*
2. It wasn't difficult to find their house. → *Finding their house wasn't difficult.*
3. Voting in every election is important.
4. It was exciting to meet the king and queen.
5. Hearing the other side of the story would be interesting.
6. It is unusual to see Joan awake early in the morning.
7. If you know how, it is easy to float in water for a long time.

8. Mastering a second language takes time and patience.

9. Driving to Atlanta will take us ten hours.

10. It takes courage to dive into the sea from a high cliff.

☐ **EXERCISE 20—ORAL:** **STUDENT A:** Complete the sentence with an infinitive phrase. **STUDENT B:** Give a sentence with the same meaning by using a gerund phrase as the subject.

1. It is fun . . . .
   A: . . . *to ride a horse.*
   B: *Riding a horse is fun.*
2. It's dangerous . . . .
3. It's easy . . . .
4. It's impolite . . . .

5. It is important . . . .
6. It is wrong . . . .
7. It takes a lot of time . . . .
8. It's a good idea . . . .
9. Is it difficult . . . ?

☐ **EXERCISE 21—ORAL:** The phrase "*for (someone)*" may precede an infinitive to identify exactly who the speaker is talking about. Add "*for (someone)*" to the following sentences and any other words to give a more specific meaning.

1. It's important to take advanced math courses. → *It's important for science students to take advanced math courses.*
2. It isn't possible to be on time. → *It isn't possible for me to be on time to class if the bus drivers are on strike and I have to walk to class in a rainstorm.*
3. It's easy to speak Spanish.
4. It's important to learn English.
5. It's unusual to be late.
6. It is essential to get a visa.
7. It is dangerous to play with matches.
8. It's difficult to communicate.
9. It was impossible to come to class.
10. It is a good idea to study gerunds and infinitives.

4–10 INFINITIVE OF PURPOSE: *IN ORDER TO*

(a) He came here **in order to study** English. (b) He came here **to study** English.	**In order to** is used to express *purpose*. It answers the question "Why?" **In order** is often omitted, as in (b).
(c) *INCORRECT: He came here for studying English.* (d) *INCORRECT: He came here for to study English.* (e) *INCORRECT: He came here for study English.*	To express purpose, use (**in order**) **to** not **for**, with a verb.*
(f) I went to the store **for** some bread. (g) I went to the store **to buy** some bread.	**For** is sometimes used to express purpose, but it is a preposition and is followed by a noun object, as in (f).

*Exception: The phrase **be used for** expresses the typical or general purpose of a thing. In this case, the preposition **for** is followed by a gerund: A saw **is used for cutting** wood. Also possible: A saw **is used to cut** wood.
However, to talk about a particular thing and a particular situation, **be used** + an infinitive is used: A chain saw **was used to cut** down the old oak tree. (INCORRECT: A chain saw was used for cutting down the old oak tree.)

☐ **EXERCISE 22—ERROR ANALYSIS:** Correct the errors in the following.

1. Helen borrowed my dictionary for look up the spelling of "occurrence."

2. I went to the library for to study last night.

3. The teacher opened the window for getting some fresh air in the room.

4. I came to this school for learn English.

5. I need to get a part-time job for to earn some money for my school expenses.

☐ **EXERCISE 23:** Make up completions to the following. Express the *purpose* of the action.

1. I went to Chicago to _visit my relatives._

2. Tom went to Chicago for _a business conference._

3. I went to the market to _buy some food_

4. Mary went to the market for _some food_

5. I went to the doctor to _exam my heart_

6. My son went to the doctor for _____

7. I swim every day to _exercise my body_.

8. My friend swims every day for _his body exercise_.

9. I drove into the service station to _fix the wheel_.

10. They stopped at the service station for _fixing_.

4–11 ADJECTIVES FOLLOWED BY INFINITIVES

(a) We **were sorry to hear** the bad news. (b) I **was surprised to see** Tim at the meeting.	Certain adjectives can be immediately followed by infinitives, as in (a) and (b). In general, these adjectives describe a person (or persons), not a thing. Many of these adjectives describe a person's feelings or attitudes.

SOME COMMON ADJECTIVES FOLLOWED BY INFINITIVES

glad to	sorry to*	ready to	careful to	surprised to*
happy to	sad to*	prepared to	hesitant to	amazed to*
pleased to	upset to*	anxious to	reluctant to	astonished to*
delighted to	disappointed to*	eager to	afraid to	shocked to*
content to		willing to		stunned to*
relieved to	proud to	motivated to		
lucky to	ashamed to	determined to		
fortunate to				

*The expressions with asterisks are usually followed by infinitive phrases with verbs such as **see, learn, discover, find out, hear**.

☑ **EXERCISE 24:** Complete the sentences with infinitives.

1. I was glad _to get_ a letter from you.

2. I was relieved _to find out_ that I had passed the exam.

3. Sue is lucky _to be_ alive after the accident.

4. The soldiers were prepared _to fight_.

5. The children are anxious _to go_ to the circus.

6. Dick didn't feel like going anywhere. He was content _to stay at_ home and _to read_ a book.

7. The teacher is always willing _to help_ us.

hesitate (v) do dự, ngần đại
hesitation (n)

motive (n, lý do, động cơ)
motivate (v) bày tỏ động cơ, kích cơ

8. The students are motivated ___to study___ (sleep) English.

9. Be careful not ___to walk___ on the icy sidewalks!

10. Tom was hesitant ___to leave___ home alone on the dark street.

11. Sally is afraid ___to stay___ home alone.

12. Ann is proud ___to be___ the top student in her class.

13. I was surprised ___to see___ Mr. Yamamoto at the meeting.

14. We were sorry ___to hear___ the bad news.

☐ **EXERCISE 25—ORAL (BOOKS CLOSED):** Answer "yes" to the question. Use an infinitive phrase in your response.

Example: You saw your friend at the airport. Were you happy?
Response: Yes, I was happy to see my friend at the airport.

1. (. . .) has a lot of good friends. Is s/he fortunate?
2. You're leaving on vacation next week. Are you eager?
3. You met (. . .)'s wife/husband. Were you delighted?
4. You went to (*name of a faraway place in the world*) last summer. You saw (. . .) there. Were you surprised?
5. You're going to take a test tomorrow. Are you prepared?
6. You're thinking about asking (. . .) a personal question. Are you hesitant?
7. Your friend was ill. Finally you found out that she was okay. Were you relieved?
8. You heard about (. . .)'s accident. Were you sorry?

Answer the following questions in complete sentences.

9. What are you careful to do before you cross a busy street?
10. What are children sometimes afraid to do?
11. When you're tired in the evening, what are you content to do?
12. If one of your friends has a problem, what are you willing to do?
13. Sometimes when people don't know English very well, what are they reluctant to do?
14. If I announce there is a test tomorrow, what will you be motivated to do tonight?
15. What are you determined to do before you are 60 years old?
16. What are some things people should be ashamed to do?

17. Can you tell me something you were shocked to find out?/astonished to learn?
18. Can you tell me something you were disappointed to discover?/sad to hear?

[handwritten: too ... to (can't)   only too ... (to) can]

4–12   USING INFINITIVES WITH *TOO* AND *ENOUGH*

(a) That box is **too heavy** for Bob **to lift**. COMPARE: (b) That box is **very heavy**, but Bob can lift it.	In the speaker's mind, the use of **too** implies a negative result. In (a): **too heavy** = It is *impossible* for Bob to lift that box. In (b): **very heavy** = It is *possible but difficult* for Bob to lift that box.
(c) I am **strong enough** *to lift* that box. I can lift it. (d) I have **enough strength** *to lift* that box. (e) I have **strength enough** *to lift* that box.	**Enough** follows an adjective, as in (c). **Enough** may precede a noun, as in (d), or follow a noun, as in (e).

[handwritten annotations "(adj)" above "enough" in (c) and (d)]

☑ **EXERCISE 26:** Think of a negative result, and then complete the sentence with an infinitive phrase.

1. That ring is too expensive. → *Negative result: I can't buy it. That ring is too expensive for me to buy.*
2. I'm too tired. → *Negative result: I can't/don't want to go to the meeting. I'm too tired to go to the meeting.*
3. It's too late. → *Negative result:* . . . *[handwritten: I'm too late to go to school]*
4. It's too cold. *[handwritten: for me to]*
5. Nuclear physics is too difficult. *[handwritten: it's too difficult for me to understand]*
6. I'm too busy. *[handwritten: to go to the movies]*
7. My son is too young.
8. The mountain cliff is too steep. *[handwritten: to ...]*

Now think of a positive result, and complete the sentence with an infinitive phrase.

9. That ring is very expensive, but it isn't too expensive. → *Positive result: I can buy it. That ring isn't too expensive for me to buy.*
10. I'm very tired, but I'm not too tired. → *Positive result:* *[handwritten: I'm not too tired to ...]*
11. My suitcase is very heavy, but it's not too heavy.
12. I'm very busy, but I'm not too busy. *[handwritten: I'm not too busy to visit my parents]*

1. What is a child too young to do but an adult old enough to do?
2. (. . .)'s daughter is 18 months old. Is she too young or very young?
3. Who had a good dinner last night? Was it too good or very good?
4. Is it very difficult or too difficult to learn English?
5. After you wash your clothes, are they too clean or very clean?
6. Who stayed up late last night? Did you stay up too late or very late?
7. What is my pocket big enough to hold? What is it too small to hold?
8. Compare a mouse with an elephant. Is a mouse too small or very small?
9. What is the highest mountain in (*this country/the world*)? Is it too high or very high?
10. What did you have enough time/time enough to do before class today?

4–13 PASSIVE AND PAST FORMS OF INFINITIVES AND GERUNDS

PASSIVE INFINITIVE: **to be** + *past participle* (a) I didn't expect **to be invited** to his party.	In (a): **to be invited** is passive. The understood "**by** phrase" is "by him": *I didn't expect to be invited by him.*
PASSIVE GERUND: **being** + *past participle* (b) I appreciated **being invited** to your home.	In (b): **being invited** is passive. The understood "**by** phrase" is "by you": *I appreciated being invited by you.*
PAST INFINITIVE: **to have** + *past participle* (c) The rain seems **to have stopped**.	The event expressed by a past infinitive or past gerund happened before the time of the main verb. In (c): *The rain seems now to have stopped a few minutes ago.* *
PAST GERUND: **having** + *past participle* (d) I appreciate **having had** the opportunity to meet the king.	In (d): I met the king yesterday. *I appreciate now having had the opportunity to meet the king yesterday.* *
PAST-PASSIVE INFINITIVE: **to have been** + *past participle* (e) Jane is fortunate **to have been given** a scholarship.	In (e): Jane was given a scholarship last month by her government. She is fortunate. *Jane is fortunate now to have been given a scholarship last month by her government.*
PAST-PASSIVE GERUND: **having been** + *past participle* (f) I appreciate **having been told** the news.	In (f): I was told the news yesterday by someone. I appreciate that. *I appreciate now having been told the news yesterday by someone.*

*If the main verb is past, the action of the past infinitive or gerund happened before a time in the past:
*The rain **seemed to have stopped**.* = The rain seemed at six P.M. to have stopped before six P.M.
*I **appreciated having had** the opportunity to meet the king.* = I met the king in 1985. I appreciated in 1987 having had the opportunity to meet the king in 1985.

☑ **EXERCISE 28:** Supply an appropriate form for each verb in parentheses.

1. I don't enjoy (*laugh*) __being laughed__ at by other people.

2. I'm angry at him for (*tell, not*) __not telling / not having told*__ me the truth.

3. It is easy (*fool*) __to be fooled__ by his lies.

4. Jack had a narrow escape. He was almost hit by a car. He barely avoided (*hit*) __being hit__ by the speeding automobile.

5. Sharon wants us to tell her the news as soon as we hear anything. If we find out anything about the problem, she wants (*tell*) __to be told__ about it immediately.

6. Yesterday Anna wrote a check for fifty dollars, but when she wrote it she knew she didn't have enough money in the bank to cover it. Today she is very worried about (*write*) __having written__ that check. She has to find a way to put some money in her account right away.

7. A: What's the difference between ''burn up'' and ''burn down''?

   B: Hmmm. That's an interesting question. I don't recall ever (*ask*) __having been asked__ that question before.

8. Living in a foreign country has been a good experience for me. I am glad that my company sent me to another country to study. I am very pleased (*give*) __to have been given__ the opportunity to learn about another culture.

9. You must tell me the truth. I insist on (*tell*) __being told__ the truth.

10. Don't all of us want (*love*) __to be loved__ and (*need*) __needed__ by other people?

11. I enjoy (*watch*) __watching__ television in the evenings.

12. Dear Jim: I feel guilty about (*write, not*) __not having written__ to you sooner, but I've been swamped with work lately.

---

*The past gerund is used to emphasize that the action of the gerund took place *before* that of the main verb. However, often there is little difference in meaning between a simple gerund and a past gerund.

☑ **EXERCISE 29:** Supply an appropriate form for each verb in parentheses.

1. Martha doesn't like to have her picture taken. She avoids (*photograph*) _being photographed_ .

2. Tim was in the army during the war. He was caught by the enemy but he managed to escape. He is lucky (*escape*) _to have escaped_ with his life.

3. A: It's been nice talking to you. I really have enjoyed our conversation, but I have to leave now. I'm very happy (*have*) _to have had_ this opportunity to meet you and talk with you. Let's try to get together again soon.

   B: I'd like that.

4. A: Is Ted a transfer student?

   B: Yes.

   A: Where did he go to school before he came here?

   B: I'm not sure, but I think he mentioned something about (*go*) _having gone_ to UCLA or USC.

5. A: You know Jim Frankenstein, don't you?

   B: Jim Frankenstein? I don't think so. I don't recall ever (*meet*) _having met_ _____ him.

6. A: This letter needs (*send*) _to be sent_ immediately. Will you take care of it?

   B: Right away.

7. Sally is very quick. You have to tell her how to do something only once. She doesn't need (*tell*) _to be told_ twice.

8. A: I thought Sam was sick.

   B: So did I. But he seems (*recover*) _to have ⱽbeen recovered_ very quickly. He certainly doesn't seem (*be*) _to be_ sick now.

9. Last year I studied abroad. I appreciate (*have*) _having had_ . the opportunity to live and study in a foreign country.

10. This year I am studying abroad. I appreciate (*have*) ___*having had*___
    this opportunity to live and study in a foreign country.

11. Ms. Walters complained about (*tell, not*) ___*not being told*___
    about the meeting. In the future, she expects (*inform*) ___*to be informed*___
    _____ of any and all meetings.

4-14 USING GERUNDS OR PASSIVE INFINITIVES FOLLOWING *NEED*

(a) I **need to borrow** some money. (b) John **needs to be told** the truth.	Usually an infinitive follows **need**, as in (a) and (b).
(c) The house **needs painting**. (d) The house **needs to be painted**.	In certain situations, a gerund may follow **need**. In this case, the gerund carries a passive meaning. Usually the situations involve fixing or improving something. (c) and (d) have the same meaning.

☑ **EXERCISE 30:** Supply an appropriate form for the verbs in parentheses.

1. The chair is broken. I need (*fix*) ___*to fix*___ it. The chair
   needs (*fix*) ___*fixing (or to be fixed)*___

2. What a mess! This room needs (*clean*) ___*cleaning*___ up. We need
   (*clean*) ___*to clean*___ it up before the company arrives.

3. The baby's diaper needs (*change*) ___*changing*___. It's wet.

4. My shirt is wrinkled. It needs (*iron*) ___*ironing*___.

5. There is a hole in our roof. The roof needs (*repair*) ___*repairing*___.

6. I have books and papers all over my desk. I need (*take*) ___*to take*___
   some time to straighten up my desk. It needs (*straighten*) ___*straightening*___
   _____ up.

7. The apples on the tree are ripe. They need (*pick*) ___*picking (or to be picked)*___

8. The dog needs (*wash*) ___*washing*___. He's been digging in the
   mud.

4–15 USING A POSSESSIVE TO MODIFY A GERUND

We came to class late. Mr. Lee complained about that fact. (a) FORMAL: Mr. Lee complained about **our coming** *to class late.* * (b) INFORMAL: Mr. Lee complained about **us coming** *to class late.*	In formal English, a possessive pronoun (e.g., **our**) is used to modify a gerund, as in (a). In informal English, the object form (e.g., **us**) is frequently used, as in (b).
(c) FORMAL: Mr. Lee complained about **Mary's coming** *to class late.*	In very formal English, a possessive noun (e.g., **Mary's**) is used to modify a gerund.
(d) INFORMAL: Mr. Lee complained about **Mary coming** *to class late.*	The possessive form is often not used in informal English, as in (d).

"Coming to class late" occurred before "Mr. Lee complained," so a past gerund is also possible: Mr. Lee complained about **our having come to class late.*

☐ **EXERCISE 31:** Combine the following. Change *"that fact"* to a gerund phrase. Use formal English. Discuss informal usage.

1. Mary won a scholarship. We are excited about *that fact*. → *We are excited about Mary's winning a scholarship.*
2. He didn't want to go. I couldn't understand *that fact*. → *I couldn't understand his not wanting to go.*
3. You took the time to help us. We greatly appreciate *that fact*.
4. We talked about him behind his back. The boy resented *that fact*.
5. They ran away to get married. *That fact* shocked everyone.
6. You don't want to do it. I don't understand *that fact*.
7. Ann borrowed Sally's clothes without asking her first. Sally complained about *that fact*.
8. Helen is here to answer our questions about the company's new insurance plan. We should take advantage of *that fact*.

☑ **EXERCISE 32:** Supply an appropriate form for each verb in parentheses.

1. Alice didn't expect (*ask*) ___to be asked___ to Bill's party.
2. I'm not accustomed to (*drink*) ___drinking___ coffee with my meals.
3. I'll help you with your homework as soon as I finish (*wash*) ___washing___ ___ the dishes.
4. She took a deep breath (*relax*) ___to relax___ herself before she got up to give her speech.

5. I'm prepared (*answer*) _to answer_ any question that might be asked during my job interview tomorrow.

6. Matthew left without (*tell*) _telling_ anyone.

7. It's useless. Give up. Enough's enough. Don't keep (*beat*) _beating_ _____ your head against a brick wall.

8. His (*be, not*) _not being_ able to come is disappointing.

9. I hope (*award*) _to be awarded_ a scholarship for the coming semester.

10. We are very pleased (*accept*) _to accept_ your invitation.

11. I have considered (*get*) _getting_ a part-time job (*help*) _to help_ pay for my school expenses.

12. It is exciting (*travel*) _to travel_ to faraway places and (*leave*) _to leave_ one's daily routine behind.

13. (*Help*) _helping_ the disadvantaged children learn how to read was a rewarding experience.

14. He wants (*like*) _to be liked_ and (*trust*) _trusted_ by everyone.

15. I can't help (*wonder*) _wondering_ why Larry did such a foolish thing.

16. Mr. Carson is very lucky (*choose*) _to be chosen_ by the committee as their representative to the meeting in Paris.

17. (*Live*) _living_ in a city has certain advantages.

18. Keep on (*do*) _doing_ whatever you were doing. I didn't mean (*interrupt*) _to interrupt_ you.

19. It is very kind of you (*take*) _____ to take _____ care of that problem for me.

20. She opened the window (*let*) _____ to let _____ in some fresh air.

21. They agreed (*cooperate*) _____ to cooperate _____ with us to the fullest extent.

22. Did you remember (*turn*) _____ in your assignment?

23. I don't remember ever (*hear*) _____ that story before.

24. Does your son regret (*leave*) _____ leaving _____ home and (*go*) _____ going _____ _____ to a foreign country (*study*) _____?

25. I appreciate your (*ask*) _____ asking _____, my opinion on the matter.

26. You should stop (*drive*) _____ driving _____ if you get sleepy. It's dangerous (*drive*) _____ to drive _____ when you're not alert.

27. After driving for three hours, we stopped (*get*) _____ to get _____ something to eat.

28. Please forgive me for (*be, not*) _____ not being _____ here to help you yesterday.

4-16 USING VERBS OF PERCEPTION

(a) I *saw* my friend *run* down the street. (b) I *saw* my friend *running* down the street. (c) I *heard* the rain *fall* on the roof. (d) I *heard* the rain *falling* on the roof.	Certain verbs of perception are followed by either *the simple form*★ or *the -ing form*★★ of a verb. There is usually little difference in meaning between the two forms except that the *-ing* form usually gives the idea of "while." In (b): I saw my friend while she was running down the street.
(e) I *heard* a famous opera star *sing* at the concert last night. (f) When I walked into the apartment, I *heard* my roommate *singing* in the shower.	Sometimes (not always) there is a clear difference between using the simple form or the *-ing* form. In (e): I heard the singing from beginning to end. In (f): The singing was in progress when I heard it.

VERBS OF PERCEPTION FOLLOWED BY THE SIMPLE FORM OR THE *-ING* FORM			
see notice watch look at observe	hear listen to	feel	smell

★The simple form of a verb = the infinitive form without "to." *INCORRECT: I saw my friend to run down the street.*
★★The *-ing* form refers to the present participle.

□ **EXERCISE 33:** Complete the sentences with the words in the list. Use both possible forms.

✔ chase	land	shake
come	look at	sing
knock	ring	take off

1. When I was downtown yesterday, I saw the police _____chase/chasing_____ a thief.

2. There was an earthquake in my hometown last year. It was just a small one, but I could feel the ground _____shake_____.

3. Polly was working in her garden, so she didn't hear the phone _____ring_____ _____.

4. I like to listen to the birds _____sing_____ when I get up early in the morning.

5. The guard observed a suspicious-looking person _____come_____ into the bank.

6. I was almost asleep last night when I suddenly heard someone _____knocking_____ _____ on the door.

7. Did you notice Max _____look at_____ another student's paper during the exam?

8. While I was waiting for my plane, I watched other planes _____land / landing_____ and _____take off / taking off_____.

*In the following, choose the more appropriate form (either simple or **-ing**) of the verbs in parentheses.*

9. Last weekend I went to my daughter's soccer game. I enjoyed watching the children _____play_____ soccer. (*play*)

10. When I walked past the park, I saw some children _____playing_____ baseball. (*play*)

11. Do you see Mary _____walking_____ up the street? Isn't that her, the woman in the red dress? (*walk*)

12. I remember it distinctly. At 5:30 yesterday afternoon, I saw Jim _____walk_____ _____ to his car, _____open_____ the door, and _____get in_____ _____. (*walk, open, get in*)

13. When I glanced out the window, I saw Jack _____walking_____ toward my house. (*walk*)

14. Do you hear someone _____call_____ for help in the distance? I do. (*call*)

15. When I heard the principal of the school _____call_____ my name at the graduation ceremony, I walked to the front of the auditorium to receive my diploma. (*call*)

16. Last night while I was trying to fall asleep, I could hear the people in the next apartment __sing / singing__ and __laugh / laughing__. (*sing, laugh*)

17. Do you smell something __burning__? (*burn*)

18. As soon as I saw the fly _____land_____ on the table, I swatted it with a rolled up newspaper. (*land*)

4–17 USING THE SIMPLE FORM AFTER LET AND HELP

(a) My father **let** me **drive** his car. (b) I **let** my friend **borrow** my bicycle.	**Let** is always followed by the simple form of a verb, not an infinitive. (*INCORRECT: My father let me to drive his car.*)
(c) My brother **helped** me **wash** my car. (d) My brother **helped** me **to wash** my car.	**Help** is often followed by the simple form of a verb, as in (c). An infinitive is also possible, as in (d). Both (c) and (d) are correct.

☐ **EXERCISE 34:** Complete the sentences with verb phrases.

1. Don't let me _____*forget to take my keys to the house with me.*_____

2. The teacher usually lets us __make__

3. Why did you let your roommate __look__

4. You shouldn't let other people __know__

5. A stranger helped the lost child __find__

6. It was very kind of my friend to help me __press__

7. Keep working. Don't let me __remind__

8. Could you help me __do__

4–18 USING CAUSATIVE VERBS: *MAKE, HAVE, GET*

have some do something (handwritten)

(a) I **made** my brother **carry** my suitcase. (b) I **had** my brother **carry** my suitcase. *get someone to do something* (handwritten) (c) I **got** my brother **to carry** my suitcase. FORM: X *makes* Y **do** something. (simple form) X *has* Y **do** something. (simple form) X *gets* Y **to do** something. (infinitive)	**Make, have,** and **get** can be used to express the idea that "X" causes "Y" to do something. When they are used as causative verbs, their meanings are similar but not identical. In (a): My brother had no choice. I insisted that he carry my suitcase. In (b): My brother carried my suitcase simply because I asked him to. In (c): I managed to persuade my brother to carry my suitcase.
(d) Mrs. Lee **made** her son **clean** his room. (e) Sad movies **make** me **cry**.	Causative **make** is followed by the simple form of a verb, not an infinitive. (*INCORRECT: She made him to clean his room.*) **Make** gives the idea that "X" forces "Y" to do something. In (d): Mrs. Lee's son had no choice.
(f) I **had** the plumber **repair** the leak. (g) Jane **had** the waiter **bring** her some tea.	Causative **have** is followed by the simple form of a verb, not an infinitive. (*INCORRECT: I had him to repair the leak.*) **Have** gives the idea that "X" requests "Y" to do something. In (f): The plumber repaired the leak because I asked him to.
(h) The students **got** the teacher **to dismiss** class early. (i) Jack **got** his friends **to play** soccer with him after school.	Causative **get** is followed by an infinitive. **Get** gives the idea that "X" persuades "Y" to do something. In (h): The students managed to persuade the teacher to let them leave early.
(j) I **had** my watch **repaired** (by someone). (k) I **got** my watch **repaired** (by someone). *participle (passive)* (handwritten)	The past participle is used after **have** and **get** to give a passive meaning. In this case, there is usually little or no difference in meaning between **have** and **get**. In (j) and (k): I caused my watch to be repaired by someone.

☐ **EXERCISE 35:** Complete the sentences with the words in parentheses.

1. The doctor made the patient _____*stay*_____ in bed. (*stay*)

2. Mrs. Crane had her house _____*painted*_____. (*paint*)

3. The teacher had the class ___*write*___ a 2000-word research paper. (*write*)

4. I made my son ___*wash*___ the windows before he could go outside to play. (*wash*)

5. Don got some kids in the neighborhood ___*to clean*___ out his garage. (*clean*)

6. I went to the bank to have a check ___*cashed*___. (*cash*)

7. Tom had a bad headache yesterday, so he <u>got</u> his twin brother Tim _____to go_____ to class for him. The teacher didn't know the difference. (*go*)

8. When Scott went shopping, he found a jacket that he really liked. After he had the sleeves ____shortened____, it fit him perfectly. (*shorten*)

9. My boss made me ____redo____ my report because he wasn't satisfied with it. (*redo*)

10. Alice stopped at the service station to have the tank ____filled____. (*fill*)

11. I got Mary ____to lend____ me some money so I could go to a movie last night. (*lend*)

12. Mr. Fields went to a doctor to have the wart on his nose ____removed____. (*remove*)

13. Peeling onions always makes me ____cry____. (*cry*)

14. Tom Sawyer was supposed to paint the fence, but he didn't want to do it. He was a very clever boy. Somehow he got his friends ____to do____ it for him. (*do*)

15. We had a professional photographer ____take____ pictures of everyone who participated in our wedding. (*take*)

16. I spilled some tomato sauce on my suit coat. Now I need to get my suit ____cleaned____. (*clean*)

□ **EXERCISE 36:** Complete the sentences with verb phrases.

1. I got my friend _____*to translate a letter for me.*_____

2. Sometimes parents make their children ____clean____

3. When I'm at a restaurant, I sometimes have the waiter ____bring____

4. Many people take their cars to service stations to get the oil ____filled____

5. Teachers sometimes have their students ____go____

6. I'm more than willing to help you ____finish____

7. Before I left on my trip, I had the travel agent ____check____

8. My cousin's jokes always make me ____bring____

9. When I was a child, my parents wouldn't let me _go_ _____

10. We finally got our landlady _to received_ _____

4–19 SPECIAL EXPRESSIONS FOLLOWED BY THE -*ING* FORM OF A VERB

(a) We *had fun* We *had a good time* } *playing* volleyball.	*have fun* + -*ing* *have a good time* + -*ing*
(b) I *had trouble* I *had difficulty* I *had a hard time* I *had a difficult time* } *finding* his house.	*have trouble* + -*ing* *have difficulty* + -*ing* *have a hard time* + -*ing* *have a difficult time* + -*ing*
(c) Sam *spends* most of his time *studying*. (d) I *waste* a lot of time *watching* TV.	*spend* + expression of time or money + -*ing* *waste* + expression of time or money + -*ing*
(e) She *sat* at her desk *writing* a letter. (f) I *stood* there *wondering* what to do next. (g) He *is lying* in bed *reading* a novel.	*sit* + expression of place + -*ing* *stand* + expression of place + -*ing* *lie* + expression of place + -*ing*
(h) When I walked into my office, I *found* George *using* my telephone. (i) When I walked into my office, I *caught* a thief *looking* through my desk drawers.	*find* + (pro)noun + -*ing* *catch* + (pro)noun + -*ing* In (h) and (i): Both *find* and *catch* mean *discover*. *Catch* expresses anger or displeasure.

☐ **EXERCISE 37:** Complete the following.

1. We had a lot of fun ____*playing*____ games at the picnic.

2. I have trouble ____understanding____ Mrs. Maxwell when she speaks. She talks too fast.

3. I spent five hours ____doing____ my homework last night.

4. Martha is standing at the corner ____writing____ for the bus.

5. Michael is sitting in class ____taking____ notes.

6. Ms. Anderson is a commuter. Every work day, she spends almost two hours ____driving____ to and from work.

7. It was a beautiful spring day. Dorothy was lying under a tree ____listening____ _____ to the birds sing.

8. We wasted our money ____going____ to that movie. It was very boring.

9. Joe spent all day _____ *getting* _____ ready to leave on vacation.

10. Ted is an indecisive person. He has a hard time _____ *making* _____ up his mind about anything.

11. I wondered what the children were doing while I was gone. When I got home, I found them _____ *watching* _____ TV.

12. When Mr. Brown walked into the kitchen, he caught the children _____ *eating* _____ some candy even though he'd told them not to spoil their dinners.

13. A: My friend is going to Germany next month, but he doesn't speak German. What do you suppose he will have difficulty _____ *communicating* _____?
    B: Well, he might have trouble _____ *understanding* _____.

14. A: Did you enjoy your trip to New York City?
    B: Very much. We had a good time _____ *enjoying* _____.

15. A: This is your first semester at this school. Have you had any problems?
    B: Not really, but sometimes I have a hard time _____ *catching up* _____.

16. A: What did you do yesterday?
    B: I spent almost all day _____ *sleeping* _____.

☐ **EXERCISE 38:** Supply an appropriate form for each verb in parentheses.

1. Edward stood on the beach (*look*) _____ *looking* _____ out over the ocean.

2. Why don't you let him (*make*) _____ *make* _____ up his own mind?

3. Jean sat on a park bench (*watch*) _____ *watching* _____ the ducks (*swim*) _____ *swimming* _____ in the pond.

4. They refused (*pay*) _____ *to pay* _____ their taxes, so they were sent to jail.

5. It is foolish (*ignore*) _____ *to ignore* _____ physical ailments.

6. Sara is going to spend next year (*study*) _____ *studying* _____ at a university in Japan.

7. The sad expression on his face made me (*feel*) _____ *felt* _____ sorry for him.

8. I didn't know how to get to Harry's house, so I had him (*draw*) _draw_ a map for me.

9. Barbara has a wonderful sense of humor. She can always make me (*laugh*) _laugh_.

10. The little boy had a lot of trouble (*convince*) _convincing_ anyone that he had seen a mermaid.

11. The teacher had the class (*open*) _open_ their books to page 185.

12. It was a hot day and the work was hard. I could feel sweat (*trickle*) _trickle_ down my back.

13. I went to the pharmacy to have my prescription (*fill*) _filled_.

14. Mr. Flynn is good at (*tell*) _telling_ the difference between diamonds and cut glass.

15. Many people think Mr. Peel will win the election. He has a good chance of (*elect*) _electing_.

16. I found a penny (*lie*) _lying_ on the sidewalk.

17. My cousins helped me (*move*) _to move / move_ into my new apartment.

18. I was tired, so I just watched them (*play*) _playing_ volleyball instead of (*join*) _joining_ them.

19. You can lead a horse to water, but you can't make him (*drink*) _drink_.

20. You shouldn't let children (*play*) _play_ with matches.

21. I finally told him (*be*) _to be_ quiet for a minute and (*listen*) _listen_ to what I had to say.

22. Irene was lying in bed (*think*) _thinking_ about what a wonderful time she'd had.

23. When Shelley needed a passport photo, she had her picture (*take*) _taken_ by a professional photographer.

24. If you hear any news, I want (*tell*) _to be told_ immediately.

25. Let's (*have*) _have_ Ron and Maureen (*join*) _join_ us for dinner tonight, okay?

26. There's a great difference between (*be*) _being_ a freshman and (*be*) _being_ a senior.

27. My English is pretty good, but sometimes I have trouble (*understand*) _understanding_ lectures at school.

28. The illogic of his statements made me (*tear*) _tear_ my hair out.

29. Recently Jo has been spending most of her time (*do*) _doing_ research for a book on pioneer women.

30. I was getting sleepy, so I had my friend (*drive*) _drive_ the car.

☐ **EXERCISE 39:** Supply an appropriate form for each verb in parentheses.

1. Jason wouldn't let them (*take*) _take_ his picture.

2. I couldn't understand what the passage said, so I had my friend (*translate*) _translate_ it for me.

3. No, that's not what I meant (*say*) _to say_. How can I make you (*understand*) _understand_?

4. I have finally assembled enough information (*begin*) _to begin_ writing my thesis.

5. It's a serious problem. Something needs (*do*) _to be done_ about it soon.

6. I was terribly disappointed (*discover*) __to discover__ that he had lied to me.

7. I had the operator (*put*) __put__ the call through for me.

8. No one could make Ted (*feel*) __feel__ afraid. He refused (*intimidate*) __to intimidate__ by anyone.

9. I don't see how she can possibly avoid (*fail*) __failing__ the course.

10. Do something! Don't just sit there (*twiddle*) __twiddling__ your thumbs.

11. Emily stopped her car (*let*) __to let__ a black cat (*run*) __run__ across the street.

12. He's a terrific soccer player! Did you see him (*make*) __making__ that last goal?

13. We spent the entire class period (*talk*) __talking__ about the revolution.

14. Karen got along very well in France despite not (*be*) __being__ able to speak French.

15. Mary Beth suggested (*go*) __going__ on a picnic.

➤ 16. I don't like (*force*) _____ (*leave*) _____ the room (*study*) _____ whenever my roommate feels like (*have*) _____ a party.

17. He's at an awkward age. He's old enough (*have*) __to have__ adult problems but too young (*know*) __to know__ how (*handle*) __handle__ them.

18. (*Look*) __look__ at the car after the accident made him (*realize*) __realize__ that he was indeed lucky (*be*) __to be__ alive.

19. We sat in his kitchen (*sip*) __sipping__ very hot, strong tea and (*eat*) __eating__ chunks of hard cheese.

20. I admit (*be*) __being__ a little nervous about the job interview. I don't know what (*expect*) __expect__.

21. I'm tired. I wouldn't mind just (stay) __*staying*__ home tonight
    and (get) __*getting*__ to bed early.

22. It is the ancient task of the best artists among us (force) __*to force*__
    _____ us (use) __*to use*__ our ability (feel) __*to feel*__
    _____ and (share) __*to share*__ emotions.

23. Please speak softly. My roommate is in the other room (sleep) __*sleeping*__
    _____.

24. I don't anticipate (have) __*having*__ any difficulties (adjust)
    __*adjusting*__ to a different culture when I go abroad.

25. Isabel expected (admit) __*to be admitted*__ to the university, but she
    wasn't.

26. When Franco went to the barber shop (get) __*to get*__ his hair
    (cut) __*cut*__, he had his beard (trim) __*trimmed*__, too.

□ **EXERCISE 40—ERROR ANALYSIS:** Find and correct the errors in the following.

Example: I am considering to go to a show tonight.
Correction: I am considering **going** to a show tonight.

1. My parents made me to promise to write them once a week.
2. I don't mind to have a roommate.
3. Most students want return home as soon as possible.
4. When I went to shopping last Saturday, I saw a man to drive his car onto
   the sidewalk.
5. I asked my roommate to let me to use his shoe polish.
6. To learn about another country it is very interesting.
7. I don't enjoy to play card games.
8. I heard a car door to open and closing.
9. I had my friend to lend me his car.
10. I tried very hard to don't make any mistakes.
11. You should visit my country. It is too beautiful.
12. The music director tapped his baton for beginning the rehearsal.
13. Some people prefer save there money to spend it.

14. The task of find a person who could help us wasn't difficult.

15. All of us needed to went to the cashier's window.

16. I am looking forward to go to swim in the ocean.

17. When your planting a garden, it's important to be known about soils.

18. My mother always make me to be slow down if she think I am driving to fast.

19. One of our fights ended up with me having to sent to the hospital for getting stitches.

☐ **EXERCISE 41—WRITTEN:** Following are composition topics.

1. Write about your first day or week here (in this city/at this school/etc.). Did you have any unusual, funny, or difficult experiences? What were your first impressions and reactions? Whom did you meet?

2. Write about your childhood. What are some of the pleasant memories you have of your childhood? Do you have any unpleasant memories?

3. Whom do you like to spend some of your free time with? What do you enjoy doing together? Include an interesting experience the two of you have had.

☐ **EXERCISE 42—PHRASAL VERBS:** Supply appropriate prepositions. All of the sentences contain two-word verbs.

1. A: I think we should increase the membership dues from one dollar to two.

   B: That might solve some of our financial problems. Why don't you bring that _____ at the next meeting?

2. A: Did you hand _____ your composition?

   B: No. I didn't like it, so I decided to do it _____.

3. A: What time did you get _____ this morning?

   B: I slept late. I didn't drag myself out of bed until after nine.

4. A: What's the baby's name?

   B: Helen. She was named _____ her paternal grandmother.

5. A: I need to get more exercise.

   B: Why don't you take _____ tennis?

6. A: You can't go in there.

   B: Why not?

   A: Look at that sign. It says, "Keep _____. No trespassing."

7. A: I can't reach Fred. There's a busy signal.

   B: Then hang _____ and try again later.

8. A: The radio is too loud. Would you mind if I turned it _____ a little?

   B: No.

9. A: I can't hear the radio. Could you turn it _____ a little?

   B: Sure.

10. A: What are you doing Saturday night, Bob?

   B: I'm taking Virginia _____ for dinner and a show.

APPENDIX *1*

Supplementary Grammar Units

UNIT A: Basic Grammar Terminology
UNIT B: Questions
UNIT C: Negatives
UNIT D: Articles

UNIT A: Basic Grammar Terminology

A-1 SUBJECTS, VERBS, AND OBJECTS

<table>
<tr>
<td>

    S   V
(a) ***Birds   fly.***
    (NOUN) (VERB)
</td>
<td>Almost all English sentences contain a subject (**S**) and a verb (**V**). The verb may or may not be followed by an object (**O**).</td>
</tr>
<tr>
<td>

        S   V
(b) The ***baby   cried.***
      (NOUN) (VERB)
</td>
<td rowspan="4">

VERBS: Verbs that are not followed by an object, as in (a) and (b), are called *intransitive verbs.* Common intransitive verbs: *agree, arrive, come, cry, exist, go, happen, live, occur, rain, rise, sleep, stay, walk.*

Verbs that are followed by an object, as in (c) and (d), are called *transitive verbs.* Common transitive verbs: *build, cut, find, like, make, need, send, use, want.*

Some verbs can be either intransitive or transitive.
    intransitive: A student studies.
    transitive: A student studies books.
</td>
</tr>
<tr>
<td>

         S   V   O
(c) The ***student needs *** a ***pen.***
      (NOUN)   (VERB)   (NOUN)
</td>
</tr>
<tr>
<td>

      S   V   O
(d) My ***friend enjoyed *** the ***party.***
     (NOUN)   (VERB)   (NOUN)
</td>
</tr>
<tr>
<td></td>
<td>

SUBJECTS AND OBJECTS: The subjects and objects of verbs are nouns (or pronouns). Examples of nouns: *person, place, thing, John, Asia, pen, information, appearance, amusement.*
</td>
</tr>
</table>

A-2   PREPOSITIONS AND PREPOSITIONAL PHRASES

COMMON PREPOSITIONS				
about	*before*	*despite*	*of*	*to*
above	*behind*	*down*	*off*	*toward(s)*
across	*below*	*during*	*on*	*under*
after	*beneath*	*for*	*out*	*until*
against	*beside*	*from*	*over*	*up*
along	*besides*	*in*	*since*	*upon*
among	*between*	*into*	*through*	*with*
around	*beyond*	*like*	*throughout*	*within*
at	*by*	*near*	*till*	*without*

S   **V**   **PREP**   **O of PREP**
(a) The student studies ***in   the library***.
                        (NOUN)
      S   **V**   **O**   **PREP** **O of PREP**
(b) We enjoyed the party ***at   your house***.
                            (NOUN)
	An important element of English sentences is the prepositional phrase. It consists of a preposition (**PREP**) and its object (**O**). The object of a preposition is a noun or pronoun. In (a): ***in the library*** is a prepositional phrase.

(c) We went ***to the zoo in the afternoon***. (place) (time) (d) ***In the afternoon***, we went to the zoo.	In (c): In most English sentences, "place" comes before "time." In (d): Sometimes a prepositional phrase comes at the beginning of a sentence.

□ **EXERCISE 1:** Find the subjects (**S**), verbs (**V**), objects (**O**), and prepositional phrases (**PP**) in the following sentences.

                S   **V**   **O**   **PP**

1. Jack put the letter in the mailbox.

2. The children walked to school.

3. Beethoven wrote nine symphonies.

4. Mary did her homework at the library.

5. Bells originated in Asia.

6. Chinese printers created the first paper money in the world.

A-3   ADJECTIVES

(a) Mary is an ***intelligent   student***.
           (ADJECTIVE) (NOUN)
(b) The ***hungry   children*** ate fruit.
    (ADJECTIVE)(NOUN)
	Adjectives describe nouns. In grammar, we say that adjectives modify nouns. The word *modify* means "change a little." Adjectives give a little different meaning to a noun: *intelligent student, lazy student, good student.* Examples of adjectives: *young, old, rich, poor, beautiful, brown, French, modern.*

(c) I saw some ***beautiful*** pictures. *INCORRECT: beautifuls pictures*	An adjective is neither singular nor plural. A final *-s* is never added to an adjective.

A-4 ADVERBS

(a) He walks **quickly**.
(ADVERB)
(b) She opened the door **quietly**.
(ADVERB)
	Adverbs modify verbs. Often they answer the question "How?" In (a): *How does he walk?* Answer: *Quickly.*
	Adverbs are often formed by adding **-ly** to an adjective.
	    adjective: **quick**
	    adverb: **quickly**

(c) I am **extremely** *happy*. (ADVERB) (ADJECTIVE)	Adverbs are also used to modify adjectives, i.e., to give information about adjectives, as in (c).
(d) Ann will come **tomorrow**. (ADVERB)	Adverbs are also used to express time or frequency. Examples: *tomorrow, today, yesterday, soon, never, usually, always, yet.*
MIDSENTENCE ADVERBS (e) Ann **always** *comes* on time. (f) Ann *is* **always** on time. (g) Ann *has* **always** *come* on time. (h) *Does she* **always** *come* on time?	Some adverbs may occur in the middle of a sentence. Midsentence adverbs have usual positions; they (1) come in front of simple present and simple past verbs (except **be**), as in (e); (2) follow **be** (simple present and simple past), as in (f); (3) come between a helping verb and a main verb, as in (g). In a question, a midsentence adverb comes directly after the subject, as in (h).

COMMON MIDSENTENCE ADVERBS
ever, always, usually, often, frequently, generally, sometimes, occasionally, seldom, rarely, hardly ever, never, not ever, already, finally, just, probably

☐ **EXERCISE 2:** Choose the correct word (*adjective* or *adverb*) in parentheses.

1. George is a (*careless, carelessly*) writer. He writes (*careless, carelessly*).
2. Frank asked me an (*easy, easily*) question. I answered it (*easy, easily*).
3. Sally speaks (*soft, softly*). She has a (*soft, softly*) voice.
4. I entered the classroom (*quiet, quietly*) because I was late.
5. Ali speaks English very (*good, well*). He has very (*good, well*) pronunciation.★

★The word **well** can be either an adverb or an adjective.
    (a) Don *writes* **well**. In (a): **well** = an adverb meaning "in a good manner." It describes how Don writes.
    (b) Mary was sick, but now she *is* **well**. In (b): **well** = an adjective meaning "healthy, not sick." It follows the verb **be** and describes the subject "she"; i.e., Mary is a *well* person, not a sick person.
NOTE: After the linking verb **feel**, either **good** or **well** may be used:
    (c) I *feel* **good**.
    (d) I *feel* **well**.
    (c) and (d) have essentially the same meaning. However, **well** usually refers specifically to health, whereas **good** can refer to one's physical and/or emotional condition.

□ **EXERCISE 3:** Identify the adjectives (**ADJ**) and adverbs (**ADV**) in the following
sentences.

          ADJ   **ADV**

1. Jack opened the heavy door slowly.

2. Chinese jewelers carved beautiful ornaments from jade.

3. The old man carves wooden figures skillfully.

4. A busy executive usually has short conversations on the telephone.

5. The young women had a very good time at the picnic yesterday.

□ **EXERCISE 4:** Put the adverb in parentheses in its usual midsentence position.

1. (*never*)   Erica has seen snow. → *Erica has never seen snow.*
2. (*often*)   Ted studies at the library in the evening.
3. (*often*)   Ann is at the library in the evening, too.
4. (*already*)   Fred has finished studying for tomorrow's test.
5. (*seldom*)   Jack is at home.
6. (*always*)   Does he stay there?
7. (*often*)   He goes into town to hang around with his buddies.
8. (*always*)   You should tell the truth.

A-5 THE VERB *BE*

(a) John *is*   **a student.**
   (BE)   (NOUN)
(b) John *is*   **intelligent.**
   (BE) (ADJECTIVE)
(c) John *was* **at the library.**
    (BE) (PREP. PHRASE)
	A sentence with **be** as the main verb has three basic patterns:
	In (a): **be** + *a noun*
	In (b): **be** + *an adjective*
	In (c): **be** + *a prepositional phrase*

(d) Mary *is writing* a letter. (e) They *were listening* to some music. (f) That letter *was written* by Alice.	**Be** is also used as an auxiliary verb in progressive verb tenses and in the passive. In (d) *is* = *auxiliary*; **writing** = *main verb*

TENSE FORMS OF *BE*

	SIMPLE PRESENT	SIMPLE PAST	PRESENT PERFECT
	I am	*I was*	*I have been*
SINGULAR	*you are*	*you were*	*you have been*
	he, she, it is	*he, she, it was*	*he, she, it has been*
PLURAL	*we, you, they are*	*we, you, they were*	*we, you, they have been*

A-6 LINKING VERBS

(a) The soup **smells** **good**.
    (LINKING VERB)   (ADJECTIVE)
(b) This food **tastes delicious**.
(c) The children **feel happy**.
(d) The weather **became cold**.
	Other verbs like **be** that may be followed immediately by an adjective are called *linking verbs*. An adjective following a linking verb describes the subject of a sentence.*
	Common verbs that may be followed by an adjective:
	    feel, **look**, **smell**, **sound**, **taste**
	    appear, **seem**
	    become (and **get**, **turn**, **grow** when they mean "become")

*COMPARE:
    (1) *The man looks angry.* → An adjective (**angry**) follows **look**. The adjective describes the subject (**the man**). **Look** has the meaning of "appear."
    (2) *The man looked at me angrily.* → An adverb (**angrily**) follows **look at**. The adverb describes the action of the verb. **Look at** has the meaning of "regard, watch."

☐ **EXERCISE 5:** Choose the correct form (*adjective* or *adverb*) in parentheses.

    1. This math problem looks (*easy, easily*). I'm sure I can do it (*easy, easily*).
    2. That chair looks (*comfortable, comfortably*).
    3. I looked at the problem (*careful, carefully*) and then solved it.
    4. I felt (*sad, sadly*) when I heard the news.
    5. Susan smiled (*cheerful, cheerfully*). She seemed (*cheerful, cheerfully*).
    6. I tasted the soup (*careful, carefully*) because it was hot. The soup tasted (*good, well*).
    7. The room got (*quiet, quietly*) when the professor entered. The students sat (*quiet, quietly*) at their desks.
    8. The sky grew (*dark, darkly*) as the storm approached.

A-7 PERSONAL PRONOUNS

	SINGULAR	PLURAL	
SUBJECT PRONOUNS	*I* *you* *she*, *he*, *it*	*we* *you* *they*	A pronoun is used in place of a noun. It refers to a noun. The noun it refers to is called the *antecedent*. *Examples:* I read the **book**. **It** was good. (The pronoun "it" refers to the antecedent noun "book.")
OBJECT PRONOUNS	*me* *you* *her*, *him*, *it*	*us* *you* *them*	Mary said, "**I** drink tea." (The pronoun "I" refers to the speaker, whose name is Mary.)

(continued)

POSSESSIVE PRONOUNS	*mine* *your* *hers*, *his*	*ours* *yours* *theirs*	Possessive pronouns are not followed immediately by a noun; they stand alone. *Example:* That book is **mine**. Those are **yours** over there.*
POSSESSIVE ADJECTIVES	*my* name *your* name *her*, *his*, *its* name	*our* names *your* names *their* names	Possessive adjectives are followed immediately by a noun; they do not stand alone. *Example:* **My** book is here. **Your** books are over there.

*Possessive nouns require apostrophes; e.g., That book is *Mary's*. (See Chart 5-3.) Possessive pronouns do NOT take apostrophes.
    CORRECT: That book is *hers*, and those books are *theirs*.
    INCORRECT: That book is *her's* and those books are *theirs'*.

☐ **EXERCISE 6:** Identify the pronouns and their antecedents in the following sentences.

1. Jack has a part-time job. He works at a fast-food restaurant.

    (*he* = *a pronoun*; *Jack* = *the antecedent*)

2. Many monkeys don't like water, but they can swim well when they have to.
3. The teacher graded the students' papers last night. She returned them during class the next day.
4. The cormorant is a diving bird. It can stay under water for a long time. In some countries, it is used by fishermen to catch fish for them.
5. Tom took an apple with him to school. He ate it at lunch time.

☐ **EXERCISE 7:** Choose the correct word in parentheses.

1. This is (*my, mine*) umbrella. (*You, Yours*) umbrella is over there.
2. This umbrella is (*my, mine*). The other one is (*your, yours*).
3. Mary and Bob have (*their, theirs*) books. In other words, Mary has (*her, hers*) and Tom has his.
4. A honeybee has two wings on each side of (*its, it's*) body.*
5. (*Its, It's*) true that a homing pigeon will find (*its, it's*) way home even though it begins (*its, it's*) trip in unfamiliar territory.
6. I have a pet. (*Its, It's*) name is Squeak. (*Its, It's*) a turtle. (*Its, It's*) been my pet for two years.

---

*COMPARE: *its* = a possessive adjective
           it's = a contraction of *it is* or *it has*

A-8 CONTRACTIONS

> IN SPEAKING: In everyday spoken English, certain forms of **be** and auxiliary verbs are usually contracted with pronouns, nouns, and question words.
>
> IN WRITING: (1) In written English, contractions with pronouns are common in informal writing, but not generally acceptable in formal writing.
>
> (2) Contractions with nouns and question words are, for the most part, rarely used in writing. A few of these contractions may be found in quoted dialogue in stories or in very informal writing, such as a chatty letter to a good friend, but most of them are rarely if ever written.

In the following, quotation marks indicate that the contraction is frequently spoken but rarely if ever written.

	WITH PRONOUNS	WITH NOUNS	WITH QUESTION WORDS
am	*I'm* reading a book.	Ø	*"What'm"* I supposed to do?
is	*She's* studying. *It's* going to rain.	My *"book's"* on the table. *Mary's* at home.	*Where's* Sally? *Who's* that man?
are	*You're* working hard. *They're* waiting for us.	My *"books're"* on the table." The *"teachers're"* at a meeting.	*"What're"* you doing? *"Where're"* they going?
has	*She's* been here for a year. *It's* been cold lately.	My *"book's"* been stolen! *Sally's* never met him.	*Where's* Sally been living? *What's* been going on?"
have	*I've* finished my work. *They've* never met you.	The *"books've"* been sold. The *"students've"* finished the test."	*"Where've"* they been? *"How've"* you been?
had	*He'd* been waiting for us. *We'd* forgotten about it.	The *"books'd"* been sold. *"Mary'd"* never met him before.	*"Where'd"* you been before that? *"Who'd"* been there before you?
did	Ø	Ø	*"What'd"* you do last night? *"How'd"* you do on the test?
will	*I'll* come later. *She'll* help us.	The *"weather'll"* be nice tomorrow. *"John'll"* be coming soon.	*"Who'll"* be at the meeting? *"Where'll"* you be at ten?
would	*He'd* like to go there. *They'd* come if they could.	My *"friends'd"* come if they could. *"Mary'd"* like to go there, too.	*"Where'd"* you like to go?

☐ **EXERCISE 8—ORAL:** Read the sentences aloud. Practice usual contracted speech.

Example: The streets are wet. → "The streets're wet."

CONTRACTIONS WITH NOUNS:

1. My friend is here.
2. My friends are here.
3. Tom has been here since two.
4. The students have been here since one.
5. Bob had already left.
6. Bob would like to come with us.
7. Don will be here soon.
8. The window is open.
9. The windows are open.
10. Jane has never seen a ghost.
11. The boys have been there before.
12. Sally had forgotten her book.
13. Sally would forget her book if I didn't remind her to take it.

CONTRACTIONS WITH QUESTION WORDS:

14. Who is that woman?
15. Who are those people?
16. Who has been taking care of your house?
17. What have you been doing?
18. What had you been doing before that?
19. What would you like to do?

20. What did you do yesterday?
21. Why did you stay home?
22. When will I see you again?
23. How long will you be away?
24. Where am I supposed to go?
25. Where did you stay?

UNIT B: Questions

B-1 FORMS OF YES/NO AND INFORMATION QUESTIONS

A yes/no question	=	a question that may be answered by *yes* or *no*.
		Yes/no question: Does he live in Chicago?
		Answer: Yes, he does. OR No, he doesn't.

An information question	=	a question that asks for information by using a question word.
		Information question: Where does he live?
		Answer: In Chicago.

	QUESTION WORD	AUXILIARY VERB	SUBJECT	MAIN VERB		
(a) *She lives* there.		*Does*	she	*live*	there?	If the verb is in the simple present, use *does* (with *he, she, it*) or *do* (with *I, you, we, they*) in the question. If the verb is simple past, use *did*.
	Where	*does*	she	*live*?		
(b) *They live* there.		*Do*	they	*live*	there?	
	Where	*do*	they	*live*?		
(c) *He lived* there.		*Did*	he	*live*	there?	Notice: The main verb in the question is in its simple form; there is no final *-s* or *-ed*.
	Where	*did*	he	*live*?		
(d) *He is living* there.		*Is*	he	*living*	there?	If the verb has an auxiliary (a helping verb), the same auxiliary is used in the question. There is no change in the form of the main verb.
	Where	*is*	he	*living*?		
(e) *They have lived* there.		*Have*	they	*lived*	there?	
	Where	*have*	they	*lived*?		
(f) *Mary can live* there.		*Can*	Mary	*live*	there?	
	Where	*can*	Mary	*live*?		
(g) *He will be living* there.		*Will*	he	*be living*	there?	If the verb has more than one auxiliary, only the first auxiliary precedes the subject.
	Where	*will*	he	*be living*?		

(continued)

	QUESTION WORD	AUXILIARY VERB	SUBJECT	MAIN VERB		
(h) *John lives* there.	*Who*	Ø	Ø	*lives*	there?	If the question word is the subject, do not change the verb. Do not use *does*, *do*, or *did*.
(i) *Mary can come*.	*Who*	*can*	Ø	*come?*		
(j) *They are* there.		*Are*	*they*		there?	*Be* in the simple present (*am*, *is*, *are*) and simple past (*was*, *were*) precedes the subject when *be* is the main verb.
	Where	*are*	*they?*			
(k) *Jim was* there.		*Was*	*Jim*		there?	
	Where	*was*	*Jim?*			

☐ **EXERCISE 9:** For each of the following, first make a yes/no question. Then make an information question using *where*.

> *Example:* They can stay there.
> *Yes/no question:* Can they stay there?
> *Information question:* Where can they stay?

1. She stays there.
2. She is staying there.
3. She will stay there.
4. She is going to stay there.
5. They stayed there.
6. They will be staying there.
7. They should stay there.
8. He has stayed there.
9. He has been staying there.
10. John is there.
11. John will be there.
12. John has been there.
13. Judy will have been there.
14. Ann and Tom were married there.
15. This package should have been taken there.

B-2 QUESTION WORDS

	QUESTION	ANSWER	
WHEN	(a) **When** did they arrive? **When** will you come?	Yesterday. Next Monday.	**When** is used to ask questions about *time*.
WHERE	(b) **Where** is she? **Where** can I find a pen?	At home. In that drawer.	**Where** is used to ask questions about *place*.
WHY	(c) **Why** did he leave early? **Why** aren't you coming with us?	Because he's ill. I'm tired.	**Why** is used to ask questions about *reason*.
HOW	(d) **How** did you come to school? **How** does he drive?	By bus. Carefully.	**How** generally asks about *manner*.
	(e) **How much** money does it cost? **How many** people came?	Ten dollars. Fifteen.	**How** is used with **much** and **many**.
	(f) **How old** are you? **How cold** is it? **How soon** can you get here? **How fast** were you driving?	Twelve. Ten below zero. In ten minutes. 50 miles an hour.	**How** is also used with adjectives and adverbs.
	(g) **How long** has he been here?	Two years.	**How long** asks about *length of time*.
	How often do you write home?	Every week.	**How often** asks about *frequency*.
	How far is it to Miami from here?	500 miles.	**How far** asks about *distance*.
WHO	(h) **Who** can answer that question? **Who** came to visit you?	I can. Jane and Eric.	**Who** is used as the subject of a question. It refers to people.
	(i) **Who is** coming to dinner tonight? **Who wants** to come with me?	Ann, Bob, and Al. We do.	**Who** is usually followed by a singular verb even if the speaker is asking about more than one person.
WHOM	(j) **Who(m)** did you see? **Who(m)** are you visiting? (k) **Who(m)** should I talk **to**? **To whom** should I talk? (*formal*)	I saw George. My relatives. The secretary.	**Whom** is used as the object of a verb or preposition. In spoken English, **whom** is rarely used; **who** is used instead. **Whom** is used only in formal questions. Note: **Whom**, not **who**, is used if preceded by a preposition.

(continued)

A10 □ Appendix 1

		QUESTION	ANSWER	
WHOSE	(l)	*Whose book* did you borrow? *Whose key* is this? (*Whose* is this?)	David's. It's mine.	*Whose* asks questions about *possession*.
WHAT	(m)	*What* made you angry? *What* went wrong?	His rudeness. Everything.	*What* is used as the subject of a question. It refers to "things."
	(n) (o)	*What* do you need? *What* did Alice buy? *What* did he talk *about*? *About what* did he talk? (*formal*)	I need a pencil. A book. His vacation.	*What* is also used as an object.
	(p)	*What kind of* soup is that? *What kind of* shoes did he buy?	It's bean soup. Sandals.	*What kind of* asks about the particular variety or type of something.
	(q)	*What did* you *do* last night? *What is* Mary *doing*?	I studied. Reading a book.	*What* + *a form of do* is used to ask questions about activities.
	(r)	*What countries* did you visit? *What time* did she come? *What color* is his hair?	Italy and Spain. Seven o'clock. Dark brown.	*What* may accompany a noun.
	(s) (t)	*What is* Ed *like*? *What is* the weather *like*?	He's kind and friendly. Hot and humid.	*What* + *be like* asks for a general description of qualities.
	(u) (v)	*What does* Ed *look like*? *What does* her house *look like*?	He's tall and has dark hair. It's a two-story, red brick house.	*What* + *look like* asks for a physical description.
WHICH	(w) (x)	I have two pens. *Which pen* do you want? *Which one* do you want? *Which* do you want? *Which book* should I buy?	The blue one. That one.	*Which* is used instead of *what* when a question concerns choosing from a definite, known quantity or group.
	(y) (z)	*Which countries* did he visit? *What countries* did he visit? *Which class* are you in? *What class* are you in?	Peru and Chile. This class.	In some cases, there is little difference in meaning between *which* and *what* when they accompany a noun, as in (y) and (z).

☐ **EXERCISE 10:** Make questions from the following sentences. The words in parentheses should be the answer to your question.

1. I need (*five dollars*).
   → *How much money do you need?*
2. Roberto was born (*in Panama*).
3. I go out to eat (*at least once a week*).
4. I'm waiting for (*Maria*).
5. (*My sister*) answered the phone.
6. I called (*Benjamin*).
7. (*Benjamin*) called.
➤ 8. The boy has (*a ball*) in his pocket.*

9. "Deceitful" means ("*dishonest*").
10. An abyss is (*a bottomless hole*).
11. He went (*this*) way, (*not that way*).
12. These are (*Jim's*) books and papers.
13. They have (*four*) children.
14. He has been here (*for two hours*).
15. It is (*two hundred miles*) to New Orleans.

☐ **EXERCISE 11:** Make questions from the following sentences. The words in parentheses should be the answer to your question.

1. She bought (*twelve gallons of gas*).
2. The doctor can see you (*at three on Friday*).
3. Her roommate is (*Jane Peters*).
4. Her roommates are (*Jane Peters and Sue Lee*).
5. My parents have been living there (*for three years*).
6. This is (*Alice's*) book.
7. (*The soap bubbles*) made her sneeze.
8. (*Fred and Jack*) are coming over for dinner.
9. Ann's dress is (*blue*).
10. Anne's eyes are (*brown*).
11. I was late (*because the traffic was heavy*).**
12. (*Bob*) can't go on the picnic.
13. Bob can't go (*because he is sick*).
14. I didn't answer the phone (*because I didn't hear it ring*).

---

*A form of **do** is usually used in questions when the main verb is **have** (especially in American English but also commonly in British English); e.g., *Do you have a car?* Using **have** without a form of **do** is also possible but less common; e.g., *Have you a car?*

NOTE: Especially in British English but also in American English, the idiom **have got** is used to indicate possession instead of **have** alone; e.g., *Bob **has got** a car. **Have** you **got** a car?*

In informal spoken English, another way of asking **why is **how come**. Usual question word order is not used with **how come**; instead, the subject comes in front of the verb.
   Example: John isn't here (*because he is sick*). → *Why isn't John here?*
                                                    → *How come John isn't here?*

15. I like (*classical*) music.
16. I don't understand (*the chart on page 50*).
17. Janet is (*studying*) right now.
18. You spell "sitting" (*with two "t's." S-I-T-T-I-N-G*).
19. Tom (*is about medium height and has red hair and freckles*).
20. Tom is (*very serious and hardworking*).
21. Ron (*works as a civil engineer for the railroad company*).
22. Mexico is (*eight hundred miles*) from here.
23. I take my coffee (*black with sugar*).
24. Of Stockholm and Moscow, (*Stockholm*) is farther north.
25. (*Fine.*) I'm getting along (*just fine*).

☐ **EXERCISE 12—ORAL (BOOKS CLOSED):** Make questions. Use question words.

Example: I bought a book.
Response: What did you buy?

1. It is fifty-five miles to (*Springfield*).
2. Fall semester begins on September 10th.
3. I bought the red pen, not the green one.
4. The secretary typed those letters.
5. I took four courses last semester.
6. "Rapid" means "fast."
7. (. . .) went to the library.
8. (. . .) telephoned me.
9. The post office is on Seventh Avenue.
10. It is three blocks to the post office.
11. I slept eight hours last night.
12. (. . .) gave a speech.
13. (. . .) talked about his/her country.
14. (. . .) talked about his/her family.
15. I need twenty-five dollars.
16. (. . .) lives on the fifth floor, not the fourth.
17. I will be in (*the United States*) for four years.
18. This is (. . .)'s pen.
19. I go to the library every day.
20. The next test is on Tuesday.
21. I have been studying English for ten years.
22. I laughed because (. . .) made a funny face.
23. (. . .) dropped his/her pen.
24. You should give that book to (. . .).
25. I didn't come to class yesterday because I wasn't feeling well.

☐ **EXERCISE 13—ORAL (BOOKS CLOSED):** Make questions. Use question words.

1. I had a sandwich for lunch.
2. These are (. . .)'s books.
3. We are supposed to read Chapter Five, not Chapter Six.

4. I talked to (. . .).
5. I talked to (. . .) about the story in this morning's newspaper.
6. I fell asleep in class because I had only two hours of sleep last night.
7. That book belongs to (. . .).
8. "Request" means "ask."
9. It is 325 miles to (*Chicago*).
10. I can speak three languages.
11. (. . .) opened the window.
12. I didn't go to the party because I had to study.

13. I live in this house, not that one.
14. I hung my coat in the closet.
15. The letter is addressed to (. . .).
16. It took me three hours to finish my assignments.
17. Mr. Smith taught English in Japan.
18. You should be here at two o'clock.
19. I found (. . .)'s keys.
20. I visit my aunt and uncle twice a year.

B-3 NEGATIVE QUESTIONS

(a) ***Doesn't she live*** in the dormitory? (b) ***Does she not live*** in the dormitory? (*very formal*)	In a yes/no question in which the verb is negative, usually a contraction (e.g., *does + not = doesn't*) is used, as in (a). Example (b) is very formal and is usually not used in everyday speech. Negative questions are used to indicate the speaker's idea (i.e., what s/he believes is or is not true) or attitude (e.g., surprise, shock, annoyance, anger).
(c) Bob returns to his dorm room after his nine o'clock class. Dick, his roommate, is there. Bob is surprised. Bob says: "*What are you doing here?* ***Aren't you supposed to be in class now?***" (d) Alice and Mary are at home. Mary is about to leave on a trip and Alice is going to take her to the airport. Alice says: "*It's already two o'clock. We'd better leave for the airport.* ***Doesn't your plane leave at three?***"	In (c): Bob believes that Dick is supposed to be in class now. *Expected answer:* **Yes.** In (d): Alice believes that Mary's plane leaves at three. She is asking the negative question to make sure that her information is correct. *Expected answer:* **Yes.**
(e) The teacher is talking to Jim about a test he failed. The teacher is surprised that Jim failed the test because he usually does very well. The teacher says: "*What happened?* ***Didn't you study?***" (f) Barb and Don are riding in a car. Don is driving. He comes to a corner where there is a stop sign, but he does not stop the car. Barb is shocked. Barb says: "*What's the matter with you?* ***Didn't you see that stop sign?***"	In (c): The teacher believes that Jim did not study. *Expected answer:* **No.** In (f): Barb believes that Don did not see the stop sign. *Expected answer:* **No.**

☐ **EXERCISE 14:** Notice the examples in Chart B-3: Sometimes the expected answer to a negative question is *yes* and sometimes *no*. In the following dialogues, make negative questions from the words in parentheses and determine the expected response.

1. A: Why didn't you come to lunch with us? ____Weren't you hungry?____

    (*be hungry*)

   B: ___No.___ I had a late breakfast.

2. A: Did you give Linda my message when you went to class this morning?

   B: No. I didn't see her.

    A: Oh? _____ (*be in class*)

    B: _____ She didn't come today.

3. A: Do you see that woman over there, the one in the blue dress?_____

    _____ (*be Mrs. Robbins*)

   B: _____

   A: I thought so. I wonder what she is doing here.

4. A: It's almost dinner time and you haven't eaten since breakfast.

    _____ (*be hungry*)

   B: _____ I'm starving. Let's go eat.

5. A: You look tired this morning. _____

    (*sleep well last night*)

   B: _____ I tossed and turned all night.

6. A: You look pale. What's the matter? _____ (*feel well*)

   B: _____ I think I might be coming down with something.

7. A: Daddy, Tommy said that the sun rises in the west. _____

    _____ (*rise in the east*)

   B: _____, Annie. You're right. Tommy is a little mixed up.

8. A: See that man over there, the one in the green shirt?

   B: Yes. Who is he?

    A: _____ (*recognize him*)

   B: _____. Am I supposed to?

B-4 TAG QUESTIONS

(a) Jack **can** come, **can't he?** (b) Fred **can't** come, **can he?**	*A tag question* is a question added at the end of a sentence. Speakers use tag questions chiefly to make sure their information is correct or to seek agreement.*

AFFIRMATIVE SENTENCE + NEGATIVE TAG	→ AFFIRMATIVE ANSWER EXPECTED
Mary **is** here, **isn't** she?	Yes, she is.
You **like** tea, **don't** you?	Yes, I do.
They **have** left, **haven't** they?	Yes, they have.

NEGATIVE SENTENCE + AFFIRMATIVE TAG	→ NEGATIVE ANSWER EXPECTED
Mary **isn't** here, is she?	No, she isn't.
You **don't like** tea, do you?	No, I don't.
They **haven't** left, have they?	No, they haven't.

(c) **This/That** is your book, isn't **it?** **These/Those** are yours, aren't **they?**	The tag pronoun for **this/that** = **it**. The tag pronoun for **these/those** = **they**.
(d) **There is** a meeting tonight, **isn't there?**	In sentences with **there + be**, **there** is used in the tag.
(e) **Everything** is okay, isn't **it?** (f) **Everyone** took the test, didn't **they?**	Personal pronouns are used to refer to indefinite pronouns. **They** is usually used in a tag to refer to **everyone, everybody, someone, somebody, no one, nobody.**
(g) **Nothing is** wrong, **is** it? (h) **Nobody called** on the phone, **did** they? (i) You**'ve never been** there, **have** you?	Sentences with negative words take affirmative tags.
(j) **I am** supposed to be here, **am I not?** (k) **I am** supposed to be here, **aren't I?**	In (j): **am I not?** is formal English. In (k): **aren't I?** is common in spoken English.

*A tag question may be spoken:
(1) with a rising intonation if the speaker is truly seeking to ascertain that his/her information, idea, belief is correct (e.g., *Ann lives in an apartment, doesn't she?*); OR
(2) with a falling intonation if the speaker is expressing an idea with which s/he is almost certain the listener will agree (e.g., *It's a nice day today, isn't it?*).

☐ **EXERCISE 15:** Add tag questions to the following.

1. They want to come, _____*don't they*_____?

2. Elizabeth is a dentist, _____?

3. They won't be here, _____?

4. There aren't any problems, _____?

5. That is your umbrella, _____?

6. George is a student, _____?

7. He's learned a lot in the last couple of years, _____?

8. He has* a bicycle, _____?

9. Joan can't come with us, _____?

10. She'll help us later, _____?

11. Peggy would like to come with us to the party, _____?

12. Those aren't Fred's books, _____?

13. You've never been to Paris, _____?

14. Something is wrong with Jane today, _____?

15. Everyone can learn how to swim, _____?

16. Nobody cheated on the exam, _____?

17. Nothing went wrong while I was gone, _____?

18. I am invited, _____?

□ **EXERCISE 16—ORAL (BOOKS CLOSED):** Add tag questions.

> *Example:* (*Carlos*) is a student....
> *Responses:* ...isn't he?

1. That's (...)'s pen....
2. (...) is living in an apartment....
3. (...) lives on (*Main Street*)....
4. There isn't a test tomorrow....
5. (...) has his/her book....
6. You had a good time....
7. (...) has been invited to the party....
8. You didn't forget your key....
9. Your parents haven't arrived yet....
10. Turtles lay eggs....
11. (...) can't speak (*Arabic*)....
12. (...) is never late to class....
13. Something will be done about that problem right away....
14. These keys don't belong to you....
15. You used to live in New York....
16. There's a better way to solve that problem....
17. (...) is going to come to class tomorrow....
18. You should leave for the airport by six....
19. (...) doesn't have a car....
20. (...) sat next to (...) yesterday....
21. We have class tomorrow....
22. You've already seen that movie....
23. (...) will help us....
24. Nobody has told you the secret....
25. I am right....
26. Class ends at (*ten*)....

---

*A form of **do** is usually used in the tag when **have** is the main verb: Tom **has** a car, **doesn't** he? Also possible, but less common: Tom **has** a car, **hasn't** he?

UNIT C: Negatives

C-1 USING *NOT* AND OTHER NEGATIVE WORDS

(a) AFFIRMATIVE: The earth is round. (b) NEGATIVE: The earth is **not** flat.	**Not** expresses a *negative* idea.
AUX + *NOT* + MAIN VERB (c) I *will* not go there. I *have* not gone there. I *am* not going there. I *was* not there. I *do* not go there. He *does* not go there. I *did* not go there.	**Not** immediately follows an auxiliary verb or *be*. (Note: If there is more than one auxiliary, **not** comes immediately after the first auxiliary: *I will not be going there.*) **Do** or **does** is used with **not** to make a simple present verb (except *be*) negative. **Did** is used with **not** to make a simple past verb (except *be*) negative.
CONTRACTIONS OF AUXILIARY VERBS WITH *NOT* *are not* = *aren't*★ *do not* = *don't* *must not* = *mustn't* *cannot* = *can't* *has not* = *hasn't* *should not* = *shouldn't* *could not* = *couldn't* *have not* = *haven't* *was not* = *wasn't* *did not* = *didn't* *had not* = *hadn't* *were not* = *weren't* *does not* = *doesn't* *is not* = *isn't* *will not* = *won't* *would not* = *wouldn't*	

(d) I **never** go there.
 I have **hardly ever** gone there.
 	
 (e) There's **no** chalk in the drawer.
	In addition to **not**, the following are negative adverbs:
	   never, rarely, seldom
	   hardly (ever), scarcely (ever), barely (ever)
	 No also expresses a negative idea.

COMPARE: *NOT* vs. *NO* (f) I **do not have** any money. (g) I have **no money**.	**Not** is used to make a verb negative, as in (f). **No** is used as an adjective in front of a noun (e.g., **money**), as in (g). Note: (f) and (g) have the same meaning.

*Sometimes in spoken English you will hear "ain't." It means *am not, isn't,* or *aren't.* "Ain't" is not considered proper English, but many people use "ain't" regularly, and it is also frequently used for humor.

☐ **EXERCISE 17:** Change the following into the negative in two ways: use **not . . . any** in one sentence and **no** in the other.

1. I have some problems. → *I don't have any problems. I have no problems.*
2. There was some food.
3. I received some letters from home.
4. I need some help.
5. We have some time to waste.
6. You should have given the beggar some money.
7. I trust someone. → *I don't trust anyone. I trust no one.*★
8. I saw someone.
9. There was someone in his room.
10. She can find somebody who knows about it.

---

*In American English, **no one** is written without a hyphen. In British English, it is written either **no one** (without a hyphen) or **no-one** (with a hyphen).

C-2 AVOIDING "DOUBLE NEGATIVES"

(a) *INCORRECT: I don't have no money.* (b) CORRECT: I **don't** have **any** money. CORRECT: I have **no** money.	(a) is an example of a "double negative," i.e., a confusing and grammatically incorrect sentence that contains two negatives in the same clause.* One clause should contain only one negative.

*NOTE: Negatives in two different clauses in the same sentence cause no problems; for example:
  *A person who **doesn't** have love **can't** be truly happy.*
  *I **don't** know why he **isn't** here.*

☐ **EXERCISE 18—ERROR ANALYSIS:** Correct the following sentences, all of which contain double negatives.

1. I don't need no help.
2. I didn't see nobody.
3. I can't never understand him.
4. He doesn't like neither coffee nor tea.
5. I didn't do nothing.
6. I can't hardly hear the radio. Would you please turn it up?
7. The beach was deserted. We couldn't see nothing but sand.
8. Methods of horse training haven't barely changed at all in the last eight centuries.

C-3 BEGINNING A SENTENCE WITH A NEGATIVE WORD

(a) ***Never will I do*** that again. (b) ***Rarely have I eaten*** better food. (c) ***Hardly ever does he come*** to class on time.	When a negative word begins a sentence, the subject and verb are inverted (i.e., question word order is used).*

*Beginning a sentence with a negative word is relatively uncommon in everyday usage, but is used when the speaker/writer wishes to emphasize the negative element of the sentence.

☐ **EXERCISE 19:** Change each sentence so that it begins with a negative word.

1. We rarely go to movies. → *Rarely do we go to movies.*
2. I seldom sleep past seven o'clock.
3. I hardly ever agree with her.
4. I will never forget the wonderful people I have met here.
5. I have never known Pat to be dishonest.
6. The mail scarcely ever arrives before noon.

UNIT D: Articles

D-1   BASIC ARTICLE USAGE

	I. USING *A* or Ø: GENERIC NOUNS	
SINGULAR COUNT NOUN	(a) ***A** banana* is yellow.*	A speaker uses generic nouns to make generalizations. A generic noun represents a whole class of things; it is not a specific, real, concrete thing but rather a symbol of a whole group.
PLURAL COUNT NOUN	(b) *Ø Bananas* are yellow.	In (a) and (b): The speaker is talking about any banana, all bananas, bananas in general. In (c), the speaker is talking about any and all fruit, fruit in general.
NONCOUNT NOUN	(c) *Ø Fruit* is good for you.	Notice that no article (Ø) is used to make generalizations with plural count nouns and noncount nouns, as in (b) and (c).

	II. USING *A* or *SOME*: INDEFINITE NOUNS	
SINGULAR COUNT NOUN	(d) I ate ***a** banana*.	Indefinite nouns are actual things (not symbols), but they are not specifically identified.
		In (d): The speaker is not referring to "this banana" or "that banana" or "that banana you gave me." The speaker is simply saying that s/he ate one banana. The listener does not know nor need to know which specific banana was eaten; it was simply one banana out of that whole group of things in this world called bananas.
PLURAL COUNT NOUN	(e) I ate ***some** bananas*.	
NONCOUNT NOUN	(f) I ate ***some** fruit*.	In (e) and (f): ***Some*** is often used with indefinite plural count nouns and indefinite noncount nouns. In addition to *some*, a speaker might use ***two**, **a few**, **several**, **a lot of***, etc., with plural count nouns, or ***a little**, **a lot of***, etc., with noncount nouns. (See Chart 5-8.)

	III. USING *THE*: DEFINITE NOUNS	
SINGULAR COUNT NOUN	(g) Thank you for ***the** banana*.	A noun is definite when both the speaker and the listener are thinking about the same specific thing.
		In (g): The speaker uses ***the*** because the listener knows which specific banana the speaker is talking about, i.e., that particular banana which the listener gave to the speaker.
PLURAL COUNT NOUN	(h) Thank you for ***the** bananas*.	
NONCOUNT NOUN	(i) Thank you for ***the** fruit*.	Notice that ***the*** is used with both singular and plural count nouns and with noncount nouns.

*Usually ***a/an*** is used with a singular generic count noun. Examples:
    A window *is made of glass*. ***A doctor*** *heals sick people. Parents must give* ***a child*** *love*. ***A box*** *has six sides*. ***An apple*** *can be red, green, or yellow*.
The is sometimes used with a singular generic count noun (not a plural generic count noun, not a generic noncount noun). "Generic ***the***" is commonly used with, in particular:
    (1) species of animals: ***The whale*** *is the largest mammal on earth*.
                          The elephant *is the largest land mammal*.
    (2) inventions: *Who invented* ***the telephone***? ***the wheel***? ***the refrigerator***? ***the airplane***?
                         The computer *will play an increasingly large role in all of our lives*.
    (3) musical instruments: *I'd like to learn to play* ***the piano***.
                         Do you play ***the guitar***?

D-2 GENERAL GUIDELINES FOR ARTICLE USAGE

(a) **The sun** is bright today. Please hand this book to **the teacher**. Please open **the door**. Jack is in **the kitchen**.	GUIDELINE: Use **the** when you know or assume that your listener is familiar with and thinking about the same specific thing or person you are talking about.
(b) Yesterday I saw *some dogs*. **The dogs** were chasing *a cat*. **The cat** was chasing *a mouse*. **The mouse** ran into *a hole*. **The hole** was very small.	GUIDELINE: Use **the** for the second mention of an indefinite noun*; in (b): first mention = *some dogs, a cat, a mouse, a hole* second mention = *the dogs, the cat, the mouse, the hole*

(c) *INCORRECT:* *The apples are my favorite fruit.*
     CORRECT: **Apples** are my favorite fruit.
 (d) *INCORRECT:* *The gold is a metal.*
     CORRECT: **Gold** is a metal.
	GUIDELINE: Do not use **the** with a plural count noun (e.g., *apples*) or a noncount noun (e.g., *gold*) when you are making a generalization.

(e) *INCORRECT:* *I drove car.*
     CORRECT: I drove **a car**.
                I drove **the car**.
                I drove **that car**.
                I drove **his car**.
	GUIDELINE: Do not use a singular count noun (e.g., *car*) without:
	 (1) an article (**a/an** or **the**); OR
	 (2) **this/that**; OR
	 (3) a possessive pronoun.

*__The__ is not used for the second mention of a generic noun. COMPARE:
   (1) What color is **a banana** (*generic noun*)? **A banana** (*generic noun*) is yellow.
   (2) Tom offered me **a banana** (*indefinite noun*) or an apple. I chose **the banana** (*definite noun*).

☐ **EXERCISE 20:** In the following dialogues, try to decide whether the speakers would probably use *a/an* or *the*.

  1. A: I have _____*an*_____ idea. Let's go on _____*a*_____ picnic Saturday.

     B: Okay.

  2. A: Did you have fun at _____*the*_____ picnic yesterday?

     B: Sure did. And you?

  3. A: You'd better have _____ good reason for being late!

     B: I do.

  4. A: Did you think _____ reason Jack gave for being late was

       believable?

     B: Not really.

  5. A: Where's my blue shirt?

     B: It's in _____ washing machine. You'll have to wear _____

       different shirt.

6. A: I wish we had _____ washing machine.

   B: So do I. It would make it a lot easier to do our laundry.

7. A: What happened to your bicycle? _____ front wheel is bent.

   B: I ran into _____ parked car when I swerved to avoid _____ big pothole in the street.

   A: Did you damage _____ car?

   B: A little.

   A: What did you do?

   B: I left _____ note for _____ owner of _____ car.

   A: What did you write on _____ note?

   B: My name and address. I also wrote _____ apology.

8. A: Can you repair my car for me?

   B: What's wrong with it?

   A: _____ radiator has _____ leak, and one of _____ windshield wipers doesn't work.

   B: Can you show me where _____ leak is?

9. A: Have you seen my boots?

   B: They're in _____ closet in _____ front hallway.

□ **EXERCISE 21:** Complete the sentences with *a/an*, *the*, or ∅.

1. _____∅_____ beef is a kind of _____∅_____ meat.

2. _____*The*_____ beef we had for dinner last night was excellent.

3. Jack is wearing _____*a*_____ straw hat today.

4. Jack likes to wear _____ hats.

5. _____ hat is _____ article of clothing.

6. _____ hats are _____ articles of clothing.

7. _____ brown hat on that hook over there belongs to Mark.

8. Everyone has _____ problems in _____ life.

9. My grandfather had _____ long life.

10. That book is about _____ life of Helen Keller.

11. Tommy wants to be _____ engineer when he grows up.

12. The Brooklyn Bridge was designed by _____ engineer.

13. John Roebling is _____ name of _____ engineer who designed the Brooklyn Bridge. He died in 1869 from _____ infection. He died before _____ bridge was completed.

14. _____ people wear _____ jewelry to make themselves more attractive.

15. _____ jewelry Diana is wearing today is beautiful.

16. Mary is wearing _____ beautiful ring today. It is made of _____ gold and _____ rubies. _____ gold in her ring was mined in Canada. _____ rubies came from Burma.

17. One of the first things you need to do when you move to _____ new city is to find _____ place to live. Most _____ newspapers carry _____ advertisements (called ''want ads'') for _____ apartments that are for rent. If you find _____ ad for _____ furnished apartment, _____ apartment will probably contain _____ stove and _____ refrigerator. It will also probably have _____ furniture such as _____ beds, _____ tables, _____ chairs, and maybe _____ sofa.

18. My wife and I have recently moved to this city. Since we're going to be here for only _____ short time, we're renting _____ furnished apartment. We decided that we didn't want to bring our own furniture with us. _____ apartment is in _____ good location, but that's about the only good thing I can say about it. Only one burner on _____ stove works. _____ refrigerator is noisy, and _____ refrigerator door won't stay closed unless we tape it shut. _____ bed sags in the middle and creaks. All of the rest of _____ furniture is old and decrepit too. Nevertheless, we're still enjoying living in this city. We may have to look for _____ another apartment, however.

APPENDIX 2
Preposition Combinations

Appendix 2 contains two lists of preposition combinations. The first list consists of preposition combinations with adjectives and verbs. The second list contains phrasal verbs.

These lists contain only those preposition combinations used in the exercises in the text and in the accompanying workbooks.

PREPOSITION COMBINATIONS WITH ADJECTIVES AND VERBS

A   *be* absent from
      accuse of
      be accustomed to
      be aquainted with
      be addicted to
      be afraid of
      agree with
      be angry at, with
      be annoyed with
      apologize for
      apply to, for
      approve of
      argue with, about
      arrive in, at
      be associated with
      be aware of

B   believe in
      blame for
      be blessed with
      be bored with

C   *be* capable of
      care about, for
      be cluttered with
      be committed to
      compare to, with
      complain about
      be composed of
      be concerned about
      be connected to
      consist of
      be content with
      contribute to
      be convinced of
      be coordinated with
      count (up)on
      cover with
      be crowded with

D   decide (up)on
      be dedicated to
      depend (up)on

be devoted to
be disappointed in, with
be discriminated against
distinguish from
be divorced from
be done with
dream of, about
be dressed in

E *be* engaged to
be envious of
be equipped with
escape from
excel in
be excited about
excuse for
be exposed to

F *be* faithful to
be familiar with
feel like
fight for
be filled with
be finished with
be fond of
forget about
forgive for
be friendly to, with
be furnished with

G *be* grateful to, for
be guilty of

H hide from
hope for

I *be* innocent of
insist (up)on
be interested in
be involved in

J *be* jealous of

K *be* known for

L *be* limited to
look forward to

M *be* made of, from
be married to

O object to
be opposed to

P participate in
be patient with
be polite to
pray for
be prepared for
prevent from
prohibit from
protect from
be provided with
be proud of
provide with

R recover from
be related to
be relevant to
rely (up)on
be remembered for
rescue from
respond to
be responsible for

S *be* satisfied with
be scared of
stare at
stop from
subscribe to
substitute for
succeed in

T take advantage of
take care of
be terrified of
thank for
be tired of, from

U *be* upset with
be used to

V vote for

W *be* worried about

PHRASAL VERBS (TWO-WORD AND THREE-WORD VERBS)

The term *phrasal verb* refers to a verb and preposition which together have a special meaning. For example, ***put + off*** means "postpone." Sometimes a phrasal verb consists of three parts. For example, ***put + up + with*** means "tolerate." Phrasal verbs are also called *two-word verbs* or *three-word verbs*.

SEPARABLE PHRASAL VERBS (a) I **handed** *my paper* **in** yesterday. (b) I **handed in** *my paper* yesterday.	A phrasal verb may be either *separable* or *nonseparable*. With a separable phrasal verb, a noun may come either between the verb and the preposition or after the preposition, as in (a) and (b).
(c) I **handed** *it* **in** yesterday. (*INCORRECT: I handed in it yesterday.*)	A pronoun comes between the verb and the preposition if the phrasal verb is separable, as in (c).
NONSEPARABLE PHRASAL VERBS (d) I **ran into** *an old friend* yesterday. (e) I **ran into** *her* yesterday. (*INCORRECT: I ran an old friend into.*) (*INCORRECT: I ran her into yesterday.*)	With a nonseparable phrasal verb, a noun or pronoun must follow the preposition, as in (d) and (e).

Phrasal verbs are especially common in informal English. Following is a list of common phrasal verbs and their usual meanings. This list contains only those phrasal verbs used in the exercises in the text. The phrasal verbs marked with an asterisk (*) are nonseparable.

A ask out . . . . *ask someone to go on a date*

B bring about, bring on . . . . *cause*
    bring up . . . . *(1) rear children; (2) mention or introduce a topic*

C call back . . . . *return a telephone call*
    call in . . . . *ask to come to an official place for a specific purpose*
    call off . . . . *cancel*
    *call on . . . . *(1) ask to speak in class; (2) visit*
    call up . . . . *call on the telephone*
    *catch up (with) . . . . *reach the same position or level*
    *check in, check into . . . . . *register at a hotel*
    *check into . . . . *investigate*
    check out . . . . *(1) take a book from the library; (2) investigate*
    *check out (of) . . . . *leave a hotel*
    cheer up . . . . *make (someone) feel happier*
    clean up . . . . *make clean and orderly*
    *come across . . . . *meet by chance*
    cross out . . . . *draw a line through*
    cut out . . . . *stop an annoying activity*

D do over . . . . *do again*
    *drop by, drop in (on) . . . . *visit informally*
    drop off . . . . *leave something/someone at a place*
    *drop out (of) . . . . *stop going to school, to a class, to a club, etc.*

F figure out . . . . *find the answer by reasoning*
    fill out . . . . *write the completions of a questionnaire or official form*
    find out . . . . *discover information*

G *get along (with) . . . . *exist satisfactorily*
    get back (from) . . . . *(1) return from a place; (2) receive again*
    *get in, get into . . . . *(1) enter a car; (2) arrive*
    *get off . . . . *leave an airplane, a bus, a train, a subway, a bicycle*
    *get on . . . . *enter an airplane, a bus, a train, a subway, a bicycle*
    *get out of . . . . *(1) leave a car; (2) avoid work or an unpleasant activity*
    *get over . . . . *recover from an illness*
    *get through . . . . *finish*
    *get up . . . . *arise from bed, a chair*
    give back . . . . *return an item to someone*
    give up . . . . *stop trying*
    *go over . . . . *review or check carefully*
    *grow up (in) . . . . *become an adult*

H hand in . . . . *submit an assignment*
    hang up . . . . *(1) conclude a telephone conversation; (2) put clothes on a hanger or a hook*
    have on . . . . *wear*

K keep out (of) . . . . *not enter*
    *keep up (with) . . . . *stay at the same position or level*
    kick out (of) . . . . *force (someone) to leave*

L *look after . . . . *take care of*
    *look into . . . . *investigate*
    *look out (for) . . . . *be careful*
    look over . . . . *review or check carefully*
    look up . . . . *look for information in a reference book*

M make up . . . . *(1) invent; (2) do past work*

N name after, name for . . . . *give a baby the name of someone else*

P *pass away . . . . *die*
    pass out . . . . *(1) distribute; (2) lose consciousness*
    pick out . . . . *select*
    pick up . . . . *(1) go to get someone (e.g., in a car); (2) take in one's hand*
    point out . . . . *call attention to*

```
put away . . . . . . . . . . . . . .  remove to a proper place
put back . . . . . . . . . . . . . .  return to original place
put off . . . . . . . . . . . . . . .  postpone
put on . . . . . . . . . . . . . . .  put clothes on one's body
put out. . . . . . . . . . . . . . .  extinguish a cigarette or cigar
*put up with . . . . . . . . . . .  tolerate
```

R *run into, *run across . . . . meet by chance
   *run out (of). . . . . finish a supply of something

S *show up. . . . . appear, come
   shut off . . . . stop a machine, light, faucet

T *take after. . . . . resemble
```
take off . . . . . . . . . . . . . .  (1) remove clothing; (2) leave on a trip
take out . . . . . . . . . . . . . .  (1) take someone on a date; (2) remove
take over . . . . . . . . . . . . .  take control
take up . . . . . . . . . . . . . .  begin a new activity or topic
tear down . . . . . . . . . . . .  demolish; reduce to nothing
tear up . . . . . . . . . . . . . . .  tear into many little pieces
think over . . . . . . . . . . . .  consider carefully
throw away, throw out . . .  discard; get rid of
throw up . . . . . . . . . . . . .  vomit; regurgitate food
try on. . . . . . . . . . . . . . . .  put on clothing to see if it fits
turn down . . . . . . . . . . . .  decrease volume or intensity
turn in . . . . . . . . . . . . . . .  (1) submit an assignment; (2) go to bed
turn off . . . . . . . . . . . . . .  stop a machine, light, faucet
turn on . . . . . . . . . . . . . .  begin a machine, light, faucet
turn out. . . . . . . . . . . . . .  extinguish a light
turn up . . . . . . . . . . . . . .  increase volume or intensity
```

APPENDIX *3*
Guide for Correcting Writing Errors

To the student: Each number represents an area of usage. Your teacher will use these numbers when marking your writing to indicate that you have made an error. Refer to this list to find out what kind of error you have made and then make the necessary correction.

1	SINGULAR-PLURAL	He have been here for six month. *He has been here for six months.*
2	WORD FORM	I saw a beauty picture. *I saw a beautiful picture.*
3	WORD CHOICE	She got on the taxi. *She got into the taxi.*
4	VERB TENSE	He is here since June. *He has been here since June.*
5+	ADD A WORD	I want ∧ go to the zoo. *I want to go to the zoo.*
5−	OMIT A WORD	She entered to the university. *She entered the university.*
6	WORD ORDER	I saw five times that movie. *I saw that movie five times.*
7	INCOMPLETE SENTENCE	I went to bed. Because I was tired. *I went to bed because I was tired.*

8	SPELLING	An accident occured.⁽⁸⁾ *An accident occurred.*
9	PUNCTUATION	What did he say.⁽⁹⁾ *What did he say?*
10	CAPITALIZATION	I am studying english.⁽¹⁰⁾ *I am studying English.*
11	ARTICLE	I had a accident.⁽¹¹⁾ *I had an accident.*
12?	MEANING NOT CLEAR	He borrowed some smoke.⁽¹²?⁾ *(? ? ?)*
13	RUN-ON SENTENCE★	My roommate was sleeping, we didn't want to wake her up.⁽¹³⁾ *My roommate was sleeping. We didn't want to wake her up.*

★A run-on sentence occurs when two sentences are incorrectly connected: the end of one sentence and the beginning of the next sentence are not properly marked by a period and a capital letter or by a semicolon. (See Charts 8-3 and 8-9.)

Index—Volume A

Able to, 107, 109, 112 *(Look on pages 107, 109, and 112.)*	The numbers following the words listed in the index refer to page numbers in the main text.
Be, A4 *(Look in the back part of this book on the fourth page of the Appendixes.)*	The index numbers preceded by the letter "A" (e.g., A4) refer to pages in the Appendixes, which are found in the last part of the text. The main text ends on page 196, and the appendixes immediately follow. Page 196 is followed by page A1.
Continuous tenses, 3*fn.* *(Look at the footnote on page 3.)*	Information given in footnotes to charts or exercises is noted by the page number plus the abbreviation *fn.*